The College Panda

ACT Math

Advanced Guide and Workbook

ISBN: 978-0-9894964-7-6

*ACT is a registered trademark of ACT, Inc., which does not endorse this product.

For more information, visit thecollegepanda.com

Discounts available for teachers and companies. Please contact thecollegepanda@gmail.com for details.

To Tina

Introduction

The best way to do well on any test is to be experienced with the material. Nowhere is this more true than on the ACT, which is standardized to repeat the same question types again and again. The purpose of this book is to teach you the concepts and battle-tested approaches you need to know for all these questions types. If it's not in this book, it's not on the test. The goal is for every ACT question to be a simple reflex, something you know how to handle instinctively because you've seen it so many times before.

You won't find any cheap tricks in this book, simply because there aren't any that work consistently. Don't buy into the idea that you can improve your score significantly without hard work.

Format of the Test

There is only one math section on the ACT (it's the second section). It contains 60 questions to be done in 60 minutes and a calculator is permitted.

How to Read this Book

For a complete understanding, this book is best read from beginning to end. That being said, each chapter was written to be independent of the others as much as possible. After all, you may already be proficient in some topics yet weak in others. If so, feel free to jump around, focusing on the chapters that are most relevant to your improvement.

All chapters come with exercises. Do them. You won't master the material until you think through the questions yourself.

About the Author

Nielson Phu graduated from New York University, where he studied actuarial science. He has obtained perfect scores on the SAT and on the SAT math subject test. As a teacher, he has helped hundreds of students throughout Boston and Hong Kong perform better on standardized tests. Although he continues to pursue his interests in education, he is now an engineer in the Boston area.

Table of Contents

1   Absolute Value   7

2   Exponents & Radicals   9

    Laws of exponents
    Evaluating expressions with exponents
    Solving equations with exponents
    Simplifying square roots

3   Manipulating and Solving Equations   15

    Common mistakes to avoid
    Tools for isolating variables

4   Expressions   21

    Combining like terms
    Expansion and factoring
    Combining and splitting fractions
    Modeling real-life scenarios

5   Numbers and Operations   27

    Fraction arithmetic
    Arithmetic word problems

6   Properties of Numbers   32

    Types of numbers
    Notations and values
    Factors, multiples, and LCM
    Scientific notation

7   Complex Numbers   38

8   Rates   42

    Conversion factors
    Working with the distance formula

9   Ratio & Proportion   47

    Interpreting ratios
    Direct and indirect proportion

10 Percent   52

    Percent word problems
    Percent change

11 Functions   57

    What is a function?
    Composite functions
    Graphing functions

Zeros and solutions
Domain and range
Rational functions
Horizontal and vertical asymptotes
Inverse functions
Function transformations

12 Lines   70
Slope, x-intercept, and y-intercept
Equations of lines: slope-intercept form and point-slope form
Finding the intersection of two lines
Parallel and perpendicular lines
Horizontal and vertical lines

13 Quadratics   78
Tactics for finding the roots
The vertex and vertex form
The discriminant
The quadratic formula
Completing the square

14 Coordinate Geometry   88
Finding coordinates
The midpoint formula
The distance formula
Translations, reflections, rotations, and projections

15 Angles   96
Exterior angle theorem
Parallel lines
Polygons

16 Triangles   103
Isosceles and equilateral triangles
Right triangles
Special right triangles
Similar triangles

17 Circles   114
Properties of circles
Arc length
Area of a sector
Central and inscribed angles
Equations of circles

18 Area & Perimeter   123

19 Volume   132

20 Systems of Equations   137

Substitution
Elimination
Systems with no solutions and infinite solutions
Word problems

21 Inequalities   143

Solving inequalities
"And" vs. "Or"
Number lines
Graphs of systems of inequalities
Dealing with absolute value in inequalities

22 Trigonometry   152

Sine, cosine, and tangent
Law of sines, law of cosines
Inverse trig functions
Radians
Trigonometry in the coordinate plane
Graphs of trig functions
Trigonometric identities

23 Permutations & Probability   169

24 Data & Statistics   174

Interpreting tables and graphs
Mean, median, and mode
Range and standard deviation
Stem-and-leaf plots and scatterplots

25 Logarithms   183

26 A Mix of Algebra Topics   187

Word problems
Modeling questions
Linear programming

27 Miscellaneous Topics I   192

Sequences
Venn diagrams
Brute force/trial and error strategies

28 Miscellaneous Topics II   198

Matrices
Logic
Visualizations
Ellipses

29 Answers to the Exercises   206

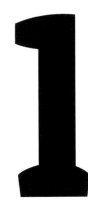

Absolute Value

The absolute value of x, denoted by $|x|$, is the distance x is from 0. In other words, absolute value makes everything positive. If it's positive, it stays positive. If it's negative, it becomes positive.

EXAMPLE 1: $|11(-3) + 5(4)| = ?$

A. -11 B. 11   C. 13   D. 17   E. 53

$|11(-3) + 5(4)| = |-33 + 20| = |-13| = 13$. Answer $\boxed{(C)}$.

EXAMPLE 2: If $x \geq -2$, then $|x + 2| = ?$

A. 0   B. $-x - 2$ C. $-x + 2$ D. $x - 2$ E. $x + 2$

One of the best strategies to use when dealing with absolute value expressions is to make up a number. If we let $x = 3$, then $|x + 2| = 5$, which is the value we now look for in the answer choices. Plugging $x = 3$ into each answer choice gives

A. 0   B. -5 C. -1 D. 1   E. 5

As you can see, only $\boxed{(E)}$ results in 5.

EXAMPLE 3: The solution set of which of the following equations is the set of real numbers that are 4 units from 2?

A. $|x + 2| = 4$ B. $|x - 2| = 4$ C. $|x + 4| = 2$ D. $|x - 4| = 2$ E. $|x + 4| = -2$

This question might seem complicated but it's not. What are the numbers that are 4 units from 2? Well, there's only two: $2 - 4 = -2$ and $2 + 4 = 6$. The correct answer must be the equation for which $x = -2$ and $x = 6$ are solutions. Plugging those values into each of the answer choices, we see that only $\boxed{(B)}$ holds true for both values.

CHAPTER EXERCISE: Answers for this chapter start on page 206.

1. $|3 - 6| - |8 - 2| = ?$

   A. -9
   B. -3
   C. 3
   D. 6
   E. 9

2. $|-4(6) - (4)(-3)| = ?$

   A. -12
   B. 12
   C. 16
   D. 24
   E. 36

3. If $-|x| = x$, which of the following statements *must* be true?

   A. $x \leq 0$
   B. $x \geq 0$
   C. $x = 0$
   D. $x \neq 0$
   E. x is not a real number.

4. If $|x - 7| = 18$, what are the possible values for x ?

   A. -25 and -11
   B. -25 and 11
   C. -11 and 25
   D. -7 and 7
   E. 11 and 25

5. For which of the following values of x and y is $|x| \, |y| = -xy$?

   A. $x = -2$ and $y = -3$
   B. $x = 2$ and $y = 3$
   C. $x = -3$ and $y = -2$
   D. $x = 3$ and $y = -2$
   E. $x = 3$ and $y = 2$

6. For all real numbers x, $|-x| + |x| = ?$

   A. 0
   B. x
   C. $|x|$
   D. $2x$
   E. $|2x|$

7. For all $b \geq 0$, $|-4b|^2 - |-b|^3 = ?$

   A. $8b^2 + b^3$
   B. $-8b^2 - b^3$
   C. $16b^2 - b^3$
   D. $-16b^2 + b^3$
   E. $16b^2 + b^3$

8. For all real numbers x, $|-2x| - 2|x| = ?$

   A. 0
   B. $2x$
   C. $2|x|$
   D. $4x$
   E. $4|x|$

9. The solution set of which of the following equations is the set of real numbers that are 3 units from -7 ?

   A. $|x - 3| = 7$
   B. $|x + 3| = 7$
   C. $|x + 3| = -7$
   D. $|x - 7| = 3$
   E. $|x + 7| = 3$

Exponents & Radicals

Here are the laws of exponents you should know:

Law	Example
$x^1 = x$	$3^1 = 3$
$x^0 = 1$	$3^0 = 1$
$x^m \cdot x^n = x^{m+n}$	$3^4 \cdot 3^5 = 3^9$
$\dfrac{x^m}{x^n} = x^{m-n}$	$\dfrac{3^7}{3^3} = 3^4$
$(x^m)^n = x^{mn}$	$(3^2)^4 = 3^8$
$(xy)^m = x^m y^m$	$(2 \cdot 3)^3 = 2^3 \cdot 3^3$
$\left(\dfrac{x}{y}\right)^m = \dfrac{x^m}{y^m}$	$\left(\dfrac{2}{3}\right)^3 = \dfrac{2^3}{3^3}$
$x^{-m} = \dfrac{1}{x^m}$	$3^{-4} = \dfrac{1}{3^4}$

Many students don't know the difference between

$$(-3)^2 \text{ and } -3^2$$

Order of operations (PEMDAS) dictates that parentheses take precedence. So,

$$(-3)^2 = (-3) \cdot (-3) = 9$$

Without parentheses, exponents take precedence:

$$-3^2 = -3 \cdot 3 = -9$$

The negative is not applied until the exponent operation is carried through. Make sure you understand this so you don't make this common mistake. Sometimes, the result turns out to be the same, as in:

$$(-2)^3 \text{ and } -2^3$$

Make sure you understand why they yield the same result.

EXAMPLE 1: $4x^3 \cdot 5x^5$ is equivalent to:

A. $9x^2$ **B.** $9x^8$ **C.** $9x^{15}$ **D.** $20x^8$ **E.** $20x^{15}$

We multiply the coefficients and add the exponents:

$$4x^3 \cdot 5x^5 = 20x^8$$

Answer (D).

EXAMPLE 2: For all nonzero values of x, $\dfrac{12x^6 - 8x^3}{4x^3} = ?$

A. $3x^2 - 2x$ **B.** $3x^2 - 2$ **C.** $-5x^3$ **D.** $3x^3 - 2x$ **E.** $3x^3 - 2$

First, we split the fraction into two. Then, we divide the coefficients and subtract the exponents.

$$\frac{12x^6 - 8x^3}{4x^3} = \frac{12x^6}{4x^3} - \frac{8x^3}{4x^3} = 3x^3 - 2$$

Answer (E).

EXAMPLE 3: Which of the following expressions is equivalent to $(4x^2)^3$?

A. $4x^5$ **B.** $4x^6$ **C.** $16x^5$ **D.** $16x^6$ **E.** $64x^6$

The exponent of 3 applies to both the 4 and the x^2.

$$(4x^2)^3 = 4^3 \cdot (x^2)^3 = 64x^6$$

Answer (E).

Square roots are just fractional exponents:

$$x^{\frac{1}{2}} = \sqrt{x}$$

$$x^{\frac{1}{3}} = \sqrt[3]{x}$$

But what about $x^{\frac{2}{3}}$? The 2 on top means to square x. The 3 on the bottom means to cube root it:

$$\sqrt[3]{x^2}$$

We can see how this works more clearly if we break it down:

$$x^{\frac{2}{3}} = (x^2)^{\frac{1}{3}} = \sqrt[3]{x^2}$$

The order in which we do the squaring and the cube-rooting doesn't matter.

$$x^{\frac{2}{3}} = (x^{\frac{1}{3}})^2 = (\sqrt[3]{x})^2$$

The end result just looks prettier with the cube root on the outside. That way, we don't need the parentheses.

EXAMPLE 4: For positive values of x, which of the following is equivalent to $\sqrt[4]{x^5}$?

A. x **B.** $x^5 - x^4$ **C.** $x^{\frac{5}{4}}$ **D.** $x^{\frac{4}{5}}$ **E.** $\dfrac{x^5}{4}$

The fourth root equates to a fractional exponent of $\dfrac{1}{4}$, so

$$\sqrt[4]{x^5} = (x^5)^{\frac{1}{4}} = x^{\frac{5}{4}}$$

Answer $\boxed{(C)}$.

The ACT will also test you on simplifying square roots (also called "surds"). To simplify a square root, factor the number inside the square root and take out any pairs:

$$\sqrt{48} = \sqrt{2 \cdot 2 \cdot 2 \cdot 2 \cdot 3} = \sqrt{\boxed{2 \cdot 2} \cdot \boxed{2 \cdot 2} \cdot 3} = (2 \cdot 2)\sqrt{3} = 4\sqrt{3}$$

In the example above, we take a 2 out for the first $\boxed{2 \cdot 2}$. Then we take another 2 out for the second $\boxed{2 \cdot 2}$. Finally, we multiply the two 2's outside the square root to get 4. Of course, a quicker route would have looked like this:

$$\sqrt{48} = \sqrt{\boxed{4 \cdot 4} \cdot 3} = 4\sqrt{3}$$

Here's one more example:

$$\sqrt{72} = \sqrt{\boxed{2 \cdot 2} \cdot \boxed{3 \cdot 3} \cdot 2} = (2 \cdot 3)\sqrt{2} = 6\sqrt{2}$$

To go backwards, put the number outside back under the square root as a pair:

$$6\sqrt{2} = \sqrt{6 \cdot 6 \cdot 2} = \sqrt{72}$$

EXAMPLE 5: Which of the following is a simplified form of $\sqrt{72} + \sqrt{18}$?

A. $3\sqrt{6}$ **B.** $3\sqrt{10}$ **C.** $9\sqrt{2}$ **D.** $9\sqrt{10}$ **E.** $12\sqrt{3}$

Square roots cannot be added unless the numbers under them are the same, so the following is WRONG:

$$\sqrt{72} + \sqrt{18} = \sqrt{90}$$

Instead, first simplify each square root individually.

$$\sqrt{72} + \sqrt{18} = \sqrt{6 \cdot 6 \cdot 2} + \sqrt{3 \cdot 3 \cdot 2} = 6\sqrt{2} + 3\sqrt{2}$$

Now that each term has a $\sqrt{2}$ in common, we can add them. It's no different than adding $6x$ and $3x$. You can think of the $\sqrt{2}$ as x.

$$6\sqrt{2} + 3\sqrt{2} = 9\sqrt{2}$$

Answer $\boxed{(C)}$.

EXAMPLE 6: If j and k are positive integers such that $3^j = 9^{k+1}$, which of the following relationships holds between j and k ?

A. $2j = k+1$ **B.** $j = 2k+1$ **C.** $j = 2k+2$ **D.** $j = 3k+3$ **E.** $j = 9k+9$

To find the relationship between j and k, we have to first come up with a relationship between the exponents, which we can equate only if the two terms have the same base. Fortunately, 9 is just 3^2, which gives us a nice substitution we can use:

$$3^j = 9^{k+1}$$
$$3^j = (3^2)^{k+1}$$
$$3^j = 3^{2k+2}$$
$$j = 2k+2$$

Answer $\boxed{(C)}$.

CHAPTER EXERCISE: Answers for this chapter start on page 207.

1. $-5a^2b^3 \cdot -3a^2b$ is equivalent to:

   A. $-15a^4b^3$
   B. $-8a^4b^3$
   C. $-8a^4b^4$
   D. $15a^4b^3$
   E. $15a^4b^4$

2. Which of the following expressions is equivalent to $(2ab^3)(3a^7b^2)$?

   A. $5a^7b^6$
   B. $5a^8b^5$
   C. $6a^7b^5$
   D. $6a^7b^6$
   E. $6a^8b^5$

3. For any nonzero value of x, $(x^4)^{-3} = $?

   A. $\dfrac{1}{x^{12}}$
   B. $\dfrac{1}{x}$
   C. x^7
   D. x^{12}
   E. x^{64}

4. In a given month in 2015, the population of the state of Texas was estimated to be 26,962,481. Which of the following values is closest to this estimate?

   A. 2.7×10^6
   B. 2.6×10^7
   C. 2.7×10^7
   D. 2.6×10^8
   E. 2.7×10^8

5. Which of the following is equivalent to $(-b^6)^{32}$?

   A. $-192b$
   B. $-b^{38}$
   C. b^{38}
   D. $-b^{192}$
   E. b^{192}

6. For all real values of x, which of the following expressions is equal to $x^4 \cdot x^4 \cdot x^4 \cdot x^4$?

   A. x^{16}
   B. x^{256}
   C. $4x^4$
   D. $4x^{16}$
   E. $(4x)^4$

7. Which of the following is a factored form of $6x^3y^2 + 6x^2y^3$?

   A. $6x^3y^3(x^2 + y^2)$
   B. $6x^2y^2(x + y)$
   C. $12x^2y^2(x + y)$
   D. $6x^3y^3$
   E. $12x^5y^5$

8. For which of the following values of b will $\left(-\dfrac{1}{2}\right)^b$ represent a real number greater than 1?

   A. -2
   B. -1
   C. 0
   D. 1
   E. 2

9. If m and n are positive integers such that $(\sqrt{2})^m = 8^n$, what is the value of $\dfrac{m}{n}$?

   A. $\dfrac{1}{6}$
   B. $\dfrac{3}{2}$
   C. 3
   D. 4
   E. 6

10. Which of the following is a simplified form of $\sqrt{75} - \sqrt{12}$?

    A. $-3\sqrt{7}$
    B. $3\sqrt{3}$
    C. $3\sqrt{7}$
    D. $7\sqrt{3}$
    E. $\sqrt{87}$

11. For nonzero $a, b,$ and c, the expression

$\dfrac{a^6 b^4 c}{4a^3 b^7 c^3}$ is equivalent to:

A. $\dfrac{a^3}{4b^3 c^2}$

B. $\dfrac{a^3}{4b^3 c^3}$

C. $\dfrac{a^3 bc}{4ab^3 c^3}$

D. $\dfrac{(abc)^{10}}{(4abc)^{13}}$

E. $4a^9 b^{11} c^4$

12. Which of the following fractions is equal to

$\dfrac{1}{7^{30}} - \dfrac{1}{7^{31}}$?

A. $\dfrac{1}{7^{31}}$

B. $\dfrac{1}{7^{32}}$

C. $\dfrac{1}{7^{60}}$

D. $\dfrac{6}{7^{31}}$

E. $\dfrac{6}{7^{61}}$

14

3

Manipulating and Solving Equations

On the ACT, there will be quite a few questions that involve equations. To get these types of questions right, you must know how to isolate the variables you want. The examples in this chapter will show you several key techniques.

EXAMPLE 1: If $x = \frac{1}{2}z$ and $3y = 5z$, which of the following relationships holds between x and y for each nonzero value of z ?

A. $2x = 15y$ **B.** $3x = 10y$ **C.** $5x = 6y$ **D.** $6x = 5y$ **E.** $10x = 3y$

Our overall strategy will be to isolate z in the first equation so we can substitute for z in the second equation. Doing so allows us to see how x and y relate without z getting in the way. First, multiply both sides of the first equation by 2,

$$2x = z$$

Substituting for z in the second equation,

$$3y = 5(2x) = 10x$$

Therefore, $10x = 3y$. Answer $\boxed{(E)}$.

EXAMPLE 2: Whenever $\sqrt{x} - y = 1$ for positive values of x, which of the following equations gives x in terms of y ?

A. $x = 1 - y^2$ **B.** $x = 1 + y^2$ **C.** $x = (1 + y)^2$ **D.** $x = (1 - y)^2$ **E.** $x = y^2 - 1$

In this particular example, we know we want to remove the square root, but we can't square both sides just yet. If we did, we would get

$$(\sqrt{x} - y)^2 = 1$$

which only brings us further away from isolating x.

Instead, we have to move the y to the right side first, isolating the square root to one side.

$$\sqrt{x} = 1 + y$$

Now we can square both sides, but watch out! The common mistake is to square each individual element:

$$x = 1^2 + y^2$$

However, this is WRONG. When squaring equations to remove a square root, you must remember that you're not squaring individual elements—you're squaring the entire side. If it helps, wrap each side in parentheses before squaring, like so:

$$(\sqrt{x})^2 = (1 + y)^2$$
$$x = (1 + y)^2$$

Answer $\boxed{(C)}$.

This rule of applying any given operation to the entirety of each side holds true for all operations, including multiplication and division. When you multiply or divide both sides of an equation, what you're actually doing is wrapping each side in parentheses first, but because of the distributive property, it just so happens that multiplying or dividing each individual element gets you the same result. For example, if we had the equation

$$x + 2 = y$$

and we wanted to multiply both sides by 3, what we're actually doing is

$$3(x + 2) = 3(y)$$

which turns out to be the same as

$$3x + 6 = 3y$$

When it comes to taking the square root of an equation, most students forget the plus or minus ($\pm$). Always remember that an equation such as $x^2 = 25$ has two solutions:

$$\sqrt{x^2} = \sqrt{25}$$
$$x = \pm 5$$

However, this only applies when you're taking the square root to **solve an equation**. By definition, square roots always refer to the positive root. So, $\sqrt{9} = 3$, NOT ± 3. And $\sqrt{x} = -3$ is not possible (except when working with non-real numbers, which we'll look at in a future chapter). The plus or minus is only necessary when the square root is used as a tool to solve an equation. That way, we get all the possible solutions.

EXAMPLE 3: If $(x+3)^2 = 121$, what is the sum of the two possible values of x ?

A. -14 B. -6 C. 2 D. 6 E. 8

$$(x+3)^2 = 121$$

$$\sqrt{(x+3)^2} = \pm\sqrt{121}$$

$$x+3 = \pm 11$$

$$x = -3 \pm 11$$

So x could be either 8 or -14. The sum of these two possibilities is -6. Answer $\boxed{(B)}$.

EXAMPLE 4: If $\dfrac{a-b}{a+b} = \dfrac{3}{5}$, which of the following equations gives a in terms of b ?

A. $a = \dfrac{b}{8}$ B. $a = \dfrac{b}{4}$ C. $a = 2b$ D. $a = 4b$ E. $a = 8b$

Whenever a fraction is equal to another fraction (e.g. $\dfrac{a}{b} = \dfrac{c}{d}$), you can cross-multiply: $ad = bc$. So for our example,

$$\frac{a-b}{a+b} = \frac{3}{5}$$

$$5(a-b) = 3(a+b)$$

$$5a - 5b = 3a + 3b$$

$$2a = 8b$$

$$a = 4b$$

Answer $\boxed{(D)}$.

EXAMPLE 5: If $\dfrac{pq}{p+q} = 2$, which of the following equations gives p in terms of q ?

A. $\dfrac{2q}{q-2}$ B. $\dfrac{q}{q-2}$ C. $\dfrac{q-2}{2q}$ D. $\dfrac{q-2}{q}$ E. $2q^2 - 2$

Some equations, like the one in this example, have variables that are tougher to isolate. For these equations, you will have to do some shifting around to factor out the variable you want.

$$\frac{pq}{p+q} = 2$$

$$pq = 2(p+q)$$

$$pq = 2p + 2q$$

$$pq - 2p = 2q$$

$$p(q-2) = 2q$$

$$p = \frac{2q}{q-2}$$

See what we did? We expanded everything out and moved every term containing p to the left side. Then we were able to factor out p and isolate it. The answer is $\boxed{(A)}$.

18

CHAPTER EXERCISE: Answers for this chapter start on page 208.

1. What is the largest value of a for which there exists a real value of b such that $a^2 + b^2 = 64$?

   A. 6
   B. 8
   C. 10
   D. 32
   E. 64

2. If $\dfrac{(x-1)(10-6)}{3(5)} = 2$, then $x = ?$

   A. $4\dfrac{1}{2}$

   B. $5\dfrac{1}{2}$

   C. $6\dfrac{1}{2}$

   D. $7\dfrac{1}{2}$

   E. $8\dfrac{1}{2}$

3. For all nonzero values of a, b, and c, which of the following is the solution for x of the equation $b - ax = c$?

   A. $\dfrac{b+c}{a}$

   B. $\dfrac{c}{a} - b$

   C. $b - \dfrac{c}{a}$

   D. $\dfrac{b-c}{a}$

   E. $\dfrac{c-b}{a}$

4. If x and y are positive integers and $x - y = 7$, what is the least possible value of xy ?

   A. 7
   B. 8
   C. 9
   D. 12
   E. 18

5. If $7 + (x - 7) = 7 - (7 + y)$ and $y \neq 0$, what is the value of $\dfrac{x}{y}$?

   A. -1
   B. 0
   C. 1
   D. 7
   E. 14

6. For what value of x is the equation $5.7x + 8.85 = 1.02 - 3.3x$ true?

   A. -3.26
   B. -0.87
   C. 0.87
   D. 3.26
   E. 8.7

7. What value of a will make the equation $\dfrac{3-a}{4-a} = \dfrac{3}{5}$ true?

   A. $-\dfrac{3}{2}$

   B. $-\dfrac{2}{3}$

   C. $-\dfrac{3}{8}$

   D. $\dfrac{2}{3}$

   E. $\dfrac{3}{2}$

8. If $\dfrac{a}{b} = \dfrac{3}{4}$ and $\dfrac{b}{c} = \dfrac{8}{9}$, then $\dfrac{c}{a} = ?$

   A. $\dfrac{2}{3}$

   B. $\dfrac{27}{32}$

   C. $\dfrac{32}{27}$

   D. $\dfrac{3}{2}$

   E. 3

9. What are the possible values of x such that $xy^2 = 48$, and x and y are integers?

    A. $2, 3$
    B. $2, 4$
    C. $1, 12, 48$
    D. $3, 12, 48$
    E. $1, 3, 12, 48$

10. For positive real numbers x, y, and z such that $5x = 2y$ and $\frac{1}{6}y = \frac{2}{3}z$, which of the following inequalities is true?

    A. $z < x < y$
    B. $x < z < y$
    C. $z < y < x$
    D. $x < y < z$
    E. $y < x < z$

11. If $\dfrac{x + 2y}{3x - y} = \dfrac{4}{3}$, then $\dfrac{x}{y} = ?$

    A. $\dfrac{1}{5}$
    B. $\dfrac{2}{15}$
    C. $\dfrac{2}{9}$
    D. $\dfrac{2}{3}$
    E. $\dfrac{10}{9}$

Expressions

Algebraic expressions are just combinations of numbers and variables. Both $x^2 + y$ and $\dfrac{3m - k}{2}$ are examples of expressions. In this chapter, we'll cover some fundamental techniques that will allow you to deal with questions involving expressions quickly and effectively.

1. Combining Like Terms

When combining like terms, the most important mistake to avoid is putting terms together that look like they can go together but can't. For example, you cannot combine $b^2 + b$ to make b^3, nor can you combine $a + ab$ to make $2ab$. To add or subtract, the variables have to match completely.

EXAMPLE 1: What is the sum of the 3 binomials listed below?

$$x^2 - 5x, \ 3x^2 + x, \ -2x - 3$$

A. $3x^2 - 2x - 3$ **B.** $4x^2 - 2x - 3$ **C.** $4x^2 - 6x - 3$ **D.** $3x^4 - 6x^3 - 3$ **E.** $4x^4 - 6x^3 - 3$

Handle the x^2 terms separately from the x terms.

$$(x^2 - 5x) + (3x^2 + x) + (-2x - 3) = 4x^2 - 6x - 3$$

Answer $\boxed{(C)}$.

2. Expansion and Factoring

EXAMPLE 2: Which of the following expressions is equivalent to $-(3x+5)(2x-3)$?

A. $-7x+15$ **B.** $-7x+3$ **C.** $-6x^2+15$ **D.** $-6x^2-x+15$ **E.** $-6x^2-10x+15$

Some people like to expand using a method called FOIL (first, outer, inner, last). If you haven't heard of it, that's totally fine. After all, it's the same thing as distributing each term. Instead of handling the negative at the end, we'll distribute it upfront.

$$-(3x+5)(2x-3) = (-3x-5)(2x-3)$$

Notice that the negative is applied to just one of the two factors. Either one is fine, but NOT both.

$$(-3x-5)(2x-3) = -6x^2+9x-10x+15 = -6x^2-x+15$$

Answer $\boxed{(D)}$.

EXAMPLE 3: The expression $2x^2-x-6$ is equivalent to:

A. $(2x-3)(x-2)$ **B.** $(2x-3)(x+2)$ **C.** $(2x+3)(x-2)$ **D.** $2(x+3)(x-1)$

E. $2(x-3)(x+1)$

A complete review of factoring is beyond the scope of this book, but no matter what method you use, it will require some trial and error. We know the result will be of the form $(ax+b)(cx+d)$. For a and c, we only have the factors 1 and 2 to work with. For b and d, we have the factors 1 and 6, 2 and 3, and a negative to work with.

After a little trial and error, you should be able to get $(2x+3)(x-2)$. Answer $\boxed{(C)}$. If you want to double check, you can expand this factored form to see if you get the original expression.

When it comes to factoring and expansion, there are several key formulas you should know:

- $(a+b)^2 = a^2 + 2ab + b^2$
- $(a-b)^2 = a^2 - 2ab + b^2$
- $a^2 - b^2 = (a+b)(a-b)$

Memorizing these forwards and backwards will really help.

EXAMPLE 4: For $x^2 \neq 4$, $\dfrac{x^2 - 4}{x^2 - 4x + 4} = ?$

A. $x - 2$ B. $x + 2$ C. $\dfrac{1}{x - 2}$ D. $\dfrac{x - 2}{x + 2}$ E. $\dfrac{x + 2}{x - 2}$

Using the formula $a^2 - b^2 = (a + b)(a - b)$ gives $x^2 - 4 = (x + 2)(x - 2)$. Factoring $x^2 - 4x + 4$ gives $(x - 2)^2$ (the second formula, backwards). Therefore,

$$\frac{x^2 - 4}{x^2 - 4x + 4} = \frac{(x + 2)(x - 2)}{(x - 2)^2} = \frac{x + 2}{x - 2}$$

Answer $\boxed{(E)}$.

3. Combining Fractions

When you're adding simple fractions,

$$\frac{1}{3} + \frac{1}{4}$$

the first step is to find the least common multiple of the denominators. We do this so that we can get a common denominator. In a lot of cases, it's just the product of the denominators, as it is here, $3 \times 4 = 12$.

$$\frac{1}{3} + \frac{1}{4} = \left(\frac{1}{3} \cdot \frac{4}{4}\right) + \left(\frac{1}{4} \cdot \frac{3}{3}\right) = \frac{4}{12} + \frac{3}{12} = \frac{7}{12}$$

Now when we're adding fractions with expressions in the denominator, the idea is the same.

EXAMPLE 5: Which of the following is the least common denominator for $\dfrac{1}{x^2 - 1} + \dfrac{1}{3x + 3}$?

A. $(x + 1)$ B. $3(x - 1)$ C. $(x + 1)(x - 1)$ D. $3(x + 1)(x - 1)$ E. $3(x + 1)^2(x - 1)$

First, let's factor each denominator:

$$\frac{1}{x^2 - 1} + \frac{1}{3x + 3} = \frac{1}{(x + 1)(x - 1)} + \frac{1}{3(x + 1)}$$

As you can see, both fractions have $(x + 1)$ in common. When things are in common, you go with the highest power. Since $(x + 1)$ is raised to the power of 1 in both fractions, our least common denominator will only need one $(x + 1)$, one $(x - 1)$, and one "3". Putting these terms all together, we get $3(x + 1)(x - 1)$. Answer $\boxed{(D)}$.

To actually add the two fractions, multiply the top and bottom of each fraction by the factors they need to get the denominator above.

$$\frac{1}{(x + 1)(x - 1)} + \frac{1}{3(x + 1)} = \frac{1}{(x + 1)(x - 1)} \cdot \frac{3}{3} + \frac{1}{3(x + 1)} \cdot \frac{(x - 1)}{(x - 1)}$$

$$= \frac{3}{3(x + 1)(x - 1)} + \frac{(x - 1)}{3(x + 1)(x - 1)} = \frac{3 + x - 1}{3(x + 1)(x - 1)} = \frac{x + 2}{3(x + 1)(x - 1)}$$

4. Splitting fractions

EXAMPLE 6: For all x, $\dfrac{12x^2 + 3}{3} = ?$

A. $4x^2$ **B.** $4x^2 + 1$ **C.** $4x^2 + 3$ **D.** $12x^2$ **E.** $12x^2 + 1$

We can split the fraction into two:

$$\frac{12x^2 + 3}{3} = \frac{12x^2}{3} + \frac{3}{3} = 4x^2 + 1$$

Answer (B) . This is just the reverse of adding fractions.

Note that while you can split up the numerators of fractions, you cannot do so with denominators. So,

$$\frac{3}{x + y} \neq \frac{3}{x} + \frac{3}{y}$$

In fact, you cannot break up a fraction like $\dfrac{3}{x + y}$ any further.

5. Modeling Real-Life Scenarios

On the ACT, you'll get at least one or two questions asking you to represent a "real-life" calculation as an expression. These questions aren't hard. The key is to walk through them one step at a time, thinking in terms of numbers instead of variables if it helps.

EXAMPLE 7: James had c cookies. He received 12 more cookies as a gift. He then gave 18 cookies away to his coworkers. James now decides to package his cookies by dividing them evenly among 6 boxes. Which of the following expressions gives the number of cookies in each box?

A. $(c + 12) - 18 \div 6$ **B.** $c + (12 - 18) \div 6$ **C.** $c + 12 - (18 \div 6)$ **D.** $c + (12 - 18 \div 6)$

E. $(c + 12 - 18) \div 6$

When James receives 12 more cookies, his total cookie count is $c + 12$. When he gives 18 away, the total count is then $c + 12 - 18$. Finally, there are 6 boxes so we divide by 6 to get the number of cookies in each box:

$$(c + 12 - 18) \div 6$$

Answer (E) . Note that answer A, in which only the 18 would have been divided by 6, is not the same as answer E. The placement of the parentheses, as you may remember from order of operations, does matter.

CHAPTER EXERCISE: Answers for this chapter start on page 210.

1. Which of the following expressions is equivalent to $x(3 - x) - 4(x + 2)$?

   A. $-2x^3 - 8$
   B. $-x^2 - x - 8$
   C. $-x^2 - x + 2$
   D. $-2x - 8$
   E. $-2x + 2$

2. When $(x - 1)(x + 2)(x - 3)(x + 4)(x - 5)$ is expanded and all like terms are combined, the terms of the resulting expression are ordered in descending powers of x. What are the first term and the last term of the expression?

   A. First term: $5x$, Last term: -3
   B. First term: $5x$, Last term: -120
   C. First term: x^5, Last term: -120
   D. First term: x^5, Last term: -3
   E. First term: x^5, Last term: 120

3. What is the result of the subtraction problem below?

$$\begin{array}{rrrr} (& 4x^2 & - & 3x & + & 7) \\ -(- & 2x^2 & + & 5x & - & 3) \end{array}$$

   A. $2x^2 + 2x + 4$
   B. $2x^2 - 8x + 10$
   C. $6x^2 + 2x + 4$
   D. $6x^2 - 8x + 4$
   E. $6x^2 - 8x + 10$

4. Whenever $x \neq 2$, $\dfrac{2x^2 - 3x - 2}{x - 2} = ?$

   A. $x - 4$
   B. $x + 2$
   C. $2x - 2$
   D. $2x + 1$
   E. $2x^2 + 1$

5. At John's Hot Dog Stand, the total cost of production consists of an operational cost of $250 per day, plus a food cost of $1.25 per hot dog sold. For a day when the total cost of production was d dollars, which of the following expressions gives the number of hot dogs sold that day?

   A. $0.8d - 200$
   B. $200 - 0.8d$
   C. $250 + 1.25d$
   D. $250 - 1.25d$
   E. $1.25d - 250$

6. Jane used a coupon to buy a book for D dollars less than the retail price of R. The discounted price that Jane paid represents what fraction of the retail price of the book?

   A. $\dfrac{D}{R}$
   B. $\dfrac{R}{D}$
   C. $\dfrac{R - D}{D}$
   D. $\dfrac{R - D}{R}$
   E. $\dfrac{D - R}{R}$

7. Given the equations $M = 3 - x$ and $y = N + 4$, which of the following expressions is equivalent to $M - N$ written in terms of x and y ?

   A. $-x - y - 1$
   B. $-x - y + 1$
   C. $-x - y + 7$
   D. $-x + y - 1$
   E. $-x + y + 7$

8. Which of the following expressions is equivalent to $(3x - 1)(-x - 4)$?

   A. $(-3x + 1)(x + 4)$
   B. $(-3x + 1)(-x - 4)$
   C. $(3x + 1)(x + 4)$
   D. $(3x - 1)(x + 4)$
   E. $(3x - 1)(x - 4)$

9. Whenever $x \neq 3$, $\dfrac{4x^2 + 4x - 8}{2x + 4} = ?$

    A. $(x - 2)$
    B. $(x - 1)$
    C. $2(x - 2)$
    D. $2(x - 1)$
    E. $2(x + 1)$

10. For a given show, a theater charges $80 for a premium ticket and $30 for a regular ticket. If a total of n tickets were sold and p of them were premium tickets, what is the total amount, in dollars, from the sale of regular tickets and premium tickets?

    A. $30n + 50p$
    B. $30n + 80p$
    C. $30n + 110p$
    D. $50n + 30p$
    E. $110np$

5

Numbers and Operations

Numbers and operations questions test you on arithmetic and problem solving without the use of algebra. These are questions that you have to get right since they cover math fundamentals that are relatively straightforward.

For example, what's the difference between $\dfrac{\frac{1}{2}}{3}$ and $\dfrac{1}{\frac{2}{3}}$?

The difference is the placement of the longer fraction line. The first is $\frac{1}{2}$ divided by 3. The second is 1 divided by $\frac{2}{3}$. They're not the same.

$$\frac{\frac{1}{2}}{3} = \frac{1}{2} \div 3 = \frac{1}{2} \times \frac{1}{3} = \frac{1}{6}$$

$$\frac{1}{\frac{2}{3}} = 1 \div \frac{2}{3} = 1 \times \frac{3}{2} = \frac{3}{2}$$

One shortcut is to flip the fraction when it is in the denominator. So,

$$\frac{a}{\frac{b}{c}} = \frac{ac}{b}$$

When the fraction is in the numerator, the following occurs:

$$\frac{\frac{a}{b}}{c} = \frac{a}{bc}$$

27

EXAMPLE 1: $\dfrac{\frac{1}{2}}{\frac{1}{3}+\frac{1}{4}} = ?$

A. $\dfrac{1}{14}$ B. $\dfrac{1}{6}$ C. $\dfrac{6}{7}$ D. $\dfrac{7}{6}$ E. $\dfrac{7}{2}$

First, add the two fractions in the denominator.

$$\frac{\frac{1}{2}}{\frac{1}{3}+\frac{1}{4}} = \frac{\frac{1}{2}}{\frac{4}{12}+\frac{3}{12}} = \frac{\frac{1}{2}}{\frac{7}{12}} = \frac{1}{2}\cdot\frac{12}{7} = \frac{6}{7}$$

Answer (C). Although you'll be able to use your calculator for these simple types of questions, it's important to understand the underlying concepts for the more advanced algebra questions that can't be solved with a calculator.

EXAMPLE 2: Upon landing in Germany, Pierre rents a phone to use during his stay for 3 days. He has budgeted $40 for the phone rental. Fast Lines Rental charges $8 per day and $0.40 per minute. Talk Europe Rental charges $5 per day and $0.50 per minute. Which company, if either, allows Pierre to talk more during his stay, and how many minutes more?
(Note: Taxes are already included in the charges.)

A. Talk Europe, 10   **B.** Fast Lines, 20   **C.** Talk Europe, 20   **D.** Fast Lines, 10

E. Pierre would get the same maximum number of minutes from each company.

Fast Lines Rental will charge a fixed $8 \times 3 = \$24$ over the 3 days, leaving Pierre with $40 - 24 = \$16$ in his budget. With this amount, he'll be able to talk for $16 \div 0.40 = 40$ minutes.

Talk Europe Rental will charge a fixed $5 \times 3 = \$15$ over the 3 days, leaving Pierre with $40 - 15 = \$25$ in his budget. With this amount, he'll be able to talk for $25 \div 0.50 = 50$ minutes.

Comparing the two companies, Pierre will get $50 - 40 = 10$ more minutes by renting from Talk Europe. Answer (A).

EXAMPLE 3: A catering company needs to make 90 chicken sandwiches for a local event. Each chicken sandwich will contain $\frac{3}{4}$ pounds of chicken. If the catering company buys its chicken in 6-pound packages, what is the minimum number of packages of chicken the company needs to buy for the event?
A. 11   **B.** 12   **C.** 15   **D.** 20   **E.** 21

To make all the sandwiches, the catering company needs $90 \times \frac{3}{4} = 67.5$ pounds of chicken. That's $67.5 \div 6 = 11.25$ packages. Because buying a fraction of a package isn't possible, the company needs to round up and buy 12 whole packages. Answer (B).

EXAMPLE 4: At the printing center, Sara made one copy of a 150-page manuscript and two copies of a 40-page article. She was charged a total of $41.40. If the printing center charges for copies at a fixed rate per page, how much did Sara have to pay to copy the 150-page manuscript?

A. $7.20   **B.** $14.40   **C.** $17.40   **D.** $27.00   **E.** $32.70

Sara copied a total of $150 + 2(40) = 230$ pages, which means she was charged $\frac{41.40}{230} = \$0.18$ per page. To copy just the 150-page manuscript, she had to pay $150 \times 0.18 = \$27.00$. Answer $\boxed{(D)}$.

EXAMPLE 5: Six members of a chess club decide to purchase new chess boards, dividing up the cost equally. Later on, four new members join the club and agree to pay their fair share of the cost, again dividing up the cost equally among all the members. This resulted in a savings of $12 for each of the original six members. What was the cost of the new chess boards, in dollars?

A. $120   **B.** $128   **C.** $144   **D.** $180   **E.** $216

If the original six members saved $12 each, then the total savings were $6 \times 12 = \$72$. That means the four new members must have paid a total of $72—what the original members saved must equal what the new members paid. So each of the four new members paid $72 \div 4 = \$18$. Since all 10 members split the cost evenly, the total cost of the chess boards must have been $18 \times 10 = \$180$. Answer $\boxed{(D)}$.

EXAMPLE 6: Nikolai has 10 matches. Each match, when lit, burns for 2 minutes before going out. Nikolai lights each match 5 seconds apart, from the first match to the tenth. For how long will all ten matches be lit at the same time, in seconds?

A. 60   **B.** 65   **C.** 70   **D.** 75   **E.** 80

The first match will burn out first. It burns out after 2 minutes (120 seconds). So 120 seconds is an upper limit on the time that all ten matches can stay lit. From here, we need to figure out how long it takes to light all ten matches, since that time cuts into the 120 seconds that the first match is lit.

It will take $(10 - 1) \times 5 = 45$ seconds (NOT 50 seconds) to light all ten matches. Why? Because the time starts once the first match is lit. So after 5 seconds, 2 matches are lit. After 10 seconds, 3 matches are lit. After 15 seconds, 4 matches are lit, and so on. After 45 seconds, all matches are lit. Therefore, all ten matches are lit at the same time for $120 - 45 = 75$ seconds. Answer $\boxed{(D)}$.

CHAPTER EXERCISE: Answers for this chapter start on page 211.

1. $\dfrac{16 - 2 \cdot 3}{1 + 4 \cdot \dfrac{1}{6}} = ?$

   A. 6
   B. 12
   C. 15
   D. $25\dfrac{1}{5}$
   E. $50\dfrac{2}{5}$

2. Mark fills up the tank of his car so that it has a total of 22 gallons of gasoline. On the way to work, he uses up $\dfrac{2}{3}$ gallon of gasoline. On the way home, he uses up $1\dfrac{1}{6}$ gallons of gasoline. How many gallons of gasoline are left in the tank at the end of the day?

   A. $1\dfrac{5}{6}$
   B. $20\dfrac{1}{6}$
   C. $20\dfrac{5}{6}$
   D. $21\dfrac{1}{6}$
   E. $21\dfrac{5}{6}$

3. If watermelons sell at $4.29 each or 4 for $14.80, how much is saved, to the nearest cent, on each watermelon by buying them 4 at a time?

   A. 36¢
   B. 43¢
   C. 48¢
   D. 59¢
   E. 68¢

4. $\dfrac{1}{1 + \dfrac{1}{1 + \dfrac{1}{3}}} = ?$

   A. $\dfrac{7}{4}$
   B. $\dfrac{3}{2}$
   C. $\dfrac{4}{3}$
   D. $\dfrac{3}{4}$
   E. $\dfrac{4}{7}$

5. Joey made two trips to the mall on the same day. On the first trip, he gave the cashier $50 and got $12 back in change. On the second trip, he gave the cashier $30 and got back $8 back in change. After these trips, he had $45 left. How many dollars did he have before his trips to the mall?

   A. 55
   B. 67
   C. 86
   D. 105
   E. 117

6. Professor Jones gives his students a 2 minute break between each section of a final exam. If the final exam has 7 sections, how many minutes do the students spend on break during the exam?

   A. 6
   B. 7
   C. 9
   D. 12
   E. 14

7. A lightbulb manufacturer is delivering an order of 6,000 lightbulbs using large boxes and small boxes. A large-size box can fit a maximum of 800 lightbulbs. A small-size box can fit a maximum of 350 lightbulbs. If the manufacturer will use 3 large-size boxes, what is the minimum number of small-size boxes needed to deliver all the lightbulbs?

   A. 10
   B. 11
   C. 12
   D. 13
   E. 14

8. Mark is deciding between two contracting jobs. Job A pays $45 per hour for the first 10 hours worked, and $60 per hour worked thereafter. Job B pays a flat $50 per hour. Mark's goal is to earn $1,350 from his next contracting job. Which job, if either, allows him to work fewer hours to meet his goal, and how many hours fewer?

   A. Job A, 2
   B. Job A, 12
   C. Job B, 2
   D. Job B, 12
   E. Mark would work the same number of hours at either job.

Use the following information to answer questions 9–11.

Sierra and May are planning a Halloween party for their school, and they are taking inventory of the food. The table below gives the numbers of boxes of food. For example, there are 30 boxes with 12 cupcakes in each box, 45 boxes with 8 candy bars in each box, and 25 boxes with 6 cans of soda in each box. All the boxes have been counted except for the 6-item boxes of cookies.

Items	Number of 6-item boxes	Number of 8-item boxes	Number of 12-item boxes
Cupcakes	0	15	30
Candy Bars	0	45	0
Cookies	?	15	5
Cans of Soda	25	0	10

9. Sierra completes the inventory assessment and tells May that the number of cupcakes is the same as the number of cookies. How many 6-item boxes of cookies are in inventory?

   A. 25
   B. 30
   C. 35
   D. 40
   E. 50

10. May takes all of the cans of soda in 6-item boxes and puts them together to make as many 8-item boxes as she can. How many whole 8-item boxes of soda can May make?

   A. 18
   B. 19
   C. 21
   D. 24
   E. 25

11. Sierra bought $\frac{1}{5}$ of the candy bars for $93.60. What was the price of an 8-item box of candy?

   A. $9.80
   B. $10.40
   C. $11.50
   D. $12.20
   E. $13.70

6

Properties of Numbers

Mathematicians use certain terms to describe different types of numbers and their properties. For the ACT, you need to know the following:

- **Whole Numbers:** $0, 1, 2, 3, \ldots$

- **Integers:** $\ldots, -3, -2, -1, 0, 1, 2, 3, \ldots$

- **Primes:** Numbers that are only divisible by 1 and itself $(2, 3, 5, 7, 11, \ldots)$

- **Positive** numbers are greater than 0. **Negative** numbers are less than 0. Zero is neither positive nor negative.

- **Even** numbers are divisible by 2. **Odd** numbers are not. Is zero even? You betcha.

- **Factor:** A number that divides another number evenly without a remainder. The factors of 12 are 1, 2, 3, 4, 6, and 12.

- The **Multiples** of 6 include $6, 12, 18, 24, 30, \ldots$

- **Least Common Multiple (LCM):** The lowest multiple that two or more numbers have in common. The least common multiple of 2 and 3 is 6. The least common multiple of 12 and 16 is 48. The least common multiple of 4 and 8 is 8.

- **Undefined:** A way of describing a mathematically meaningless operation (e.g. $\frac{3}{0}$ or $\log 0$)

- **Scientific Notation:** A compact way of expressing very large or very small numbers. When converting numbers to scientific notation, the decimal point should be moved until the leading number is between 1 and 10 (e.g. 2.8×10^{11}, NOT 28×10^{10}).

- **Rational:** Any number that can be expressed as a fraction of integers. Note that 0 is rational because it can be expressed as $\frac{0}{2}$, for example. However, $\frac{2}{0}$ is undefined: it's neither rational nor irrational because it's not even a number.

- **Irrational:** Any number that cannot be expressed as a fraction of integers (e.g. $\pi, \sqrt{2}, \sqrt{3}, \ldots$).

- **Real:** All rational and irrational numbers.

- **Complex/Imaginary:** Any expression involving the square root of a negative number (we'll cover these in the next chapter).

You also need to know your digits:

$$1 \ 2 \ 3 \ . \ 4 \ 5 \ 6$$

hundreds   tens   units/ones   tenths   hundredths   thousandths

---

EXAMPLE 1: The number 8 has exactly four different factors: 1, 2, 4, and 8. How many different factors does the number 54 have?

A. 2   **B.** 4   **C.** 6   **D.** 8   **E.** 10

There are 8 factors: 1, 2, 3, 6, 9, 18, 27, 54. Answer (D).

EXAMPLE 2: What is the least common multiple of 6, 9, and 12?

A. 3   **B.** 12   **C.** 24   **D.** 36   **E.** 72

An easy way of doing this question is to just test each answer choice. Start with the smaller answer choices and work your way up (i.e. from A to E). The first one that's divisible by 6, 9, and 12 will be the answer.

Another way is to first get the LCM of 6 and 9 by listing out their multiples until you find one in common: 18. Then get the LCM of 18 and 12 the same way to arrive at the answer: 36.

Lastly, a more mathematical way of finding the LCM is to prime-factorize each number and multiply all the factors with the highest power:

$$6 = 2 \cdot 3$$
$$9 = \boxed{3^2}$$
$$12 = \boxed{2^2} \cdot 3$$
$$\text{LCM} = 2^2 \cdot 3^2 = 4 \cdot 9 = 36$$

In any case, the answer is (D).

EXAMPLE 3: The mass of Asteroid X is 710,000,000,000,000 tons. In scientific notation, what is the mass, in tons, of Asteroid X?

A. 7.1×10^{-14} **B.** 7.1×10^{-13} **C.** 7.1×10^{12} **D.** 7.1×10^{13} **E.** 7.1×10^{14}

In scientific notation, we want the leading number to be between 1 and 10. So in this case, the leading number must be 7.1. That requires moving the decimal point 14 digits to the left. To compensate for this move, we have to multiply by 10^{14}. Answer (E).

EXAMPLE 4: Which of the following inequalities gives the 4 numbers $1\frac{3}{8}, 1.41, \sqrt{2}$ and $\frac{4}{3}$ in decreasing order?

A. $\sqrt{2} > 1.41 > 1\frac{3}{8} > \frac{4}{3}$ **B.** $\sqrt{2} > 1.41 > \frac{4}{3} > 1\frac{3}{8}$ **C.** $\frac{4}{3} > 1\frac{3}{8} > 1.41 > \sqrt{2}$

D. $1.41 > \sqrt{2} > 1\frac{3}{8} > \frac{4}{3}$ **E.** $1.41 > \sqrt{2} > \frac{4}{3} > 1\frac{3}{8}$

The best way of doing this type of question is to convert everything into decimals:

$$1\frac{3}{8} = 1.375, \quad 1.41, \quad \sqrt{2} \approx 1.4142, \quad \frac{4}{3} \approx 1.3333$$

Now we can clearly see that

$$\sqrt{2} > 1.41 > 1\frac{3}{8} > \frac{4}{3}$$

Answer $\boxed{(A)}$.

EXAMPLE 5: Given that $0 < x < y < z$, which of the following is the largest?

A. $\dfrac{x}{y+z}$ **B.** $\dfrac{z}{x+y}$ **C.** $\dfrac{y+z}{x}$ **D.** $\dfrac{x+z}{y}$ **E.** $\dfrac{x+y}{z}$

We produce the largest fraction by making the numerator (top) as large as possible and the denominator (bottom) as small as possible. Therefore, we want y and z on top and x on the bottom. Answer $\boxed{(C)}$.

This example illustrates a pretty important rule that you should know:

For any fraction, the larger the numerator is, the larger the value of the fraction. The larger the denominator is, the smaller the value of the fraction.

Make sure you understand why this is true.

EXAMPLE 6: What percent of the *even* numbers from 10 to 58, inclusive, have a tens digit that is 1 more than the units digit?

A. 5%   B. 8%   C. 10%   D. 16%   E. 20%

First, how many even numbers are there from 10 to 58? Let's list a few out.

$$10, 12, 14, \ldots, 56, 58$$

Notice that we can divide every number by 2 to get

$$5, 6, 7, \ldots, 28, 29$$

So the question becomes *how many numbers are there from 5 to 29?* The answer is $29 - 5 + 1 = 25$. Why did we add the one? Well, try figuring out how many numbers there are from 1 to 10 and see for yourself.

So there are 25 even numbers from 10 to 58. How many of them have a tens digit that is 1 more than the units digit? We can list all of them out pretty easily:

$$10, 21, 32, 43, 54$$

There are 5 of them. Therefore, the percentage is $\dfrac{5}{25} \times 100 = 20\%$. Answer $\boxed{(E)}$.

CHAPTER EXERCISE: Answers for this chapter start on page 212.

1. A positive integer is multiplied by 6, and the product is multiplied by 4. Which of the following numbers could be the result after the second multiplication?

   A. 540
   B. 552
   C. 564
   D. 588
   E. 612

2. Which of the following accurately describes the decimal representation of 4.6×10^{-80}?

   A. a decimal point, followed by 79 zeros, then the digits 4 and 6.
   B. a decimal point, followed by 80 zeros, then the digits 4 and 6.
   C. a decimal point, followed by 81 zeros, then the digits 4 and 6.
   D. a negative sign, followed by the digits 4 and 6, then 79 zeros, then a decimal point.
   E. a negative sign, followed by the digits 4 and 6, then 80 zeros, then a decimal point.

3. What is the least common denominator of the fractions $\dfrac{7}{24}, \dfrac{5}{9}, \dfrac{1}{4}$?

   A. 48
   B. 72
   C. 96
   D. 108
   E. 144

4. A number z is produced by multiplying x, which is divisible by 10, and y, which is divisible by 15. All of the following whole numbers must be factors of z EXCEPT:

   A. 2
   B. 3
   C. 6
   D. 20
   E. 30

5. Which of the following inequalities is true for the fractions $\dfrac{5}{9}, \dfrac{4}{7}$, and $\dfrac{6}{11}$?

   A. $\dfrac{4}{7} < \dfrac{5}{9} < \dfrac{6}{11}$
   B. $\dfrac{4}{7} < \dfrac{6}{11} < \dfrac{5}{9}$
   C. $\dfrac{5}{9} < \dfrac{6}{11} < \dfrac{4}{7}$
   D. $\dfrac{6}{11} < \dfrac{4}{7} < \dfrac{5}{9}$
   E. $\dfrac{6}{11} < \dfrac{5}{9} < \dfrac{4}{7}$

6. There are three alarm bells. The first alarm bell rings every 6 minutes, the second rings every 8 minutes, and the third rings every 10 minutes. At a certain instant, the 3 alarm bells ring at the same time. How many minutes elapse until the 3 alarm bells next ring at the same time?

   A. 60
   B. 90
   C. 120
   D. 160
   E. 480

7. Which of the following inequalities orders $0.4\overline{23}, 0.4\overline{23}, 0.42\overline{3}$ from smallest to largest? (Note: In this notation, the bar over a digit or block of digits indicates that the digit or block of digits repeats endlessly.)

   A. $0.42\overline{3} < 0.4\overline{23} < 0.\overline{423}$
   B. $0.42\overline{3} < 0.\overline{423} < 0.4\overline{23}$
   C. $0.4\overline{23} < 0.42\overline{3} < 0.\overline{423}$
   D. $0.4\overline{23} < 0.\overline{423} < 0.42\overline{3}$
   E. $0.\overline{423} < 0.42\overline{3} < 0.4\overline{23}$

8. If a and b are real numbers such that $6 \le a \le 18$ and $3 \le b \le 6$, then the maximum value of $\dfrac{a}{b}$ is:

   A. 2
   B. 3
   C. 4
   D. 6
   E. 9

9. There are 1,000,000 microseconds in a second. In scientific notation, 21.6 microseconds is equivalent to how many seconds?

    A. 2.16×10^{-7}
    B. 2.16×10^{-6}
    C. 2.16×10^{-5}
    D. 2.16×10^{6}
    E. 2.16×10^{7}

10. Given that x and $\dfrac{5 - x^2}{2}$ are integers, which of the following statements about x *must* be true?

    A. x is odd
    B. x is even
    C. x is divisible by 5.
    D. x is positive.
    E. x is negative.

11. Let $a < 0 < b < c < d$ be true for integers $a, b, c,$ and d. Which of the following expressions has the greatest value?

    A. $\dfrac{b}{d}$
    B. $\dfrac{c}{b}$
    C. $\dfrac{c}{d}$
    D. $\dfrac{d}{a}$
    E. $\dfrac{d}{b}$

12. The least common multiple (LCM) of 2 numbers is 96. The greater of the 2 numbers is 32. What is the greatest possible value of the other number?

    A. 3
    B. 6
    C. 16
    D. 24
    E. 28

13. A positive integer n is less than 500 and is a multiple of 10. When $\dfrac{n}{500}$ is written as a decimal number, what is the minimum number of digits to the right of the decimal point?

    A. 1
    B. 2
    C. 3
    D. 4
    E. 5

14.
$$\{2, 3, 4, 5\}$$

How many positive integers less than 600 are divisible by every number in the set above?

    A. 9
    B. 10
    C. 11
    D. 12
    E. 13

15. Suppose that x is a real number and $\dfrac{1}{x}$ is a rational number. Which of the following could be the value of x?

    I. 0
    II. $\sqrt{5}$
    III. -1

    A. None
    B. III only
    C. I and II only
    D. II and III only
    E. I, II, and III

Complex Numbers

What value of x satisfies $x^2 = -1$? There were no values until mathematicians invented the imaginary number i, which represents $\sqrt{-1}$. They defined i^2 to equal -1, and from there, any other power of i can be derived.

$$i^2 = -1$$
$$i^3 = -i$$
$$i^4 = 1$$
$$i^5 = i$$
$$i^6 = -1$$
$$i^7 = -i$$
$$i^8 = 1$$

The results repeat in cycles of 4. You can use the fact that $i^4 = 1$ to simplify higher powers of i. For example,

$$i^{50} = (i^4)^{12} \times i^2 = 1 \times i^2 = -1$$

When i is used in an expression like $3 + 2i$, the expression is called a **complex number**. We add, subtract, multiply, and divide complex numbers much like we would algebraic expressions.

EXAMPLE 1: Which of the following complex numbers is a sum of $\sqrt{-2}$ and $\sqrt{-8}$?

  A. $4i$ **B.** $10i$ **C.** $2i\sqrt{2}$ **D.** $3i\sqrt{2}$ **E.** $4i\sqrt{2}$

$$\sqrt{-2} = \sqrt{2} \cdot \sqrt{-1} = i\sqrt{2}$$
$$\sqrt{-8} = \sqrt{8} \cdot \sqrt{-1} = \sqrt{8} \cdot i = 2\sqrt{2} \cdot i = 2i\sqrt{2}$$

Therefore, $\sqrt{-2} + \sqrt{-8} = i\sqrt{2} + 2i\sqrt{2} = 3i\sqrt{2}$. Answer $\boxed{(D)}$. In these arithmetic operations, you can think of i almost like a variable.

EXAMPLE 2: Which of the following complex numbers is equal to $(3 + 5i) - (2 - 3i)$?

   A. $9i$ **B.** $1 - 2i$ **C.** $1 + 2i$ **D.** $1 + 8i$ **E.** $5 + 8i$

Just expand and combine like terms.

$$(3 + 5i) - (2 - 3i) = 3 + 5i - 2 + 3i = 1 + 8i$$

Answer $\boxed{(D)}$.

EXAMPLE 3: Which of the following complex numbers is a product of $4 + i$ and $5 - 2i$?

   A. $18 - 3i$ **B.** $22 - 3i$ **C.** $18 + 3i$ **D.** $22 + 3i$ **E.** 22

Expanding,

$$(4 + i)(5 - 2i) = 20 - 8i + 5i - 2i^2 = 20 - 3i + 2 = 22 - 3i$$

Answer $\boxed{(B)}$.

EXAMPLE 4: Which of the following complex numbers is equal to $\dfrac{2 + 3i}{1 + i}$?

   A. $\dfrac{1}{2} - \dfrac{1}{2}i$ **B.** $\dfrac{1}{2} + \dfrac{1}{2}i$ **C.** $\dfrac{5}{2} - \dfrac{1}{2}i$ **D.** $\dfrac{5}{2} + \dfrac{1}{2}i$ **E.** 5

When you're faced with a fraction containing i in the denominator, multiply both the top and the bottom of the fraction by the **conjugate** of the denominator. What is the conjugate, you ask? Well, the conjugate of $1 + i$ is $1 - i$. The conjugate of $5 - 4i$ is $5 + 4i$. To get the conjugate, simply reverse the sign in between. As we'll soon see, **multiplying a complex number by its conjugate always produces a number that's real instead of imaginary**.

In this example, we multiply the top and the bottom by the conjugate $1 - i$.

$$\frac{(2 + 3i)}{(1 + i)} \cdot \frac{(1 - i)}{(1 - i)} = \frac{2 - 2i + 3i - 3i^2}{1 - i + i - i^2} = \frac{2 + i - 3i^2}{1 - i^2} = \frac{5 + i}{2} = \frac{5}{2} + \frac{1}{2}i$$

Notice that the denominators are now real numbers—i is no longer in the bottom of any fraction. That only happens when we multiply the original denominator by its conjugate, and the absence of i in the denominator is a good indicator that we did everything correctly. The answer is $\boxed{(D)}$.

You'll see complex numbers on at most one question of the exam, but sometimes that's all that separates great scores from the merely good ones. Fully understanding this chapter will ensure that you don't miss out on any easy points.

CHAPTER EXERCISE: Answers for this chapter start on page 214.

1. The *absolute value* of a complex number $a + bi$, where a and b are real numbers and $i^2 = -1$, is defined by $\sqrt{a^2 + b^2}$. Which of the following has the smallest absolute value?

    A. $-2i$
    B. $3i$
    C. $-1 + i$
    D. $1 + 2i$
    E. $2 - i$

2. The product of the complex number $3 - 5i$ and which of the following complex numbers is a real number?

    A. $-5 - 3i$
    B. $-5 + 3i$
    C. $3 - 5i$
    D. $3 + 5i$
    E. $15i$

3. Which of the following complex numbers equals $(5 + 4i)(\sqrt{2} - 9i)$?

    A. $5\sqrt{2} - 36i$
    B. $5\sqrt{2} + 36$
    C. $(5 + \sqrt{2}) - 5i$
    D. $(5\sqrt{2} - 36) + (4\sqrt{2} - 45)i$
    E. $(5\sqrt{2} + 36) + (4\sqrt{2} - 45)i$

4. Which of the following complex numbers is equal to $\sqrt{-27} - \sqrt{-12}$?

    A. $i\sqrt{3}$
    B. $i\sqrt{15}$
    C. $i\sqrt{39}$
    D. $5i\sqrt{3}$
    E. $15i$

5. Which of the following complex numbers is in the solution set of the equation $(x - 2)^2 = -16$?

    A. $-2 + 4i$
    B. $2 - 2i$
    C. $2 - 4i$
    D. $2 + 16i$
    E. $4 + 4i$

6. The solution set for the equation $(x^2 + 3)(x - 3) = 0$ contains:

    A. 1 positive real number only.
    B. 1 imaginary number and 1 positive real number.
    C. 2 imaginary numbers only.
    D. 2 imaginary numbers and 1 positive real number.
    E. 2 positive and 1 negative real number.

7. Which of the following equations has roots at $\frac{1}{3}$, $-3i$, and $3i$?

    A. $(3x - 1)(x^2 - 9) = 0$
    B. $(3x - 1)(x^2 + 3) = 0$
    C. $(3x - 1)(x^2 + 9) = 0$
    D. $(3x + 1)(x^2 + 3) = 0$
    E. $(3x + 1)(x^2 + 9) = 0$

8. The complex number $a + bi$ is graphed in the complex plane by plotting a along the real axis and b along the imaginary axis. One of the points z_1, z_2, z_3, z_4, and z_5 below represents $3 - 2i$ in the complex plane. Which one?

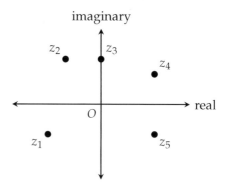

    A. z_1
    B. z_2
    C. z_3
    D. z_4
    E. z_5

9. The solution set for x of the equation $(x-2)^2 = b$ consists of the complex numbers $2 - 5i$ and $2 + 5i$. What is the value of b ?

    A. -25

    B. -10

    C. -5

    D. $\sqrt{5}$

    E. 25

10. Which of the following complex numbers is equal to $\dfrac{1+i}{3-2i}$?

    A. $\dfrac{1}{13} + \dfrac{5}{13}i$

    B. $\dfrac{3}{13} + \dfrac{3}{13}i$

    C. $\dfrac{5}{13} + \dfrac{5}{13}i$

    D. $-2 - i$

    E. $\dfrac{1}{5} + i$

8
Rates

I've found rate problems to be pretty polarizing—some students just "get" them intuitively, others get completely lost. Most of the rate problems on the ACT will be pretty straightforward, but for the ones that aren't, I highly recommend using conversion factors to setup the solution (if you've gone through chemistry, you should know what I'm talking about). Conversion factors are a fool-proof way to approach a lot of these problems, but they can be slow-going for stronger problem solvers. I'll be covering both the straightforward, intuitive approaches and the conversion factor approach throughout the examples in this chapter.

EXAMPLE 1: A tree grows at an average rate of 2.8 inches per month. By approximately how many inches does the tree grow over 5 years?

A. 14   B. 34   C. 87   D. 140   E. 168

There are $12 \times 5 = 60$ months in 5 years. Therefore, the tree grows $2.8 \times 60 = 168$ inches over 5 years. Answer $\boxed{(E)}$.

EXAMPLE 2: Joanna is paid $30 per hour to sew buttons on shirts. If she sews 840 buttons at the rate of 4 buttons per minute, how much will she be paid?

A. $90   B. $105   C. $120   D. $135   E. $150

To sew 840 buttons, Joanna will need $840 \div 4 = 210$ minutes. That's $210 \div 60 = 3.5$ hours. At $30 per hour, she will be paid a total of $30 \times 3.5 = \$105$. Answer $\boxed{(B)}$.

EXAMPLE 3: A box at the supermarket can hold 6 oranges each. Each orange costs the supermarket 20 cents. Given that the supermarket has a budget of $500 to stock oranges, how many boxes will the supermarket be able to completely fill?

A. 208   B. 312   C. 578   D. 416   E. 624

Since each orange costs 20 cents, a dollar is enough for 5 oranges, and five hundred dollars is enough for $500 \times 5 = 2,500$ oranges, which would fill $2500 \div 6 = 416.67$ boxes. Given that the question asks for full boxes, the answer is 416. Answer $\boxed{(D)}$.

The examples above were quite straightforward and didn't really call for writing out full conversion factors, but what if we had wanted to use conversion factors for Example 3? What would've the solution looked like?

$$500 \text{ dollars} \times \frac{100 \text{ cents}}{1 \text{ dollar}} \times \frac{1 \text{ orange}}{20 \text{ cents}} \times \frac{1 \text{ box}}{6 \text{ oranges}} = 416.67 \text{ boxes}$$

Most of the remaining examples in this chapter are done with conversion factors to teach you how they're used, even though there may be more "casual" solutions.

EXAMPLE 4: A recipe for 12 servings requires 5 cups of water. About how many cups of water are required for 30 servings?

A. 10.8   **B.** 12.5   **C.** 17.2   **D.** 25.4   **E.** 72.0

To solve rate problems using conversion factors, start with what the question is asking for, which is typically the thing that you need to convert. Here, we need to convert 30 servings into cups of water.

$$30 \text{ servings} \times \frac{5 \text{ cups of water}}{12 \text{ servings}} = 12.5 \text{ cups of water}$$

The units should cancel as you go along. If the units are canceling, chances are we're doing things right. Notice that the "cups of water" unit at the end is the unit we wanted to end up with. This is another sign that we've done things right. The answer is $\boxed{(B)}$.

EXAMPLE 5: A car can travel 1 mile in 1 minute and 15 seconds. At this rate, how many miles can the car travel in 1 hour?

A. 36   **B.** 42   **C.** 45   **D.** 48   **E.** 54

$$1 \text{ hour} \times \frac{60 \text{ minutes}}{1 \text{ hour}} \times \frac{60 \text{ seconds}}{1 \text{ minute}} \times \frac{1 \text{ mile}}{75 \text{ seconds}} = \frac{60 \times 60 \text{ miles}}{75} = 48 \text{ miles}$$

Answer $\boxed{(D)}$.

This is a good place to stop and point out the important formula

$$\text{Distance} = \text{Rate} \times \text{Time}$$

This formula, often written as $d = rt$, is just a specific use-case of conversion factors since "rate" in this context refers to a conversion factor that converts time to distance. So why do we even bother with this formula then? Because it provides a ready-to-use way of tackling common math questions involving distance, speed, and time. On the ACT, you're free to use whatever you find most convenient, whether it be this formula or conversion factors.

EXAMPLE 6: Tom drives 30 miles at an average rate of 50 miles per hour. If Leona drives at an average rate of 40 miles per hour, how many more minutes will it take her to travel the same distance?

A. 7   **B.** 8   **C.** 9   **D.** 10   **E.** 11

Using $t = \dfrac{d}{r}$, Tom took $\dfrac{30}{50} = 0.6$ hours, or $0.6 \times 60 = 36$ minutes. Leona will take $\dfrac{30}{40} = 0.75$ hours, or $0.75 \times 60 = 45$ minutes. That's $45 - 36 = 9$ minutes more than Tom. Answer $\boxed{(C)}$.

If we had instead used conversion factors to solve this problem, it would've looked like this:

$$\text{Tom: } 30 \text{ miles} \times \frac{1 \text{ hour}}{50 \text{ miles}} \times \frac{60 \text{ minutes}}{1 \text{ hour}} = 36 \text{ minutes}$$

$$\text{Leona: } 30 \text{ miles} \times \frac{1 \text{ hour}}{40 \text{ miles}} \times \frac{60 \text{ minutes}}{1 \text{ hour}} = 45 \text{ minutes}$$

$45 - 36 = 9$ minutes.

EXAMPLE 7: The Russell family has a pet dog. The dog eats a cans of pet food every 4 days. At this rate, how many *weeks* will it take the dog to eat b cans of pet food?

A. $\dfrac{4a}{7b}$ **B.** $\dfrac{4b}{7a}$ **C.** $\dfrac{7a}{4b}$ **D.** $\dfrac{7b}{4a}$ **E.** $\dfrac{28b}{a}$

$$b \text{ cans} \times \frac{4 \text{ days}}{a \text{ cans}} \times \frac{1 \text{ week}}{7 \text{ days}} = \frac{4b}{7a} \text{ weeks}$$

Answer $\boxed{(B)}$.

CHAPTER EXERCISE: Answers for this chapter start on page 215.

1. A squirrel has gathered enough acorns to last 20 days if it eats 6 acorns each day. How many acorns should it eat each day if the same number of acorns is to last 24 days?

   A. 3
   B. 4
   C. 5
   D. 6
   E. 7

2. Sarah wants to buy 30 staplers. Shop A sells staplers at 6 for $10. Shop B sells staplers at 5 for $8. How many dollars will Sarah save by going to the store with the better deal?

   A. $2
   B. $5
   C. $6
   D. $9
   E. $12

3. A recipe recommends fermenting a certain type of vegetable for 5 hours per ounce of the vegetable's weight. Based on this recipe, how long should an 18-ounce vegetable of this type be fermented?

   A. 2 days 12 hours
   B. 2 days 18 hours
   C. 3 days 6 hours
   D. 3 days 12 hours
   E. 3 days 18 hours

4. In one week, a master tailor can make 15 suits whereas his apprentice can only make one-third as many. If they alternate weeks (i.e. the master works this week and the apprentice works the next), how many weeks would it take them to make 180 suits altogether?

   A. 3
   B. 6
   C. 9
   D. 18
   E. 24

5. An empty aquarium can hold 18,000 gallons of water when full. It will be filled by 5 hoses, each of which pumps 3 gallons of water per minute. How many hours will it take to fill the aquarium?

   A. 10
   B. 15
   C. 20
   D. 25
   E. 30

6. The total charge for a hotel room includes a fixed upfront fee plus a daily rate for the room. If the total charge for the room is $400 for a 4-day stay and $570 for a 6-day stay, what is the total charge for a 10-day stay?

   A. $850
   B. $880
   C. $910
   D. $940
   E. $970

7. In a cycling race, Hugo finished a course 2.4 miles long in 7 minutes and 12 seconds. About how many miles per hour did he average for the race?

   A. 60
   B. 36
   C. 30
   D. 20
   E. 15

8. A recycling machine processes 10 plastic bottles in 3 minutes. At this rate, how many plastic bottles does the recycling machine process in $3 + m$ minutes?

   A. $\dfrac{10}{3} + m$

   B. $\dfrac{10}{3} + \dfrac{m}{3}$

   C. $\dfrac{10}{3} + \dfrac{10}{3m}$

   D. $10 + \dfrac{m}{3}$

   E. $10 + \dfrac{10m}{3}$

9. A baking company hires employees to make and package cookies. Each employee assigned to baking can make 30 cookies per hour. Each employee assigned to packaging can pack 5 cookies every 12 minutes. The company currently has 15 employees who are all assigned to baking. How many employees should be hired and assigned to packaging so that the company makes and packages the same number of cookies in 1 hour?

    A. 12
    B. 16
    C. 18
    D. 20
    E. 21

10. Megan and Kristie are working together to grade 65 essays. Megan can grade 5 essays per hour and Kristie can grade 6 essays per hour. If Megan starts grading first and Kristie joins her two hours later, how many essays will Kristie have graded by the time they finish?

    A. 25
    B. 28
    C. 30
    D. 35
    E. 36

9

Ratio & Proportion

A ratio is just a way of expressing a proportion: how different quantities relate to the whole. As an example, if the ratio of red apples to green apples is 1:2, then there is 1 red apple for every 2 green apples. This ratio also means that for every 3 apples, there is one red one and two green ones. Be aware that ratios are sometimes written as fractions (i.e. $1:2 = \frac{1}{2}$).

EXAMPLE 1: Only drama, thriller, and comedy movies are available in Charlotte's Video Store. The ratio of drama movies to thriller movies to comedy movies is 3:4:5. There are 180 thriller movies available in the store. How many movies are available in the entire store?

A. 180   **B.** 360   **C.** 432   **D.** 540   **E.** 720

Solution 1: The ratio 3:4:5 means that there are 4 thriller movies for every $3 + 4 + 5 = 12$ movies available in the store. In other words, the number of movies available in the store is $12 \div 4 = 3$ times the number of thriller movies. Therefore, the number of movies available must be $180 \times 3 = 540$. Answer $\boxed{(D)}$.

Solution 2: The ratio 3:4:5 means that there are 3 drama movies and 5 comedy movies for every 4 thriller movies. Because there are $180 \div 4 = 45$ "groups of 4" thriller movies, there must be $3 \times 45 = 135$ drama movies and $5 \times 45 = 225$ comedy movies. The total number of movies available is then $135 + 180 + 225 = 540$. Answer $\boxed{(D)}$.

EXAMPLE 2: The instructions for coconut milk call for 2 cups of coconut juice and 3 cups of whole milk. Under these instructions, how many cups of whole milk will be needed to make 90 cups of coconut milk?

A. 30   **B.** 36   **C.** 45   **D.** 48   **E.** 54

3 cups of whole milk are required for every $2 + 3 = 5$ cups of coconut milk. Using this as a conversion factor,

$$90 \text{ cups of coconut milk} \times \frac{3 \text{ cups of whole milk}}{5 \text{ cups of coconut milk}} = 54 \text{ cups of whole milk}$$

Answer $\boxed{(E)}$. This question was simple enough that I didn't have to write everything out using a conversion factor, but I decided to do it this way for the sake of variety.

> **EXAMPLE 3:** When Pamela fills a box with only red blocks, 36 of them fit. When she fills the same box with only blue blocks, 48 of them fit. If she then empties out the box and puts 40 blue blocks inside, what is the greatest possible number of red blocks she can fit in the remaining space inside the box?
>
> **A.** 4   **B.** 5   **C.** 6   **D.** 7   **E.** 8

Think of 36 red blocks as being equivalent to 48 blue blocks, which boils down to 3 red blocks being equivalent to 4 blue blocks. Now if there are already 40 blue blocks in the box, there's room for $48 - 40 = 8$ more blue blocks. "Converting" these blue blocks to red blocks,

$$8 \text{ blue blocks } \times \frac{3 \text{ red blocks}}{4 \text{ blue blocks}} = 6 \text{ red blocks}$$

Answer $\boxed{(C)}$.

Two variables x and y are **directly proportional** if when one goes up, the other also goes up. Representing this mathematically,

$$y = kx \text{ where } k \text{ is a constant}$$

For example, the circumference of a circle is directly proportional to the diameter: $C = \pi d$. As the diameter increases, the circumference also increases. For every unit increase in the length of the diameter, the circumference increases by π units.

Two variables x and y are **indirectly/inversely proportional** if when one goes up, the other goes down. Mathematically, the product of the two variables always remains the same:

$$xy = k \text{ where } k \text{ is a constant}$$

For example, density is inversely proportional to volume. As an object gets bigger, it becomes less dense.

I like to remember the difference between direct and inverse by where the variables are positioned. In a direct variation, the variables are on opposite sides ($y = kx$). In an inverse variation, the variables are on the same side ($xy = k$).

> **EXAMPLE 4:** The number of cars at a mall parking lot is directly proportional to the number of people in the mall. If there are 120 cars in the mall parking lot when there are 400 people in the mall, how many cars are in the parking lot when there are 1400 people in the mall?
>
> **A.** 360   **B.** 390   **C.** 420   **D.** 450   **E.** 480

This is just a rate problem reworded as a direct proportion problem. We'll solve it using the direct proportion equation but we could just as easily use conversion factors. Let p be the number of people and c be the number of cars.

$$p = kc$$
$$400 = k \cdot 120$$
$$k = \frac{400}{120} = \frac{10}{3}$$

Now that we've found the constant k, we can use it in the same equation to find the answer:

$$p = \frac{10}{3}c$$

$$1400 = \frac{10}{3}c$$

$$c = 1400 \cdot \frac{3}{10} = 420 \text{ cars}$$

Answer $\boxed{(C)}$.

EXAMPLE 5: The number of workers it takes to build a house varies inversely with the number of days it takes to build that house. If 20 workers are needed to build a house in 15 days, how many workers are needed to build a house in 50 days?

A. 4   **B.** 6   **C.** 8   **D.** 10   **E.** 12

Let w be the number of workers and d be the number of days. Since w and d are inversely proportional,

$$wd = k$$
$$20 \cdot 15 = k$$
$$k = 300$$

Now that we've found k, we can use it in the same equation to get the answer:

$$wd = 300$$
$$w \cdot 50 = 300$$
$$w = \boxed{6}$$

It takes 6 workers to build a house in 50 days, which makes sense. The more days you have, the less workers you need. Answer $\boxed{(B)}$.

CHAPTER EXERCISE: Answers for this chapter start on page 216.

1. There are 36 pears and 54 oranges on a dining hall table. What is the ratio of pears to oranges?

   A. 1:2
   B. 1:3
   C. 2:3
   D. 2:5
   E. 3:5

2. At a restaurant, the number of burgers sold is in direct proportion to the number of hours the restaurant is open. If the restaurant sells b burgers in t hours, how many burgers are sold per hour, in terms of b and t ?

   A. $\dfrac{b}{t}$

   B. $\dfrac{t}{b}$

   C. $b - t$
   D. $b + t$
   E. bt

3. Let x and y be inversely proportional to each other. When $x = 4$, $y = 6$. What is the value of y when $x = 8$?

   A. 1
   B. 2
   C. 3
   D. 4
   E. 5

4. At a certain school, $\dfrac{3}{7}$ of the boys and $\dfrac{6}{7}$ of the girls play tennis. If the number of male and female tennis players is the same, which of the following must be true?

   A. There are seven times as many girls as boys.
   B. There are twice as many girls as boys.
   C. There are as many girls as boys.
   D. There are twice as many boys as girls.
   E. There are seven times as many boys as girls.

5. A blueprint drawing of a rectangular room is 10 inches wide and 8 inches long. The actual room is 25 feet wide. If the blueprint drawing is proportional to the actual room, what is the perimeter of the room, in feet?

   A. 40
   B. 50
   C. 70
   D. 80
   E. 90

6. The time it takes to transfer a file is directly proportional to the file's size. If a 280 megabyte file takes 50 seconds to transfer, how many seconds will it take to transfer a 700 megabyte file?

   A. 100
   B. 125
   C. 130
   D. 140
   E. 145

7. The perimeter of rectangle $ABCD$ is 108 inches. The ratio of the side lengths $AB:BC$ is 4:5. What is the area, in square inches, of rectangle $ABCD$?

   A. 720
   B. 960
   C. 1,280
   D. 1,440
   E. 2,880

8. Clarissa makes beaded necklaces in two different sizes. A large necklace consists of 24 blue beads and 36 red beads. A small necklace consists of a total of 20 beads in the same ratio of blue beads and red beads as the large necklace. How many red beads does Clarissa put in the small necklace?

   A. 6
   B. 8
   C. 12
   D. 14
   E. 15

9. Jody is a pharmacist who is tasked with mixing a solution for a new medication. The original recipe calls for $3\frac{1}{2}$ milliliters of water and $1\frac{3}{4}$ milligrams of calcium phosphate. Jody will use the entire contents of a beaker that contains $5\frac{1}{4}$ milliliters of water and will use the same ratio of ingredients called for in the original recipe. How many milligrams of calcium phosphate will Jody use?

   A. $2\frac{3}{8}$

   B. $2\frac{1}{2}$

   C. $2\frac{5}{8}$

   D. $3\frac{1}{4}$

   E. $3\frac{1}{2}$

10. A recipe that makes 5 servings of salad dressing requires 2 cups of balsamic vinegar and $\frac{2}{3}$ cup of sesame oil. Brianna has 20 cups of balsamic vinegar and 6 cups of sesame oil. If she maintains the same ratio of ingredients, what is the greatest number of servings of salad dressing she can make?

   A. 9
   B. 10
   C. 20
   D. 45
   E. 50

11. There are 210 students at Salem High School, where the ratio of juniors to seniors is 3:4. There are 140 students at Swampscott High School, where the ratio of juniors to seniors is 4:3. The two schools hold a sports competition and all the juniors and seniors from both schools attend. What fraction of the students at the competition are seniors?

   A. $\frac{2}{5}$

   B. $\frac{3}{7}$

   C. $\frac{4}{7}$

   D. $\frac{17}{35}$

   E. $\frac{18}{35}$

12. An apartment building has only one-bedroom and two-bedroom apartments. A construction company was asked to renovate all the apartments to modernize their design. Renovation costs averaged $3,200 for each one-bedroom apartment and $4,000 for each two-bedroom apartment. If the ratio of one-bedroom apartments to two-bedroom apartments in the building is 5:3, renovation costs averaged how many dollars per apartment?

   A. $3,400
   B. $3,500
   C. $3,600
   D. $3,700
   E. $3,800

10 Percent

First, let's find the total number of questions he got correct:

$$50\% \times 30 = \frac{1}{2} \times 30 = 15$$

$$90\% \times 50 = \frac{9}{10} \times 50 = 45$$

So he got $15 + 45 = 60$ questions correct out of a total of $30 + 50 = 80$ questions. $\frac{60}{80} = \frac{3}{4} = 75\%$. Answer $\boxed{(D)}$.

First, never just add/subtract all the percentages. That's wrong. Here's the correct technique for dealing with these "series of percent change" questions. Let the original price be p. When p is increased by 20%, you multiply by 1.20 because it's the original price plus 20%. When it's decreased by 40%, you multiply by 0.60 because 60% is what's left after you take away 40%. Our final price is then

$$p \times 1.20 \times 0.60 \times 1.25 = 0.90p$$

The final price is 90% of the original price. Answer $\boxed{(D)}$.

Example 2 shows an important percent concept. Never ever calculate the prices at each step. String all the changes together and multiply to get the end result.

It's important to understand why this works. Imagine again that the original price is p and we want to increase it by 20%. Normally, we would just take p and add 20% of it on top:

$$p + 0.20p$$

But realize that

$$p + 0.20p = p(1 + 0.20) = 1.20p$$

And now we want to decrease this new price by 40%:

$$1.20p - (0.40)(1.20p) = (1.20p)(1 - 0.40) = (1.20p)(0.60) = (1.20)(0.60)p$$

This proves we can directly calculate the final price by using this technique.

EXAMPLE 3: This year, the chickens on a farm laid 30% less eggs than they did last year. If they laid 3,500 eggs this year, how many did they lay last year?

A. 4,000   **B.** 4,200   **C.** 4,500   **D.** 4,800   **E.** 5,000

$$\text{This Year} = (0.70)(\text{Last Year})$$
$$3,500 = (0.70)(\text{Last Year})$$
$$5,000 = \text{Last Year}$$

Answer $\boxed{(E)}$.

Percent change (a.k.a. percent increase/decrease) is calculated as follows:

$$\% \text{ change} = \frac{\text{new value} - \text{old value}}{\text{old value}} \times 100$$

For example, if the price of a dress starts out at 80 dollars and rises to 90 dollars, the percent change is:

$$\frac{90 - 80}{80} \times 100 = 12.5\%$$

If percent change is positive, it's a percent increase. Negative? Percent decrease. It's important to remember that percent change is always based on the original value.

EXAMPLE 4: In a particular store, the number of TVs sold the week of Black Friday was 685. The number of TVs sold the following week was 500. TV sales the week following Black Friday were about what percent less than TV sales the week of Black Friday?

A. 17%   **B.** 27%   **C.** 37%   **D.** 47%   **E.** 57%

$$\frac{500 - 685}{685} \approx -0.27$$

The way the question is worded, the week of Black Friday is the "original" basis for comparison, so we put the difference over 685, NOT 500. Answer $\boxed{(B)}$.

EXAMPLE 5: In a particular store, the number of computers sold the week of Black Friday was 470. The number of computers sold the previous week was 320. Which of the following is closest to the percent increase in computer sales from the previous week to the week of Black Friday?

A. 17%   **B.** 27%   **C.** 37%   **D.** 47%   **E.** 57%

$$\frac{470 - 320}{320} \approx 0.47$$

This time, the previous week, not the week of Black Friday, is the "original" basis for the percent change. Therefore, we put the difference over the previous week's number, 320. The answer is $\boxed{(D)}$.

A few more examples involving percent:

EXAMPLE 6: The number of students at a school decreased 20% from 2010 to 2011. If the number of enrolled students in 2011 was k, which of the following expresses the number of enrolled students in 2010 in terms of k ?

A. $0.75k$ **B.** $1.20k$ **C.** $1.25k$ **D.** $1.5k$ **E.** $1.75k$

The answer is NOT $1.20k$. Percent change is based off of the original value (from 2010) and not the new value. Let x be the number of students in 2010,

$$0.80x = k$$

$$x = 1.25k$$

Therefore, there were 25% more students in 2010 than in 2011. Answer $\boxed{(C)}$.

EXAMPLE 7: Among 10th graders at a school, 40% of the students take Chemistry. Among those that take Chemistry, 20% also take Physics. What percent of the 10th graders at the school take both Chemistry and Physics?

A. 8%   **B.** 10%   **C.** 12%   **D.** 20%   **E.** 25%

We don't know the number of 10th graders at the school so let's suppose that it's 100.

$$\text{Chemistry students} = 40\% \text{ of } 100 = 40$$

$$\text{Chemistry \& Physics students} = 20\% \text{ of } 40 = 8$$

The answer is then $\frac{8}{100} = 8\%$. Answer $\boxed{(A)}$.

A common strategy in percent questions is to make up a number to represent the total, typically 100.

CHAPTER EXERCISE: Answers for this chapter start on page 218.

1. The price of a pair of shoes decreased from $80 to $50. The price decreased by what percent?

   A. 12.5%
   B. 25%
   C. 30%
   D. 37.5%
   E. 60%

2. A store purchased a pair of jeans that had a wholesale price of $30.00. The store increased the wholesale price of the jeans by 70% to get the sale price. Quinn bought the pair of jeans and paid a 5% sales tax on the sale price. How much did Quinn pay for the jeans, including tax?

   A. $40.95
   B. $51.00
   C. $52.50
   D. $53.55
   E. $63.75

3. Amy's Appliance Store is offering a special deal on a toaster. A customer who buys the toaster at the regular price of p dollars can get an additional one at a 20% discount. Which of the following gives the total cost, in dollars, a customer will pay for two toasters?

   A. $0.8p$
   B. $1.2p$
   C. $1.6p$
   D. $1.8p$
   E. $2.2p$

4. At one particular garden, 0.08 percent of all flowers grown are tulips. On the average, there will be 6 tulips out of how many flowers grown?

   A. 75
   B. 480
   C. 750
   D. 4800
   E. 7500

5. An advertisement for Bill's Butcher Shop reads, "40% off, today only: a half-pound of beef for just $3." What is the regular price for a *full* pound of beef at Bill's Butcher Shop?

   A. $5
   B. $6
   C. $8
   D. $10
   E. $12

6. A restaurant offers lunch specials that consist of one drink and one slice of pizza. The menu is shown below.

Drinks	
Water	$1.00
Soda	$1.25
Tea	$1.50
Coffee	$2.00

Pizza Slices	
Cheese	$1.25
Pepperoni	$1.75
Vegetable	$2.25

   About what percent of the lunch special options cost a total of $3.25?

   A. 8%
   B. 17%
   C. 25%
   D. 33%
   E. 57%

7. A jar contains three different colors of gumballs: 30% are blue, 25% are red, and the rest are green. If there are 36 green gumballs in the jar, how many red gumballs are in the jar?

   A. 20
   B. 24
   C. 28
   D. 32
   E. 80

8. Kendra took a test that consisted of two sections. The first section contained 35 questions and the second section contained 25 questions. Kendra answered 80% of the questions in the first section correctly. After the test, her teacher determined that Kendra answered 75% of all the questions on the test correctly. How many questions did Kendra answer correctly in the second section of the test?

    A. 14
    B. 15
    C. 16
    D. 17
    E. 18

9. Two puppies, Max and Boxer, once weighed the same number of pounds. Since then Max's weight has increased by 15% while Boxer has gained half as many pounds as Max. Max now weighs 46 pounds. What is Boxer's current weight, in pounds?

    A. 38
    B. 40
    C. 41
    D. 43
    E. 46

10. During a sale, Eli's Electronics offered a 40% discount on the original price of a computer. Walter bought the computer during the sale but the cashier made a mistake. After applying the discount, the cashier calculated the 5% sales tax using the original price of the computer instead of the discounted price. The amount by which Walter overpaid represents what percent of the original price of the computer?

    A. 1%
    B. 1.5%
    C. 2%
    D. 2.5%
    E. 3%

11

Functions

A function is a machine that takes an input, transforms it, and spits out an output. In math, functions are denoted by $f(x)$, with x being the input. So for the function

$$f(x) = x^2 + 1$$

each input is squared and then added to one to get the output. It's important to understand that x is a completely arbitrary label—it's just a placeholder for the input. In fact, I can put in whatever I want as the input, including values with x in them:

$$f(2x) = (2x)^2 + 1$$
$$f(a) = a^2 + 1$$
$$f(b + 1) = (b + 1)^2 + 1$$
$$f(\star) = (\star)^2 + 1$$
$$f(\text{Panda}) = (\text{Panda})^2 + 1$$

Notice the careful use of parentheses. In the first equation, for example, $(2x)^2$ is not the same as $2x^2$. Wrap each input in parentheses and you'll never go wrong.

EXAMPLE 1: For the function $g(x) = 2^x + 3x^2$, what is the value of $g(-2)$?

A. 1   B. 8   C. $8\dfrac{1}{4}$ D. $12\dfrac{1}{4}$ E. 16

Just plug in the input of -2:

$$g(-2) = 2^{(-2)} + 3(-2)^2 = \frac{1}{2^2} + 3(4) = 12\frac{1}{4}$$

Answer $\boxed{(D)}$.

EXAMPLE 2: Suppose the operation ✠ is defined by $x ✠ y = x^2 - y$. What is the value of $(5 ✠ 5) ✠ 5$?

A. 5   B. 125   C. 225   D. 395   E. 620

In the same way that $f(x) = x^2$ tells us to square the input, some ACT questions will define their own functions with their own notation. Don't be thrown off by the weird symbols. They're just functions in disguise. Here, the ✠ means to take two inputs, square the first one, and then subtract the second one from the result. For example,

$$3 ✠ 2 = 3^2 - 2 = 7$$

Back to the question, we do what's inside the parentheses first:

$$(5 ✠ 5) ✠ 5 = (5^2 - 5) ✠ 5 = 20 ✠ 5 = 20^2 - 5 = 395$$

Answer $\boxed{(D)}$.

EXAMPLE 3: Functions f and g are defined by $f(x) = x^2 - 1$ and $g(x) = 3x + 4$.

Part 1: What is the value of $g(f(3))$?

A. 16   B. 25   C. 28   D. 31   E. 168

Part 2: Which of the following expressions is equal to $f(g(x))$?

A. $3x^2 + 1$ B. $3x^2 + 15$ C. $9x^2 + 3$ D. $9x^2 + 15$ E. $(3x + 4)^2 - 1$

Part 1 Solution: Whenever you see composite functions (functions of other functions), start from the inside and work your way out:

$$f(3) = 3^2 - 1 = 8$$

$$g(f(3)) = g(8) = 3(8) + 4 = 28$$

Answer $\boxed{(C)}$.

Part 2 Solution: Again, we start from the inside.

$$f(g(x)) = f(3x + 4) = (3x + 4)^2 - 1$$

Note the importance of the parentheses in the final result. Answer $\boxed{(E)}$.

As we've mentioned, a function takes an input and returns an output. Well, given that we can generate pairs of inputs and outputs using a function, we can also graph them as points in the standard (x, y) plane, with x as the input and y as the output. In fact,

$$y = x^2 + 1$$

is the same as $f(x) = x^2 + 1$. Both $f(x)$ and y are the same thing—they're used to denote the output. The only reason we use y sometimes is that the naming is consistent with the y-axis.

Anytime $f(x)$ is used in a graphing question, think of it as the y. So if a question states that $f(x) > 0$, that means all y values are positive and the graph is always above the x-axis. It's extremely important that you learn to think of the points on a graph as the inputs and outputs of a function.

EXAMPLE 4: Let $f(x) = bx - 8$. In the standard (x, y) coordinate plane, $y = f(x)$ passes through $(2, 6)$. What is the value of b ?

A. 6   B. 7   C. 8   D. 9   E. 10

Remember—a point just represents an input and an output, an x and a y. Since we know $(2, 6)$ is on the graph of the function, we can plug in those values as x and y.

$$y = bx - 8$$
$$6 = b(2) - 8$$
$$14 = 2b$$
$$b = 7$$

Answer $\boxed{(B)}$.

EXAMPLE 5: The function f is defined by $f(x) = \dfrac{4}{x^2 - 10x + 25}$. For what value of x is the function f undefined?

A. -25 B. -5 C. 0   D. 5   E. 10

Because we can't divide by 0, the function f is undefined when its denominator is zero. Setting the denominator to zero,

$$x^2 - 10x + 25 = 0$$
$$(x - 5)^2 = 0$$
$$x = 5$$

The function f is undefined when $x = 5$. Answer $\boxed{(D)}$.

This would be a good time to talk about domain and range:

- **Domain:** The set of all possible input values (x) to a function.

- **Range:** The set of all possible output values (y) from a function.

In Example 5, $x = 5$ leads to $f(x)$ being undefined. However, all other numbers for x give real number outputs. Therefore, the domain of f is all real numbers except 5. To verify, we can take a look at the graph of f:

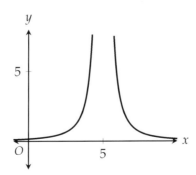

As you can see, the graph has no value when $x = 5$. In fact, $x = 5$ is like an invisible line that the graph approaches but never crosses. We call these lines **vertical asymptotes**. To summarize, the function f has one vertical asymptote with equation $x = 5$.

You might've also noticed that the graph never goes below the x-axis. It's another line that the graph approaches but never crosses. The x-axis, in this case, is a **horizontal asymptote**. The function f has one horizontal asymptote with equation $y = 0$.

Because there are no points on the graph that have a y-value of 0 or below, the range of f is all positive real numbers. Put mathematically, $f(x) > 0$. By the way, this makes sense. Because of the square in the denominator of $f(x) = \dfrac{4}{x^2 - 10x + 25} = \dfrac{4}{(x-5)^2}$, you always get a positive output for any value of x in the domain.

Lastly, the function f is what's called a **rational function** because of the variable in the denominator. A defining characteristic of rational functions is that they typically have horizontal and vertical asymptotes.

To summarize, find the domain by first thinking about all the values of x for which the function is invalid or undefined. For example, the domain of $y = \sqrt{x}$ is $x \geq 0$ because we can't take the square root of a negative number.

To find the range, graph the function on your calculator and figure out the possible values of y, taking note of any horizontal asymptotes. There are ways of directly getting the equations of the horizontal asymptotes but they're not worth knowing given how rarely horizontal asymptotes show up on the ACT. Just graph the function!

EXAMPLE 6: If $f(x) = x^3 - x$, how many different zeros does f have?

A. 0   **B.** 1   **C.** 2   **D.** 3   **E.** 4

The **zeros** of a function are just another term for x-intercepts. They're the values of x that make $f(x) = 0$. Before we solve this question, we can guess the number of zeros by looking at the **degree** of f, which refers to the highest exponent of x among the terms. In this case, $f(x)$ is a polynomial of degree 3 because of the x^3 term. Because it's a third-degree polynomial, f has AT MOST 3 zeros.

To find the exact number of zeros, we can set up an equation and factor f:

$$f(x) = 0$$
$$x^3 - x = 0$$
$$x(x^2 - 1) = 0$$
$$x(x+1)(x-1) = 0$$
$$x = -1, 0, 1$$

Therefore, f has 3 different zeros: $-1, 0$, and 1. Answer $\boxed{(D)}$.

To confirm this answer, let's take a quick look at the graph of f:

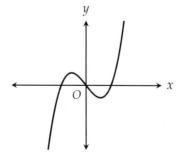

The graph crosses the x-axis in 3 different places, which confirms it has 3 different zeros. Sometimes, graphing is the only way to find the zeros so make sure you have it in your mental toolbox.

Here's one last tip. Notice that the graph of f has 3 "segments" (up, down, up). Indeed, a 3rd degree function will always have at most 3 "segments." A 4th degree function will always have at most 4 "segments." Knowing how the graph might look based on the function's degree will help immensely on the ACT.

EXAMPLE 7: The graph of f is shown in the standard (x, y) plane below.

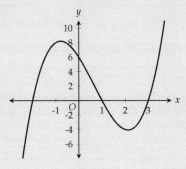

How many solutions are there to $f(x) = 3$?

A. 0   **B.** 1   **C.** 2   **D.** 3   **E.** 4

As you might expect, the term **solutions** here refers to the values of x that satisfy $f(x) = 3$. The problem is that we don't know the definition of $f(x)$, which means we have to find the number of solutions without solving for the solutions themselves. How do we do that? Well, when a question asks you for the solutions to $f(x) = g(x)$, what you really should be looking for are the intersection points. In this case, it just so happens that $g(x) = 3$, a constant. So for this question, we can think of the solutions as the places where $f(x)$ intersects $y = 3$. If we draw the line $y = 3$, we can see that there are 3 intersection points, which means there are 3 solutions.

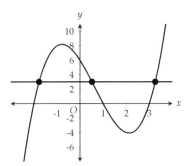

Answer $\boxed{(D)}$. In this question, we didn't care where the intersections were. We just cared about how many there were. But just for the sake of completeness, we can estimate the solutions to be $x = -1.8, 0.5$, and 3.25. Remember that the solutions are the x-values of the intersection points, not the intersection points themselves. By the way, "zeros" is just a special way of saying "the solutions to $f(x) = 0$". See how these terms all fit together?

EXAMPLE 8: If $f(x) = 3x + 4$, what is the value of $f^{-1}(1)$?

A. -1 B. 0   C. 3   D. 5   E. 7

The notation f^{-1} refers to **the inverse function** of f. It does NOT refer to the reciprocal of f, $\dfrac{1}{f(x)}$.

To find the inverse function, replace all the x's with y and all the y's with x.

$$y = 3x + 4 \quad \rightarrow \quad x = 3y + 4$$

Then solve for y:

$$x = 3y + 4$$
$$x - 4 = 3y$$
$$\frac{x - 4}{3} = y$$

This "new" y is the inverse function.

$$f^{-1}(x) = \frac{x - 4}{3}$$
$$f^{-1}(1) = \frac{1 - 4}{3} = -1$$

Answer $\boxed{(A)}$. Remember how a function takes an input and returns an output? Well, the inverse takes an output and gives us back the input. To see this in action,

$$f(1) = 3(1) + 4 = 7$$
$$f^{-1}(7) = \frac{7 - 4}{3} = 1$$

If we graph f and f^{-1}, we can see that they are symmetrical across the line $y = x$. This is true for all functions and their inverses.

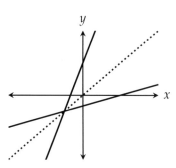

On the ACT math section, you might get one question dealing with function transformations—the ways in which a graph can move and change when its definition changes. Let's use the simple function $f(x) = x^2 - 3$ to demonstrate how certain changes affect the graph of a function.

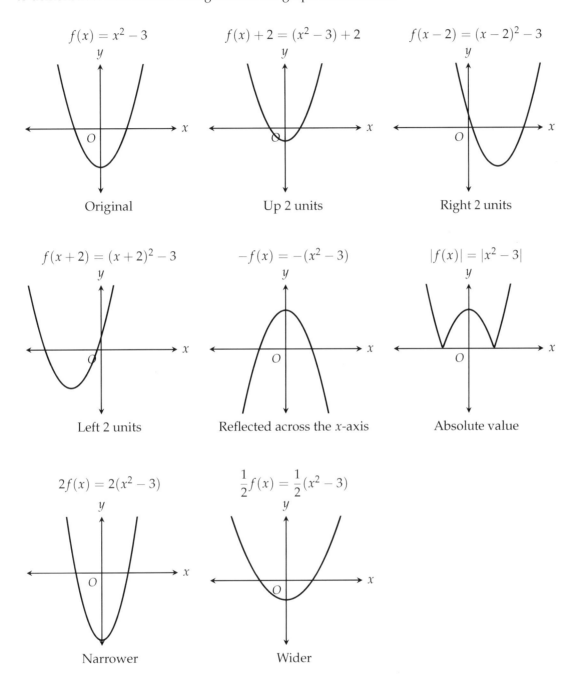

Notice how substituting $(x + 2)$ for x shifts the graph to the left 2 units, whereas substituting $(x - 2)$ for x shifts the graph to the right 2 units. It's the opposite of what a lot of students expect.

EXAMPLE 9: Consider the two functions $f(x) = x^3 + 3$ and $g(x) = x - 1$. Which of the following correctly describes the graph of $g(f(x))$ relative to the graph of $f(x)$ in the standard (x, y) coordinate plane?

A. Shifted right by 1 unit   **B.** Shifted left by 1 unit   **C.** Shifted up by 1 unit

D. Shifted down by 1 unit   **E.** Reflected across the x-axis

Since $g(f(x)) = (x^3 + 3) - 1 = f(x) - 1$, its graph is shifted down by 1 unit relative to the graph of $f(x)$. Answer $\boxed{(D)}$.

If the question had instead asked about $f(g(x)) = (x - 1)^3 + 3$, the answer would have been shifted right by 1 unit.

EXAMPLE 10: Which of the following could be the graph of $y = |2x - 1|$ in the standard (x, y) coordinate plane?

A.

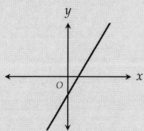

B.

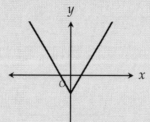

C.

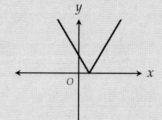

D.

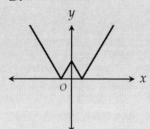

E.

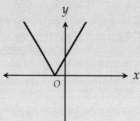

Because the absolute value of something can never be negative, y must always be greater than or equal to 0. In other words, the graph must be on or above the x-axis. That eliminates (A) and (B). Hopefully, you recognize (A) as the graph of $2x - 1$, without the absolute value. To get the answer, take all the points with negative y values in the graph of (A) and reflect them across the x-axis so that they're positive. The graph we end up with is $\boxed{(C)}$.

We could've also solved this question by determining actual points on the graph. For example, if we let $x = 0$, then $y = |2(0) - 1| = 1$. So, the point $(0, 1)$ must be on the graph, eliminating (A) and (B). Letting $y = 0$, we find that $(0.5, 0)$ must also be on the graph. This eliminates (D) because (D) has two x-intercepts whereas the graph should only have one. We can also eliminate (E). By choosing points that were easy to calculate, we very quickly narrowed down the choices to the right one.

Summary of Terms:

- A **function** is an operation that returns an output from an input. The standard notation for a function is $f(x)$ but an ACT question can define its own notation using weird symbols.

- A function can be **graphed** by plotting all possible inputs x along the x-axis and their corresponding outputs $f(x)$ along the y-axis.

- A **composite function** $f(g(x))$ is created when one function $g(x)$ is used as an input to another function $f(x)$.

- The **domain** is the set of all possible input values x to a function.

- The **range** is the set of all possible output values y from a function.

- **Vertical & Horizontal asymptotes** are lines that a function's graph approaches but never crosses.

- **Rational functions** typically have a variable in the denominator $\left(\text{e.g. } \dfrac{x-2}{x^3}\right)$.

- The **zeros** of a function $f(x)$ are the values of x such that $f(x) = 0$. Graphically, the zeros are where a function intersects the x-axis.

- The **solutions** to $f(x) = g(x)$ are the values of x where the graph of $f(x)$ intersects the graph of $g(x)$.

- The **degree** of a polynomial is the value of the greatest exponent among all its terms (except the constants). The degree determines the maximum number of zeros a polynomial can have. It also determines the maximum number of "segments" its graph can have (e.g. up, down, up for a 3rd degree polynomial).

- The **inverse** function f^{-1} takes any output from f and returns the input. The inverse function can be found by solving for y after all the x's are swapped with y's and all the y's are swapped with x's in the equation definition. The graphs of f and f^{-1} are symmetrical about the line $y = x$.

CHAPTER EXERCISE: Answers for this chapter start on page 220.

1. A function $f(x)$ is defined as $f(x) = -3x^3$. What is $f(-2)$?

   A. -24
   B. -18
   C. 9
   D. 18
   E. 24

2. Suppose the operation Φ is defined by $m\Phi n = \dfrac{m}{n}$. What is the value of $3\Phi(2\Phi 4)$?

   A. $\dfrac{1}{4}$
   B. $\dfrac{3}{8}$
   C. $\dfrac{3}{2}$
   D. 6
   E. 12

3. In the standard (x, y) coordinate plane, how many times does the graph of $y = x(x+1)(x-3)^2$ intersect the x-axis?

   A. 1
   B. 2
   C. 3
   D. 4
   E. 5

4. The domain of the function $f(x) = \dfrac{1}{49 - x^2}$ contains all real values of x EXCEPT:

   A. 0
   B. 7
   C. $-\dfrac{1}{7}$ and $\dfrac{1}{7}$
   D. 0 and 7
   E. -7 and 7

5. Given the function f and g defined by $f(x) = x^2 - 3$ and $g(x) = -\sqrt{x+1}$, what is the value of $f(g(3))$?

   A. $-\sqrt{7}$
   B. -1
   C. 1
   D. 4
   E. 5

6. The operation, $\boxdot$, is defined on pairs of ordered pairs of integers as follows:

   $$(a, b) \boxdot (c, d) = \dfrac{a + d}{b + c}$$

   If $(2, n) \boxdot (-4, n) = 3$, what is the value of n ?

   A. -7
   B. -5
   C. 5
   D. 7
   E. 9

Use the following information to answer questions 7–8.

The graph of the rational function $f(x) = \dfrac{x^2 - 4}{x + 1}$ is shown in the standard (x, y) coordinate plane below.

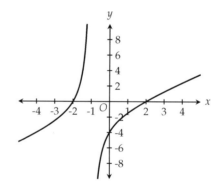

7. For what values of x does $f(x) = 0$?

   A. -4 only
   B. 2 only
   C. -2 and 0
   D. -2 and 2
   E. $-4, -2,$ and 2

8. What is the equation of the vertical asymptote of the graph of $f(x)$?

   A. $x = -1$
   B. $y = -1$
   C. $x = 1$
   D. $y = 1$
   E. $y = x$

9. The graph in the standard (x, y) coordinate plane below is the graph of $y = f(x)$. One of the following graphs is the graph of $y = |f(x)|$. Which one?

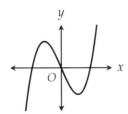

A.

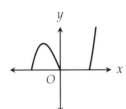

B.

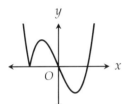

C.

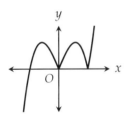

D.

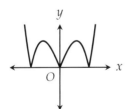

E.

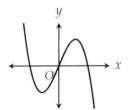

10. Given $g(x) = \sqrt[3]{x} - 2$, which of the following expressions is equal to $g^{-1}(x)$ for all real numbers x ?

   A. $x^3 - 8$
   B. $x^3 + 8$
   C. $(x + 2)^3$
   D. $2 - \sqrt[3]{x}$
   E. $\sqrt[3]{x + 2}$

Use the following information to answer questions 11–12.

Values for the 2 functions $f(x)$ and $g(x)$ are given in the tables below.

x	$f(x)$	x	$g(x)$
-3	0	-3	5
-1	3	1	2
2	-3	2	-1
7	5	3	4

11. What is the value of $f(g(2))$?

   A. -3
   B. 0
   C. 3
   D. 4
   E. 5

12. What is the value of $g(f^{-1}(-3))$?

   A. -1
   B. 0
   C. 2
   D. 5
   E. 7

13. Which of the following statements describes the function h defined by $h(x) = -\dfrac{1}{x}$ for all $x \neq 0$?

   A. h is increasing for $x < 0$ and increasing for $x > 0$
   B. h is decreasing for $x < 0$ and decreasing for $x > 0$
   C. h is increasing for $x < 0$ and decreasing for $x > 0$
   D. h is decreasing for $x < 0$ and increasing for $x > 0$
   E. h is constant for all $x \neq 0$

14. The graphs of $f(x) = x^2 - 2$ and $g(x) = x^3 - 3x$ are shown in the standard (x, y) coordinate plane below. How many solutions does $f(x) = g(x)$ have?

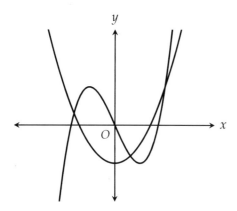

   A. 0
   B. 2
   C. 3
   D. 4
   E. 5

15. Consider the two functions $f(x) = 3x - 8$ and $g(x) = 2x + k$, where k is a real number. If $f(g(x)) = g(3x)$, then $k = ?$

   A. -16
   B. -4
   C. 4
   D. 16
   E. Any real number

16. The polynomial $f(x) = 2x^3 - 10x$ has m rational zeros and n irrational zeros. What is the value of $\dfrac{m}{n+1}$?
   (Note: *Zeros* are values of x such that $f(x) = 0$)

   A. 0
   B. $\dfrac{1}{3}$
   C. $\dfrac{1}{2}$
   D. 1
   E. 3

17. The graph of $f(x) = \dfrac{x - 3}{x^2 - 2x}$ is shown in the standard (x, y) coordinate plane below. What is the domain of $f(x)$?

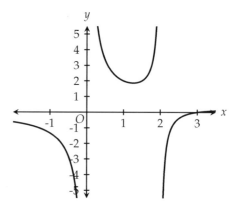

   A. All real values of x except 1
   B. All real values of x except 0 and 2
   C. All real values of x except 3
   D. All real values of x except 0, 2, and 3
   E. All real values of x where $0 < x < 2$

18. One of the following functions is graphed in the standard (x, y) coordinate plane below. Which one?

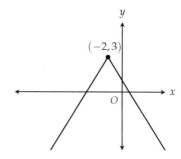

   A. $y = -|x - 2| + 3$
   B. $y = -|x + 2| + 3$
   C. $y = -|x - 2| - 3$
   D. $y = |x + 2| - 3$
   E. $y = |x + 3| + 2$

19. The function $g(x)$ is defined by $g(x) = ax(x + b)(x + c)$, where $a, b,$ and c are constants. The value of $g(x)$ is 0 when x is 0, -1, or 3. If $g(2) = -30$, what is the value of $a + b + c$?

   A. 3
   B. 4
   C. 5
   D. 6
   E. 7

68

20. The graph of $y = f(x)$ is shown in the standard (x, y) coordinate plane below. One of the following graphs is that of $y = f(x - 2) + 1$. Which graph is it?

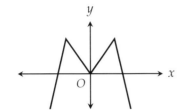

A.

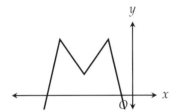

B.

C.

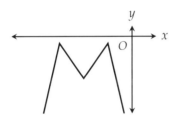

D.

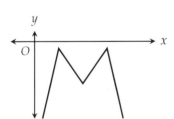

E.

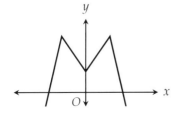

21. A polynomial function $P(x)$ has a degree of 4. The graph of $y = P(x)$ in the standard (x, y) coordinate plane crosses the x-axis at n different points. All of the following could be the value of n EXCEPT:

    A. 1
    B. 2
    C. 3
    D. 4
    E. 5

22. In the standard (x, y) coordinate plane, the graph of $g(x) = \dfrac{3x + 6}{x - 4}$ has a *horizontal* asymptote at:

    A. $y = -4$
    B. $y = -2$
    C. $y = -\dfrac{3}{2}$
    D. $y = 3$
    E. $y = 4$

12
Lines

Lines are just functions in the form $f(x) = mx + b$, which is why they are often referred to as linear functions. Despite being functions, they present a whole slew of concepts that don't necessarily apply to other types of functions. That's why we're covering them separately in this chapter. Let's dive in!

Given any two points (x_1, y_1) and (x_2, y_2) on a line,

$$\text{Slope of line} = \frac{\text{rise}}{\text{run}} = \frac{y_2 - y_1}{x_2 - x_1}$$

The slope is a measure of the steepness of a line—the bigger the slope, the more steep the line is. The rise is the distance between the y coordinates and the run is the distance between the x coordinates. A slope of 2 means the line goes 2 units up for every 1 unit to the right, or 2 units down for every 1 unit to the left. A slope of $-\frac{2}{3}$ means the line goes 2 units down for every 3 units to the right, or 2 units up for every 3 units to the left.

Lines with positive slope always go up and to the right as in the graph above.

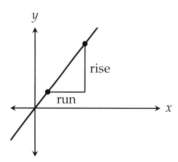

Lines with negative slope go down and to the right:

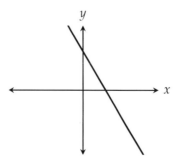

EXAMPLE 1: A line in the standard (x, y) coordinate plane passes through the points $(1, -2)$ and $(-4, 8)$. The slope of the line is:

A. -2 **B.** $-\dfrac{1}{2}$ **C.** $\dfrac{1}{2}$ **D.** 2 **E.** $\dfrac{10}{3}$

$\text{Slope} = \dfrac{y_2 - y_1}{x_2 - x_1} = \dfrac{8 - (-2)}{-4 - 1} = \dfrac{10}{-5} = -2.$ Answer $\boxed{(A)}$.

In addition to slope, you also need to know what x and y intercepts are. The x-intercept is where the graph crosses the x-axis. Likewise, the y-intercept is where the graph crosses the y-axis.

Let's say we have the line

$$2x + 3y = 12$$

To find the x-intercept, set y equal to 0.

$$2x + 3(0) = 12$$
$$2x = 12$$
$$x = 6$$

The x-intercept is 6.

To find the y-intercept, set x equal to 0.

$$2(0) + 3y = 12$$
$$3y = 12$$
$$y = 4$$

The y-intercept is 4.

EXAMPLE 2: In the standard (x, y) coordinate plane, what is the x-intercept of the line represented by $y = ax + b$, where a and b are constants?

A. $-\dfrac{a}{b}$ **B.** $-\dfrac{b}{a}$ **C.** $\dfrac{a}{b}$ **D.** $\dfrac{b}{a}$ **E.** b

To find the x-intercept, set $y = 0$ and solve for x:

$$y = ax + b$$
$$0 = ax + b$$
$$-ax = b$$
$$x = -\dfrac{b}{a}$$

Answer $\boxed{(B)}$.

All lines can be expressed in **slope-intercept form**:

$$y = mx + b$$

where m is the slope and b is the y-intercept. So for the line $y = 2x - 3$, the slope is 2 and the y-intercept is -3:

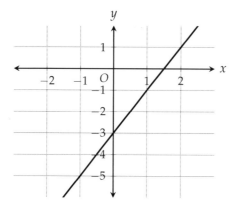

While all lines can be expressed in slope-intercept form, sometimes it'll take some work to get there. If you're given a slope and a y-intercept, then of course it's really easy to get the equation of the line. But what if we're handed a slope and a point on the line instead of a slope and a y-intercept? Then it'll be more convenient to use **point-slope form**:

$$y - y_1 = m(x - x_1)$$

where (x_1, y_1) is the given point. For example, let's say we want to find the equation of a line that has a slope of 3 and passes through the point $(1, -2)$. The equation of the line is then

$$y - (-2) = 3(x - 1)$$

Once it's in point-slope form, we can then expand and shift things around to get to slope-intercept form if we need to.

$$y - (-2) = 3(x - 1)$$
$$y + 2 = 3x - 3$$
$$y = 3x - 5$$

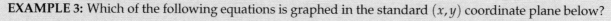

EXAMPLE 3: Which of the following equations is graphed in the standard (x, y) coordinate plane below?

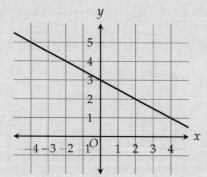

A. $y = -\dfrac{1}{2}x - 3$ **B.** $y = -\dfrac{1}{2}x + 3$ **C.** $y = \dfrac{1}{2}x + 3$ **D.** $y = -2x + 3$ **E.** $y = 2x - 3$

To get the equation of the line $y = mx + b$, we need to find the slope m and the y-intercept b. The line crosses the y-axis at 3, so $b = 3$. The line goes downward from left to right, down 1 for every 2 to the right, so the slope m is $-\dfrac{1}{2}$. Therefore, the equation of the line is $y = -\dfrac{1}{2}x + 3$. Answer $\boxed{(B)}$.

EXAMPLE 4: Which of the following is the y-intercept of the line that passes through $(-2, 3)$ and $(3, 13)$ in the standard (x, y) coordinate plane?

   A. 5   **B.** 6   **C.** 7   **D.** 8   **E.** 9

$$\text{Slope} = \frac{y_2 - y_1}{x_2 - x_1} = \frac{13 - 3}{3 - (-2)} = 2$$

Using point-slope form, our line is

$$y - 13 = 2(x - 3)$$

Note that we could've used the other point $(-2, 3)$ and the result would've been the same. Now,

$$y - 13 = 2(x - 3)$$
$$y = 2x - 6 + 13$$
$$y = 2x + 7$$

After putting the equation into slope-intercept form, we can easily see that the y-intercept is 7. Answer $\boxed{(C)}$.

EXAMPLE 5: When graphed in the standard (x, y) coordinate plane, the lines $y = 3x - 5$ and $y = -2x + 10$ intersect at which of the following points?

   A. $(-1, -8)$ **B.** $(2, 1)$ **C.** $(3, 4)$ **D.** $(4, 8)$ **E.** $(5, 10)$

To find the point where two lines intersect, put them in $y = mx + b$ form and set their equations equal to each other. You're essentially solving a system of equations using substitution. In this case, the two lines are already in $y = mx + b$ form. Setting them equal to each other,

$$3x - 5 = -2x + 10$$
$$5x = 15$$
$$x = 3$$

When $x = 3$, $y = 3(3) - 5 = 4$. So the two lines intersect at $(3, 4)$. Answer $\boxed{(C)}$.

Two lines are parallel if they have the same slope.

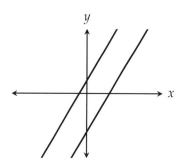

Two lines are perpendicular if the product of their slopes is -1. In other words, if one slope is the negative reciprocal of the other (e.g. 2 and $-\dfrac{1}{2}$).

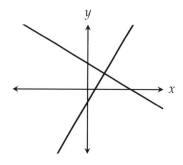

EXAMPLE 6: Line l in the standard (x, y) coordinate plane passes through the points $(6, -1)$ and $(-3, 2)$. Which of the following is an equation of a line that is perpendicular to line l ?

A. $-6x + 2y = 5$ **B.** $-3x + 2y = 5$ **C.** $-2x + 6y = 5$ **D.** $2x + 6y = 5$ **E.** $6x + 2y = 5$

The slope of line l is $\dfrac{2 - (-1)}{-3 - 6} = \dfrac{3}{-9} = -\dfrac{1}{3}$. The slope of a line that is perpendicular to line l must then be 3. When each of the answer choices are put into slope-intercept form, only answer $\boxed{(A)}$ has a slope of 3: $y = 3x + \dfrac{5}{2}$.

Finally, you'll need to know the equations of horizontal and vertical lines. The equation of the vertical line that passes through $(3, 0)$ is $x = 3$. The equation of the horizontal line that passes through $(0, 3)$ is $y = 3$.

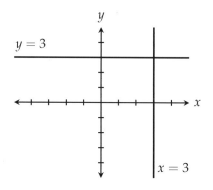

CHAPTER EXERCISE: Answers for this chapter start on page 223.

1. What is the slope of the line that passes through $(-2, 4)$ and $(4, 2)$ in the standard (x, y) coordinate plane?

    A. -3
    B. -1
    C. $-\dfrac{1}{3}$
    D. $\dfrac{1}{3}$
    E. 1

2. An elevator is lowered at a constant speed towards the ground. The table below shows the height, h meters, of the elevator at 1-second intervals from $t = 0$ seconds to $t = 4$ seconds.

t	0	1	2	3	4
h	120	112	104	96	88

    Which of the following equations represents this data?

    A. $h = -t + 120$
    B. $h = -8t + 120$
    C. $h = -8t + 128$
    D. $h = 112t$
    E. $h = 120t - 8$

3. A line in the standard (x, y) coordinate plane is parallel to the y-axis and 4 units to the left of it. Which of the following is an equation of this line?

    A. $y = -4$
    B. $x = -4$
    C. $x = 4$
    D. $y = 4x$
    E. $y = x - 4$

4. What is the slope-intercept equation of the line that passes through the points $(2, 2)$ and $(-1, -4)$?

    A. $y = -6x + 14$
    B. $y = -2x - 2$
    C. $y = -2x + 6$
    D. $y = 2x - 2$
    E. $y = 6x - 10$

5. What is the slope of a line that is perpendicular to the line graphed below in the standard (x, y) coordinate plane?

    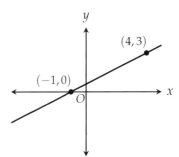

    A. $-\dfrac{5}{3}$
    B. -1
    C. $-\dfrac{3}{5}$
    D. $-\dfrac{1}{2}$
    E. $\dfrac{3}{5}$

6. Which of the following is an equation of the line that passes through $(-4, -3)$ and $(5, -6)$ in the standard (x, y) coordinate plane?

    A. $y = -\dfrac{1}{3}x - \dfrac{13}{3}$
    B. $y = -\dfrac{1}{3}x - \dfrac{5}{3}$
    C. $y = -\dfrac{1}{3}x - 2$
    D. $y = \dfrac{1}{3}x - \dfrac{5}{3}$
    E. $y = \dfrac{1}{3}x + \dfrac{13}{3}$

7. At her last gas station visit, Janelle pumped air into one of her car's tires. The relationship between the tire pressure, y pounds per square inch, and the time she spent pumping air into the tire, x seconds, was given by the equation $5y - 2x = 50$. One of the following graphs in the standard (x, y) coordinate plane models the equation for positive values of y and x. Which one?

A.

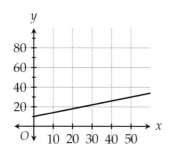

B.

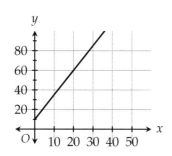

C.

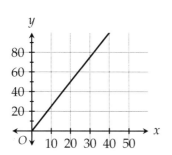

D.

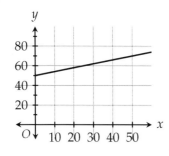

E.

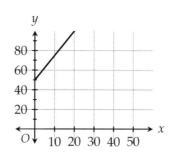

8. Line m in the standard (x, y) coordinate plane has equation $3x - 2y = 8$. Line n is parallel to line m and has a y-intercept that is 4 more than the y-intercept of m. Line n has which of the following equations?

A. $y = -\dfrac{3}{2}x$

B. $y = \dfrac{3}{2}x - 4$

C. $y = \dfrac{3}{2}x$

D. $y = \dfrac{2}{3}x - 4$

E. $y = \dfrac{2}{3}x + 12$

9. A meteorologist graphed the temperature y, in degrees Fahrenheit, over the course of x hours for two different towns. The temperature in Town A started at 50° F and increased by 2° F every hour. The temperature in Town B started at 70° F and decreased by 2° F every hour. Which of the following correctly describes the meteorologist's graph for all positive values of x in the standard (x, y) coordinate plane?

A. Two perpendicular lines
B. Two parallel lines
C. Two intersecting lines that are not perpendicular
D. Two lines with positive slope
E. Two lines with the same y-intercept

10. While doing a math assignment, Lia encountered a question that required her to graph the line $y = 2x - 4$ in the standard (x, y) coordinate plane. However, she mistakenly swapped the x and y coordinates of all her points. For example, she plotted $(2, 3)$ instead of $(3, 2)$. What is the equation of the line that Lia mistakenly graphed for this question?

    A. $y = -\dfrac{1}{2}x + 4$

    B. $y = \dfrac{1}{2}x + 2$

    C. $y = \dfrac{1}{2}x + 4$

    D. $y = -2x + 4$

    E. $y = 4x - 2$

11. In the standard (x, y) coordinate plane, the region bounded by the lines $x = c$, $y = 0$ and $y = 4x$ has an area of 32 if $c = ?$

    A. 4
    B. 5
    C. 6
    D. 8
    E. 16

12. The equations below are linear equations of a system where a and b are integers.

    $$y = ax + b$$
    $$y = a^2x + b^2$$

    If these equations are graphed in the standard (x, y) coordinate plane, which of the following graphs are possible?

    I. Two distinct parallel lines
    II. Two perpendicular lines
    III. A single line

    A. I only
    B. II only
    C. III only
    D. I and III only
    E. I, II, and III

13. A parallelogram is shown in the standard (x, y) coordinate plane below. Line l crosses the y-axis and divides the parallelogram into 2 smaller parallelograms of equal area. Which of the following is an equation of line l ?

    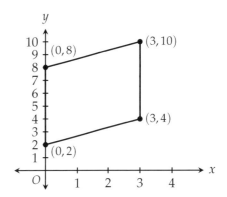

    A. $y = \dfrac{1}{2}x + 5$

    B. $y = \dfrac{2}{3}x + 5$

    C. $y = \dfrac{8}{3}x + 5$

    D. $y = \dfrac{3}{5}x + 2$

    E. $y = \dfrac{3}{7}x + 4$

13
Quadratics

Just as lines were one group of functions that have their own properties, quadratics are another. A quadratic is a function in the form

$$f(x) = ax^2 + bx + c$$

in which the highest power of x is 2. The graph of a quadratic is a parabola.

To review quadratics, we'll walk through a few examples to demonstrate the various properties you need to know.

QUADRATIC 1:

$$f(x) = x^2 - 4x - 21$$

The Roots

The roots refer to the values of x that make $f(x) = 0$. They're also called x-intercepts and solutions. We'll mainly use the term "root" in this chapter, but the other terms are just as common. Don't forget that they all mean the same thing. Here, we can just factor to find the roots:

$$x^2 - 4x - 21 = 0$$
$$(x - 7)(x + 3) = 0$$
$$x = 7, -3$$

The roots are 7 and -3. Graphically, this means the quadratic crosses the x-axis at $x = 7$ and $x = -3$.

The Sum and Product of the Roots

We already found the roots, so their sum is $7 + (-3) = 4$ and their product is $7 \times -3 = -21$. This was really easy, so why do we even care about these values? Because sometimes you'll have to find the sum or the product of the roots **without** knowing the roots themselves. How do we do that?

Given a quadratic of the form $y = ax^2 + bx + c$, the sum of the roots is equal to $-\dfrac{b}{a}$ and the product of the roots is equal to $\dfrac{c}{a}$. In our example, $a = 1, b = -4, c = -21$. So,

$$\text{Sum} = -\frac{b}{a} = -\frac{-4}{1} = 4$$

$$\text{Product} = \frac{c}{a} = -\frac{-21}{1} = -21$$

See how we were able to determine these values without needing to know the roots themselves? You can confirm these values are the same ones we found earlier.

The Vertex

The vertex is the midpoint of a parabola.

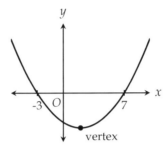

The x-coordinate of the vertex is always the midpoint of the two roots, which can be found by averaging them. Because the roots are 7 and -3, the vertex is at $x = \dfrac{7 + (-3)}{2} = 2$. When $x = 2, f(x) = (2)^2 - 4(2) - 21 = -25$. Therefore, the vertex is at $(2, -25)$. Note that the maximum or minimum of a quadratic is always at the vertex. In this case, it's a minimum of -25.

Vertex Form

Just as slope-intercept form ($y = mx + b$) is one way of representing a line, vertex form is one way of representing a quadratic function. We've already seen two different ways quadratics can be represented, namely standard form ($y = ax^2 + bx + c$) and factored form ($y = (x - a)(x - b)$). Vertex form looks like $y = a(x - h)^2 + k$. The ACT will never ask you to find the vertex form of a quadratic such as $3x^2 - 5x + 2$, where the coefficient of the x^2 term is greater than 1. However, it will ask you to put simpler quadratics into vertex form, albeit very rarely.

To get a quadratic function into vertex form, we have to do something called completing the square. Let's walk through it step-by-step:

$$y = x^2 - 4x - 21$$

See the middle term? The -4. That's the key. The first step is to divide it by 2 to get -2. Then write the following:

$$y = (x - 2)^2 - 21$$

See where we put the -2? The first part is done. Now the second step is to take that -2 and square it. We get 4.

$$y = (x - 2)^2 - 21 - 4$$

See where we put the 4? We subtracted it at the end. The vertex form is then

$$y = (x - 2)^2 - 25$$

To recap, divide the middle coefficient by 2 to get the number inside the parentheses. Subtract the square of that number at the end. Completing the square takes some time and practice, so if you didn't catch all of this, first prove to yourself that the result is indeed the same quadratic by expanding it. Then repeat the process of completing the square yourself. If you've been taught a slightly different way, feel free to use it. We'll do many more examples in this chapter.

Now why do we care about vertex form? Well, look at the numbers! It's called vertex form for a reason. The vertex $(2, -25)$ can be found just by looking at the numbers in the equation. But we already found the vertex, you say! Yes, that's true, but we had to find the roots to do so earlier, and finding the roots is not always so easy. Vertex form allows us to find the vertex without knowing the roots of a quadratic.

One final note—one of the most common mistakes students make is to look at $y = (x - 2)^2 - 25$ and think the vertex is at $(-2, -25)$ instead of $(2, -25)$. One pattern of thinking I use to avoid this mistake is to ask, *What value of x would make the expression inside the parentheses equal to zero?* Well, $x = 2$ would make $x - 2$ equal to 0. Therefore, the vertex is at $x = 2$. This is the same type of thinking you would use to get the roots from the factored form $y = (x - a)(x - b)$.

The Discriminant

If a quadratic is in the form $ax^2 + bx + c$, then the discriminant is equal to $b^2 - 4ac$. As we'll explain later, the discriminant is a component of the quadratic formula. Before we explain its significance, let's calculate the discriminant for our first example,

$$f(x) = x^2 - 4x - 21$$

$$\text{Discriminant} = b^2 - 4ac = (-4)^2 - 4(1)(-21) = 100$$

Now, what does the discriminant mean? Well, the value of the discriminant does not matter. What matters is the **sign** of the discriminant—whether it's positive, negative, or zero. In other words, we don't care that it's 100, we just care that it's positive. Letting D be short for discriminant,

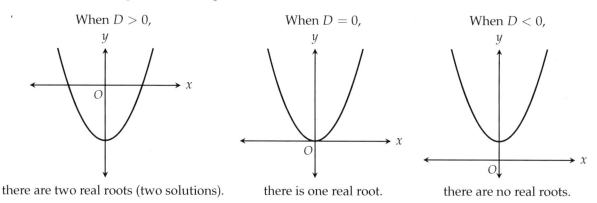

| When $D > 0$, | When $D = 0$, | When $D < 0$, |
| there are two real roots (two solutions). | there is one real root. | there are no real roots. |

Because the first example has a discriminant greater than 0, it has two real roots, which we've already determined to be -3 and 7.

The Quadratic Formula

As we've seen, the roots are the most important aspect of a quadratic. Once you have the roots, concepts like vertex form and the discriminant may not be needed. Unfortunately, the roots aren't always easy to find or work with, and that's when vertex form, the discriminant, and the sum/product of the roots can get us to the answer faster.

But if we must find the roots, there is always one surefire way to do so—the quadratic formula.

$$x = \frac{-b \pm \sqrt{b^2 - 4ac}}{2a}$$

for $ax^2 + bx + c = 0$. For learning purposes, let's apply it to our example.

$$f(x) = x^2 - 4x - 21$$

The roots, or solutions, are

$$x = \frac{-(-4) \pm \sqrt{(-4)^2 - 4(1)(-21)}}{2(1)} = \frac{4 \pm \sqrt{100}}{2} = \frac{4 \pm 10}{2} = 7 \text{ or } -3$$

And we get the same values as we did through factoring.

Notice that the discriminant, $b^2 - 4ac$, is tucked under the square root in the quadratic formula. How does this help us to understand what we know about the discriminant?

Well, when $b^2 - 4ac > 0$, the "$\pm$" takes effect and we end up with two different roots. When $b^2 - 4ac = 0$, the "$\pm$" does not have an effect since we're essentially adding and subtracting 0, both of which give us the same root. When $b^2 - 4ac < 0$, we end up adding and subtracting the square root of a negative number, which results in two imaginary roots.

Hopefully, the quadratic formula helps you understand where the discriminant comes from. Understanding this connection will help you remember the concepts.

Now that we've taken you on a thorough tour through the properties of quadratics, we'll demonstrate a few more examples to illustrate some important variations, but we'll do so at a much faster pace.

QUADRATIC 2:
$$f(x) = -x^2 + 6x - 10$$

The Roots

This quadratic cannot be factored. And in fact, if we look at the discriminant,

$$b^2 - 4ac = (6)^2 - 4(-1)(-10) = -4$$

it's negative, which means there are no real roots or solutions. The graph of the quadratic provides further confirmation:

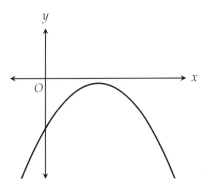

When the coefficient of the x^2 term is negative, the parabola is in the shape of an upside-down "U."

81

The Sum and Product of the Roots

$$f(x) = -x^2 + 6x - 10$$

$$\text{Sum} = -\frac{b}{a} = -\frac{6}{-1} = 6$$

$$\text{Product} = \frac{c}{a} = \frac{-10}{-1} = 10$$

Wait, what!? We already determined that there were no roots. How can there be a sum and a product of roots that don't exist? Well, the quadratic doesn't have any *real* roots, but it does have *imaginary* roots. The values above are the sum and product of these imaginary roots, which we'll find using the quadratic formula in just a moment.

Vertex Form

Because the roots are imaginary, we can't use their midpoint to find the vertex. In these cases, we must get the quadratic in vertex form by completing the square.

$$y = -x^2 + 6x - 10$$

First, multiply everything by negative 1 to get the negative out of the x^2 term. Having the negative there makes things needlessly complicated. We'll multiply everything back by -1 later.

$$-y = x^2 - 6x + 10$$

Divide the middle term by 2 to get -3 and square this result to get 9. Remember that we put the -3 inside the parentheses with x and subtract the 9 at the end. Putting these pieces in place,

$$-y = (x - 3)^2 + 10 - 9$$

$$-y = (x - 3)^2 + 1$$

Multiplying everything by -1 again,

$$y = -(x - 3)^2 - 1$$

Now it's easy to see that the vertex is at $(3, -1)$. And because the graph is an upside-down "U," -1 is the maximum value of $f(x)$.

The Quadratic Formula

The roots are imaginary, so expect i to show up. Using the quadratic formula for $-x^2 + 6x - 10 = 0$,

$$x = \frac{-6 \pm \sqrt{(6)^2 - 4(-1)(-10)}}{2(-1)} = \frac{-6 \pm \sqrt{-4}}{-2} = \frac{-6 \pm 2i}{-2} = 3 \pm i$$

QUADRATIC 3:
$$f(x) = 4x^2 - 12x + 9$$

The Roots

We could factor this, but let's use the quadratic formula instead.

$$x = \frac{-b \pm \sqrt{b^2 - 4ac}}{2a} = \frac{-(-12) \pm \sqrt{(-12)^2 - 4(4)(9)}}{2(4)} = \frac{12 \pm \sqrt{0}}{8} = \frac{3}{2}$$

As you can see, the discriminant is 0 and the quadratic has just one root, $\frac{3}{2}$.

The Sum and Product of the Roots

$$\text{Sum} = -\frac{b}{a} = -\frac{-12}{4} = 3$$
$$\text{Product} = \frac{c}{a} = \frac{9}{4}$$

If we only have one root, how is it that we can have a sum and a product of two roots? Why are they different from the one root we found?

Here's the thing. While we may say a quadratic has just one root, it really has two roots that are the same. After all, a quadratic, with an x^2 term, is expected to have two roots. When they're the same, we just refer to them as one.

So our "two" roots are $\frac{3}{2}$ and $\frac{3}{2}$. If we add them, we do indeed get 3, and if we multiply them, we get $\frac{9}{4}$.

The Vertex

When a quadratic has just one root, the x-coordinate of the vertex is the same as the root. That's because a quadratic with one root is tangent to the x-axis.

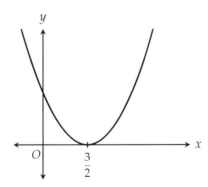

The y-coordinate is, of course, 0. Therefore, the vertex is at $\left(\frac{3}{2}, 0\right)$ and the minimum value of $f(x)$ is 0.

Because we just found the vertex, we can deduce that the vertex form of the quadratic is $y = 4\left(x - \frac{3}{2}\right)^2$.

However, finding the vertex form for this kind of quadratic (where the x^2 term has a coefficient greater than 1) is beyond the scope of the ACT, so we won't show the "completing the square" process for this one.

Wow! We just covered pretty much everything you need to know about quadratics. Unfortunately, we're not quite done yet as there are a few question variations that you should be exposed to.

EXAMPLE 1: Which of the following binomials is a factor of $x^2 - 7x + 12$?

A. $x - 4$ B. $x - 2$ C. $x + 2$ D. $x + 3$ E. $x + 4$

Through factoring, we get

$$x^2 - 7x + 12 = (x - 4)(x - 3)$$

and so both $(x - 4)$ and $(x - 3)$ are **factors** of the quadratic $x^2 - 7x + 12$ in the same way that "2" and "3" are factors of "6". Answer $\boxed{(A)}$.

It may already be intuitive to you, but notice the way in which $x = 3$ and $x = 4$, the values for which the quadratic is equal to zero (the roots), are derived from these factors. If $x - 3$ is a factor, then 3 is a root. If 3 is a root, then $x - 3$ is a factor. This concept applies not just to quadratics but to any polynomial, as we'll see in the next example.

EXAMPLE 2: What is the value of k if $x + 1$ is a factor of $2x^3 + kx^2 + 6x + 2$?

A. 4   B. 5   C. 6   D. 7   E. 8

If $x + 1$ is a factor, then -1 is a root. If -1 is a root, then the polynomial evaluates to 0 when $x = -1$:

$$2(-1)^3 + k(-1)^2 + 6(-1) + 2 = 0$$
$$-2 + k - 6 + 2 = 0$$
$$k = 6$$

Answer $\boxed{(C)}$.

EXAMPLE 3: The equation $x^2 + 5x + k = 0$ has two solutions. If one of the solutions is $x = 2$, the other solution is:

A. -10 B. -7 C. -3 D. 3   E. 5

The sum of the solutions must be $-\dfrac{5}{1} = -5$. So if we let the other solution be x, then $x + 2 = -5$ and $x = -7$.

Answer $\boxed{(B)}$.

EXAMPLE 4: If the equation $kx^2 - 4x + 8 = 0$ has one real solution, then what is the value of k?

A. $\dfrac{1}{4}$ B. $\dfrac{1}{2}$ C. 2   D. 4   E. 6

If the equation has one real solution, then the discriminant of the quadratic must be 0.

$$b^2 - 4ac = 0$$

$$(-4)^2 - 4(k)(8) = 0$$

$$16 - 32k = 0$$

$$-32k = -16$$

$$k = \frac{1}{2}$$

Answer $\boxed{(B)}$.

Review:

Given a quadratic of the form, $y = ax^2 + bx + c$,

The roots, also called solutions and x-intercepts, can be found in the following ways:

- Factoring
- Graph on the calculator (look for the x-intercepts)
- The quadratic formula $x = \dfrac{-b \pm \sqrt{b^2 - 4ac}}{2a}$

Sum of the Roots $= -\dfrac{b}{a}$

Product of the Roots $= \dfrac{c}{a}$

The **discriminant** $D = b^2 - 4ac$

- When $D > 0$, there are two real solutions.
- When $D = 0$, there is one real solution.
- When $D < 0$, there are no real solutions.

The **axis of symmetry** is the equation of the line that runs down the "middle" of a parabola.

To find the **vertex**,

- Take the average of the roots to get the x-coordinate. Then plug that value into the quadratic to get the y-coordinate.
- Put the quadratic in vertex form by **completing the square**.

  1. Divide the coefficient of the middle term by 2 to get $\dfrac{b}{2}$. Square that result to get $\dfrac{b^2}{4}$. Put $\dfrac{b}{2}$ inside the parentheses with x and subtract $\dfrac{b^2}{4}$ at the end.

  $$y = \left(x + \frac{b}{2}\right)^2 + c - \frac{b^2}{4}$$

  2. It's unnecessary to memorize these steps with the variables. Practice on quadratics with actual numbers. However, do remember what **vertex form** looks like: $y = a(x - h)^2 + k$, where (h, k) is the vertex.

CHAPTER EXERCISE: Answers for this chapter start on page 226.

1. Which of the following numbers is a solution to $2x^2 = 6x + 36$?

   A. -6
   B. -3
   C. 3
   D. 4
   E. 9

2. Which of the following equations, when graphed in the standard (x, y) coordinate plane, would cross the x-axis at $x = -2$ and $x = 5$?

   A. $-2(x - 2)(x - 5)$
   B. $-2(x + 2)(x - 5)$
   C. $-2(x + 2)(x + 5)$
   D. $5(x - 2)(x + 5)$
   E. $5(x + 2)(x + 5)$

3. A parabola crosses the x-axis at $(2, 0)$ and $(8, 0)$ as shown in the standard (x, y) coordinate plane below.

   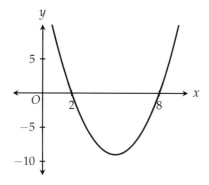

   Which of the following equations gives the axis of symmetry of the parabola?

   A. $x = 3$
   B. $y = 3$
   C. $x = 5$
   D. $y = 5$
   E. $x = 6$

4. What is the sum of the 2 solutions of the equation $2x^2 - 5x + 2 = 0$?

   A. -1
   B. 1
   C. 2
   D. $2\frac{1}{2}$
   E. 5

5. The 2 roots of an equation $ax^2 + bx + c = 0$ are given by the quadratic formula $x = \dfrac{-b \pm \sqrt{b^2 - 4ac}}{2a}$. What are the 2 roots of the equation $2x^2 - x = 15$?

   A. -3 and $\dfrac{5}{2}$
   B. $-\dfrac{5}{2}$ and 3
   C. $\dfrac{1 - 2\sqrt{30}}{4}$ and $\dfrac{1 + 2\sqrt{30}}{4}$
   D. -6 and 5
   E. 5 and 6

6. In the standard (x, y) coordinate plane, what is the vertex of the parabola with the equation $y = -2(x + 3)^2 + 1$?

   A. $(-3, -1)$
   B. $(-3, 1)$
   C. $(3, -1)$
   D. $(3, 1)$
   E. $(6, 1)$

7. Which of the following binomials is a factor of $2x^2 - 7x + 6$?

   A. $x - 3$
   B. $x - 2$
   C. $x - 1$
   D. $x + 2$
   E. $x + 3$

8. For what integer k are both solutions of the equation $x^2 + kx + 19 = 0$ negative integers?

   A. -20
   B. -18
   C. -1
   D. 18
   E. 20

9. The parabola shown in the standard (x, y) plane below is the graph of one of the following equations. Which one?

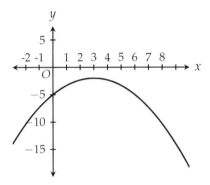

   A. $y + 2 = -(x - 3)^2$
   B. $y - 2 = -3(x + 3)^2$
   C. $y + 2 = -3(x - 3)^2$
   D. $y - 2 = -\dfrac{1}{3}(x + 3)^2$
   E. $y + 2 = -\dfrac{1}{3}(x - 3)^2$

10. A parabola crosses the point $(4, -14)$ and has x-intercepts at -3 and 5. What is the vertex of the parabola?

    A. $(1, -32)$
    B. $(1, -24)$
    C. $(1, -16)$
    D. $(2, -15)$
    E. $(2, -30)$

11. In the standard (x, y) coordinate plane, the graph of $y = x^2 + kx + 8$ crosses the x-axis at only one point. What does k equal?

    A. $2\sqrt{3}$
    B. 4
    C. $4\sqrt{2}$
    D. 6
    E. 16

12. If $(x - 3)$ and $(x + 1)$ are factors of the quadratic expression below, what is the value of $m + n$?

$$x^2 + (m - 5)x + m - n$$

    A. -3
    B. 0
    C. 3
    D. 6
    E. 9

14

Coordinate Geometry

Coordinate geometry questions typically ask you to find the coordinates of a certain point, as you'll see in our first example.

EXAMPLE 1: Three vertices of a rectangle are as given in the standard (x, y) coordinate plane below. What are the coordinates of the fourth vertex?

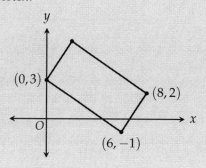

A. $(2, 3)$ **B.** $(2, 4)$ **C.** $(2, 6)$ **D.** $(3, 5)$ **E.** $(3, 6)$

In any rectangle, opposite sides are parallel and equal in length. Therefore, the two vertices on the left must have the same relative positions with respect to one another as the two vertices on the right. The point $(8, 2)$ is 2 units to the right of and 3 units up from $(6, -1)$. So the coordinates of the fourth vertex must be 2 units to the right of and 3 units up from $(0, 3)$. That gets us to $(0 + 2, 3 + 3) = (2, 6)$. Answer $\boxed{(C)}$.

Although this example question didn't demand too much from us, other question types will require you to know two formulas.

The Midpoint Formula

The midpoint of (x_1, y_1) and (x_2, y_2) consists of the average of the x-coordinates and the average of the y-coordinates. Put mathematically, the midpoint is

$$\left(\frac{x_1 + x_2}{2}, \frac{y_1 + y_2}{2} \right)$$

EXAMPLE 2: What is the midpoint of the line segment with endpoints $(3,8)$ and $(7,-10)$ in the standard (x,y) coordinate plane?

A. $(4,-1)$ **B.** $(5,-1)$ **C.** $(6,2)$ **D.** $(7,2)$ **E.** $(10,-2)$

$$\text{Midpoint} = \left(\frac{x_1+x_2}{2}, \frac{y_1+y_2}{2}\right) = \left(\frac{3+7}{2}, \frac{8-10}{2}\right) = (5,-1)$$

Answer $\boxed{(B)}$.

The Distance Formula

The straight-line distance d, in coordinate units, between two points (x_1, y_1) and (x_2, y_2) is given by the following formula:

$$d = \sqrt{(y_2-y_1)^2 + (x_2-x_1)^2}$$

EXAMPLE 3: The coordinates of the endpoints of $\overline{CD}$, in the standard (x,y) coordinate plane, are $(-2,5)$ and $(3,8)$. What is the length, in coordinate units, of $\overline{CD}$?

A. 2 **B.** 4 **C.** $\sqrt{8}$ **D.** $\sqrt{10}$ **E.** $\sqrt{34}$

$$d = \sqrt{(y_2-y_1)^2 + (x_2-x_1)^2} = \sqrt{(8-5)^2 + (3-(-2))^2} = \sqrt{3^2+5^2} = \sqrt{9+25} = \sqrt{34}$$

Answer $\boxed{(E)}$.

Just as functions can be transformed (e.g. shifting the graph of $f(x)$ down by 1 unit), so too can individual points, line segments, and geometric shapes. Let's walk through a few of these cases to illustrate the different types of transformations that can be applied.

Translation

Translation simply means moving all the points on a graph by the same amount, whether it's to the right, to the left, up, down, or some combination of the above.

EXAMPLE 4: Point P has coordinates $(-2,4)$ in the standard (x,y) coordinate plane. What are the new coordinates of point P after it is translated 12 coordinate units down and 5 coordinate units to the left?

A. $(-14,-1)$ **B.** $(-7,-8)$ **C.** $(3,16)$ **D.** $(7,8)$ **E.** $(10,9)$

Going 12 units down from P gets us to $(-2, 4-12) = (-2,-8)$. Then 5 units to the left brings us to $(-2-5, -8) = (-7,-8)$. Answer $\boxed{(B)}$.

After a transformation is performed, the result is sometimes called the **image**. You'll see this term show up occasionally on the ACT. In this example, the image of point P is $(-7,-8)$.

Reflection

A reflection always involves a line of reflection, which you can think of as a mirror. After a reflection, a point and its image must form a line segment that is perpendicular to the line of reflection, and they must each be the same distance from the line of reflection. Let's do an easy example to illustrate.

EXAMPLE 5: In the standard (x, y) coordinate plane, $A(4, -2)$ is reflected across the x-axis. What are the coordinates of the image of A ?

A. $(-4, -2)$ **B.** $(-4, 2)$ **C.** $(-2, 4)$ **D.** $(2, -4)$ **E.** $(4, 2)$

Let the image of A be B. After A is reflected across the x-axis, $\overline{AB}$ must be perpendicular to the x-axis and A and B must both be the same distance from the x-axis. This might sound complicated but if we plot it out, it's much easier to make sense of.

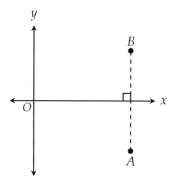

Because A is 2 units from the x-axis, point B must also be 2 units from the x-axis. Therefore, the coordinates of B are $(4, 2)$. Answer $\boxed{(E)}$.

To make sure you understand how reflections work, let's illustrate a slightly more advanced task. The graph below shows the reflection of $\overline{AB}$ across the line $y = x$.

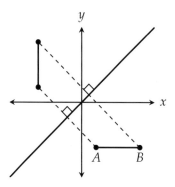

Take the time to study the graph above. Notice that we only needed to reflect the endpoints of $\overline{AB}$ to know what its full image would look like.

Rotation

Rotating something means to turn it around a center, typically the origin. Under a rotation, the distance from the center stays the same. For example, the following graph shows the image of point A after a $90°$ counterclockwise rotation about the origin.

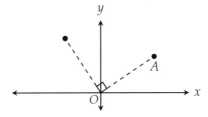

If point A has coordinates $(3, 2)$, then we can deduce from the graph that its image has coordinates $(-2, 3)$.

EXAMPLE 6: A line segment has endpoints $(0, 0)$ and $(3, 4)$ in the standard (x, y) coordinate plane. The line segment will be rotated clockwise (↻) by $90°$ about the origin. The image of the line segment will have endpoints at $(0, 0)$ and:

A. $(-4, 3)$ **B.** $(-3, 4)$ **C.** $(3, -4)$ **D.** $(4, -3)$ **E.** $(4, 3)$

Let's draw it out:

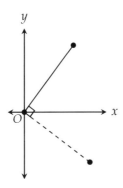

Now there isn't a mathematical method you need to know to find the coordinates of the image of the endpoint. A decently-drawn graph and your intuition are all you need to determine that the coordinates are $(4, -3)$.

Answer $\boxed{(D)}$.

Projection

Think of a projection as casting a shadow onto a line. For example, the following graph shows the projection of $\overline{AB}$ onto the x-axis. Each point on $\overline{AB}$ corresponds to its perpendicular counterpart on the x-axis.

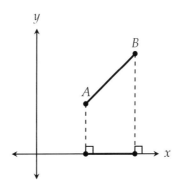

EXAMPLE 7: Which of the following points in the standard (x, y) coordinate plane below is the projection of point Z onto the line $y = x$?

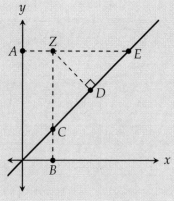

A. A **B.** B **C.** C **D.** D **E.** E

This one's easy. The projection of Z must lie on the line $y = x$ and it must form a line segment that is perpendicular to $y = x$. Therefore, the projection is point D. Answer $\boxed{(D)}$.

EXAMPLE 8: In the standard (x, y) coordinate plane shown below, $\overline{CD}$ has endpoints $C(1, 3)$ and $D(2, 5)$, and $\overline{C'D'}$ is the projection of $\overline{CD}$ onto the y-axis. By how many coordinate units is $\overline{CD}$ longer than $\overline{C'D'}$?

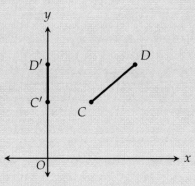

A. 3   **B.** $\sqrt{5} - 2$ **C.** $\sqrt{5} - 1$ **D.** $\sqrt{17} - 1$ **E.** $\sqrt{17} - 2$

Because $\overline{C'D'}$ is the projection of $\overline{CD}$ onto the y-axis, point C' must have coordinates $(0, 3)$, and point D' must have coordinates $(0, 5)$. The length of $\overline{C'D'}$ is then $5 - 3 = 2$.

Using the distance formula to get the length of $\overline{CD}$,

$$d = \sqrt{(y_2 - y_1)^2 + (x_2 - x_1)^2} = \sqrt{(5 - 3)^2 + (2 - 1)^2} = \sqrt{2^2 + 1^2} = \sqrt{5}$$

Therefore, $\overline{CD}$ is longer than $\overline{C'D'}$ by $\sqrt{5} - 2$ coordinate units. Answer $\boxed{(B)}$.

CHAPTER EXERCISE: Answers for this chapter start on page 228.

1. In the standard (x, y) coordinate plane, $\overline{MN}$ has endpoints $(6, -8)$ and $(-10, 20)$. What is the y-coordinate of the midpoint of $\overline{MN}$?

    A. -4
    B. -2
    C. 6
    D. 12
    E. 14

2. What is the distance, in coordinate units, between $(5, -2)$ and $(7, 1)$ in the standard (x, y) coordinate plane?

    A. $\sqrt{5}$
    B. 5
    C. $\sqrt{11}$
    D. $\sqrt{13}$
    E. 13

3. A regular hexagon is graphed in the standard (x, y) coordinate plane below. Which of the following are the coordinates of the vertex Q ?

    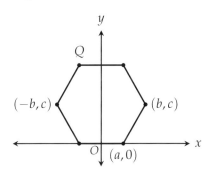

    A. $(-a, -c)$
    B. $(-a, 2b)$
    C. $(-a, 2c)$
    D. $(-b, -a)$
    E. $(-b, 2c)$

4. In the standard (x, y) coordinate plane, a diameter of a circle has endpoints $(3, 1)$ and $(11, -7)$. The center of the circle is at which of the following points?

    A. $(-4, 4)$
    B. $(4, 8)$
    C. $(7, -3)$
    D. $(8, -8)$
    E. $(14, -6)$

5. A triangle and a circle are graphed in the same standard (x, y) coordinate plane. The triangle has vertices at $(0, 2)$, $(-2, -3)$, and $(2, -3)$. The circle has radius 2 and center at $(0, 0)$. The triangle and the circle intersect at how many points?

    A. 2
    B. 3
    C. 4
    D. 5
    E. 6

6. In the standard (x, y) coordinate plane, the endpoints of $\overline{AB}$ are $(-a, a)$ and $(b, 2b)$, where a and b are distinct positive real numbers. Line segment $\overline{A'B'}$ is the image of $\overline{AB}$ after a reflection across the y-axis. What are the coordinates of the endpoints of $\overline{A'B'}$?

    A. $(-a, -a)$ and $(b, -2b)$
    B. $(-a, 0)$ and $(b, 0)$
    C. $(-a, a)$ and $(b, 2b)$
    D. $(a, -a)$ and $(-b, -2b)$
    E. (a, a) and $(-b, 2b)$

7. Judy redesigned a company webpage on a square coordinate grid marked in centimeter units. The company logo was originally located at $(4, -5)$, 4 centimeters to the right and 5 centimeters down from the center of the webpage. Judy moved the logo 6 centimeters to the left and 3 centimeters up. Which of the following is closest to the straight-line distance, in centimeters, between the new location of the logo and the center of the webpage in Judy's redesign?

    A. 3
    B. 4
    C. 7
    D. 8
    E. 10

8. In the standard (x, y) coordinate plane, the midpoint of $\overline{BC}$ is $(-4, 3)$. If B has coordinates $(2, -1)$, what are the coordinates of C ?

   A. $(-10, 7)$
   B. $(-8, 5)$
   C. $(-6, 4)$
   D. $(-2, 2)$
   E. $(-1, 1)$

9. A square with a side length of 4 coordinate units is graphed in the standard (x, y) coordinate plane. If the square has a vertex at $(3, -2)$, all of the following points could be another vertex of the square EXCEPT:

   A. $(-1, -2)$
   B. $(-1, 2)$
   C. $(3, -6)$
   D. $(3, 6)$
   E. $(7, -2)$

10. In the standard (x, y) coordinate plane shown below, quadrilateral $P'Q'R'S'$ is a reflection of quadrilateral $PQRS$ across which of the following lines?

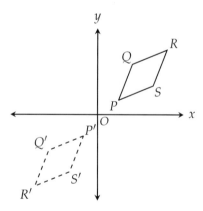

   A. $x = 0$
   B. $y = 0$
   C. $y = x$
   D. $y = x + 1$
   E. $y = -x$

11. Three points are shown in the standard (x, y) coordinate plane below. Point A has coordinates $(3, 3)$, A' is the projection of A onto the x-axis, and A'' is the image of A' after a clockwise rotation $(\circlearrowright)$ by $60°$ about the origin. What is the x-coordinate of A'' ?

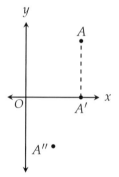

   A. $\dfrac{3}{\sqrt{2}}$

   B. $\dfrac{3}{2}$

   C. $\sqrt{3}$

   D. $\dfrac{3\sqrt{3}}{2}$

   E. 2

Use the following information to answer questions 12–13.

Triangle ABC is graphed in the standard (x, y) coordinate plane below. Vertex A is at $(1, 0)$, vertex C is at $(4, 0)$, and the length of $\overline{BC}$ is 5 coordinate units.

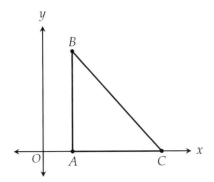

12. What are the coordinates of the midpoint of $\overline{BC}$?

    A. $(3, 1)$

    B. $\left(\dfrac{5}{2}, 2\right)$

    C. $\left(\dfrac{5}{2}, \dfrac{5}{2}\right)$

    D. $\left(2, \dfrac{5}{2}\right)$

    E. $(2, 2)$

13. Triangle ABC is rotated counterclockwise ($\circlearrowleft$) by $90°$ about the origin. The image of C is at which of the following points?

    A. $(-4, 0)$
    B. $(0, -4)$
    C. $(0, 4)$
    D. $(1, -3)$
    E. $(1, 3)$

14. What is the distance, in coordinate units, from point $(k + 1, k)$ to point $(k, -k)$ in the standard (x, y) coordinate plane?

    A. 1
    B. $4k^2 + 1$
    C. $\sqrt{2k + 1}$
    D. $\sqrt{4k^2 + 1}$
    E. $\sqrt{4k^2 + 4k + 1}$

15

Angles

Exterior Angle Theorem

An exterior angle is formed when any side of a triangle is extended. In the triangle below, $x°$ designates an exterior angle.

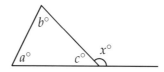

An exterior angle is always equal to the sum of the two angles in the triangle furthest from it. In this case,

$$x = a + b$$

EXAMPLE 1: Vertices C and E of triangle $\triangle CDE$ shown below lie on $\overline{AB}$. What is the value of x ?

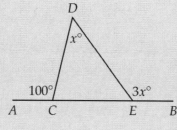

A. 30   **B.** 40   **C.** 50   **D.** 60   **E.** 80

$\angle DCE$ must be $180° - 100° = 80°$. Now we can use the exterior angle theorem to quickly solve for x:

$$80 + x = 3x$$
$$80 = 2x$$
$$x = 40$$

Answer $\boxed{(B)}$.

Parallel Lines

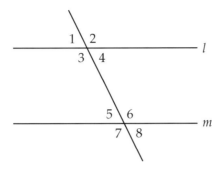

When two lines are parallel, the following are true:

- Vertical angles are equal (e.g. $\angle 1 = \angle 4$)
- Alternate interior angles are equal (e.g. $\angle 4 = \angle 5$ and $\angle 3 = \angle 6$)
- Corresponding angles are equal (e.g. $\angle 1 = \angle 5$)
- Same side interior angles are supplementary (e.g. $\angle 3 + \angle 5 = 180°$)

No need to memorize these terms. You just need to know that when two parallel lines are cut by another line, there are two sets of equal angles:

$$\angle 1 = \angle 4 = \angle 5 = \angle 8$$

$$\angle 2 = \angle 3 = \angle 6 = \angle 7$$

EXAMPLE 2: In the figure below, $\overline{AC} \parallel \overline{GD}$ and $\overline{BF} \parallel \overline{CE}$. If $\angle CAE = 70°$ and $\angle ACE = 40°$, what is the value of x ?

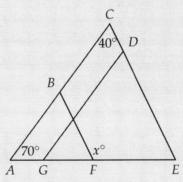

A. 100   B. 105   C. 110   D. 115   E. 120

Here is the fastest way: $\angle ACE = \angle ABF = 40°$ because they are corresponding angles ($\overline{AC}$ cuts parallel lines $\overline{BF}$ and $\overline{CE}$). Since angle x is an exterior angle to $\triangle ABF$, $x = 70 + 40 = 110°$. Answer $\boxed{(C)}$.

Polygons

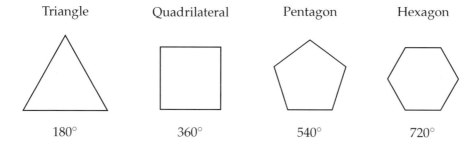

Triangle	Quadrilateral	Pentagon	Hexagon
180°	360°	540°	720°

As you can see from the polygons above, each additional side increases the sum of the interior angles by 180°. For any polygon, the sum of the interior angles is

$$180(n-2) \text{ where } n \text{ is the number of sides}$$

So for an octagon, which has 8 sides, the sum of the interior angles is $180(8-2) = 180 \times 6 = 1080°$.

A **regular polygon** is one in which all the sides and angles are equal. The polygons shown above are regular. If our octagon were regular, each interior angle would have a measure of $1080° \div 8 = 135°$.

The $180(n-2)$ formula comes from the fact that any polygon can be split up into triangles by drawing lines from any one vertex to the others.

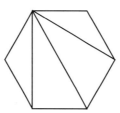

The number of triangles that results from this process is always two less than the number of sides. Count for yourself! Because each triangle contains 180°, the sum of the angles within a polygon is $180°(n-2)$, where n is the number of sides.

EXAMPLE 3: Two sides of a regular pentagon are extended until they intersect, as shown in the figure below. What is the value of x?

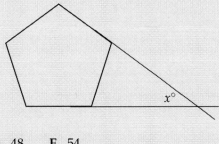

A. 30   **B.** 36   **C.** 42   **D.** 48   **E.** 54

The total number of degrees in a pentagon is $180(5-2) = 540°$. So each interior angle must measure $540° \div 5 = 108°$. The angles within the triangle formed by the intersecting lines are then $180 - 108 = 72°$.

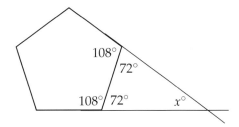

Finally, $x = 180 - 72 - 72 = 36°$. Answer $\boxed{(B)}$.

CHAPTER EXERCISE: Answers for this chapter start on page 231.

1. In the figure below, four line segments intersect at a single point. What is the value of y ?

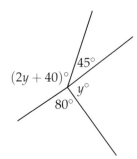

   A.   50
   B.   55
   C.   60
   D.   65
   E.   70

2. In quadrilateral $ABCD$ shown below, $\overline{AD}$ is parallel to $\overline{BC}$, and $\overline{AB}$ is perpendicular to $\overline{BC}$. What is the measure of $\angle D$?

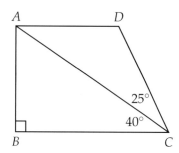

   A.   115°
   B.   120°
   C.   125°
   D.   130°
   E.   135°

3. In the diagram below, lines m and n are cut by transversal line l. The measures of the 8 angles at the intersections of these lines are labeled. Which of the following statements, when it is true, can *always* be used to prove that lines m and n are parallel?

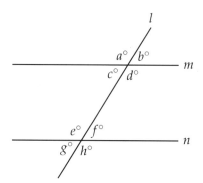

   A. $a = d$
   B. $b = g$
   C. $e = f$
   D. $c = e$
   E. $f = h$

4. In the figure below, $\angle ADC$ measures 20°, $\angle ACB$ measures 50°, and $\angle BAD$ measures 90°. What is the measure of $\angle BAC$?

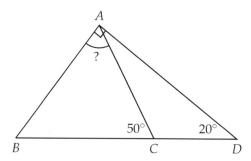

   A.   60°
   B.   65°
   C.   70°
   D.   75°
   E.   80°

5. In the figure below, lines *l* and *m* are parallel. If it can be determined, what is the sum of the degree measures of ∠1 and ∠2 ?

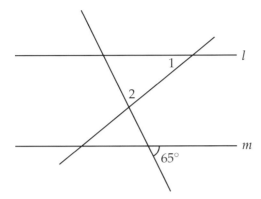

    A. 65°
    B. 90°
    C. 105°
    D. 115°
    E. Cannot be determined from the given information

6. In the figure below, *E* is a point on $\overline{BH}$ and on $\overline{CG}$, $\overline{BC}$ and $\overline{EF}$ are perpendicular to $\overline{BH}$, and $\overline{AC}$ is parallel to $\overline{EF}$ and $\overline{GI}$.

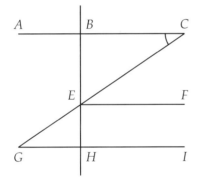

The measure of ∠CEH is 2 times the measure of ∠GEH. What is the measure of ∠BCE ?

    A. 30°
    B. 36°
    C. 40°
    D. 45°
    E. 60°

7. The hexagon shown below has 6 sides of equal length. What is the value of *x* ?

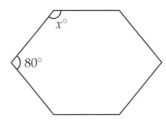

    A. 120°
    B. 135°
    C. 140°
    D. 145°
    E. 150°

8. The angle at which a ray of light strikes a mirror is equal in measure to the angle at which it is reflected. In the mirror enclosure below, what is the measure of the indicated angle?

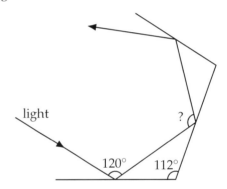

    A. 102°
    B. 104°
    C. 108°
    D. 114°
    E. 118°

9. In pentagon *ABCDE* below, $\overline{AE}$ is parallel to $\overline{BC}$, the measure of $\angle E$ is 150°, and the measure of $\angle D$ is 90°. If it can be determined, what is the measure of $\angle C$?

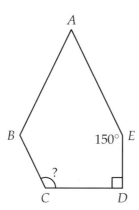

A. 120°
B. 130°
C. 140°
D. 150°
E. Cannot be determined from the given information

10. In the diagram below, $\overleftrightarrow{BA}$ is parallel to $\overleftrightarrow{CE}$, *D* lies on $\overleftrightarrow{CE}$, *E* lies on $\overleftrightarrow{AF}$, the measure of $\angle FED$ is 129°, and $\angle BAC \cong \angle CAD \cong \angle DAE$. What is the measure of $\angle ADE$?

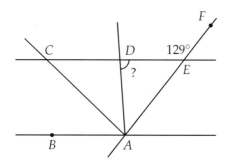

A. 51°
B. 43°
C. 71°
D. 78°
E. 86°

11. In the figure below, $\overline{AB}$ is parallel to $\overline{ED}$, the measure of $\angle CDE$ is 36°, and the measure of $\angle BCD$ is 67°. What is the measure of $\angle ABC$?

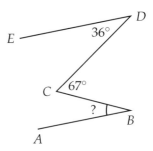

A. 29°
B. 31°
C. 33°
D. 36°
E. 38°

16

Triangles

Side and Angle Relationships

For any triangle, the largest angle is opposite the largest side. The smallest angle is opposite the smallest side.

In the triangle below, $AC > BC > AB$

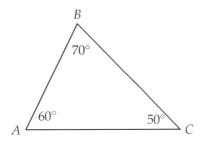

Of course, the reverse is true. The largest side is opposite the largest angle. The smallest side is opposite the smallest angle.

In the triangle below, $b > a > c$

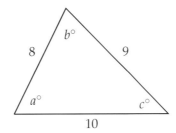

EXAMPLE 1: For $\triangle ABC$ below, the given lengths are in inches. All of the following are possible values for the length of $\overline{AB}$ EXCEPT:

A. 1   **B.** 2   **C.** 3   **D.** 4   **E.** 5

In any right triangle, the right angle is always the largest angle. Therefore, the hypotenuse is always the largest side. In this question, the hypotenuse is 5 so AB cannot also be 5. Answer (E).

Isosceles & Equilateral Triangles

An isosceles triangle has two sides of equal length. The angles opposite those sides are equal.

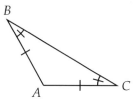

Because $AB = AC$, $\angle C = \angle B$.

In an equilateral triangle, all sides have the same length. Because equal sides imply equal angles, the angles are all $60°$.

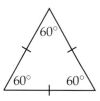

EXAMPLE 2: In the diagram below, $\triangle ABC$ is equilateral and $\triangle BCD$ is isosceles. What is the measure of $\angle BDC$?

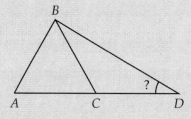

A. $10°$ **B.** $15°$ **C.** $30°$ **D.** $45°$ **E.** $60°$

Because $\triangle ABC$ is equilateral, $\angle BCA$ is $60°$ and the supplementary angle $\angle BCD$ is $180 - 60 = 120°$. Now $\triangle BCD$ is isosceles so $BC = CD$ and $\angle CBD = \angle CDB$. There's $180 - 120 = 60°$ left to split between these two angles so each of them is $60 \div 2 = 30°$. Answer (C).

Right Triangles

Right triangles are made up of two legs and a hypotenuse (the side opposite the right angle).

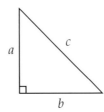

Every right triangle obeys the pythagorean theorem: $a^2 + b^2 = c^2$, where a and b are the lengths of the legs and c is the length of the hypotenuse.

EXAMPLE 3: Bryan has a rectangular piece of cardboard 18 inches wide and 14 inches long. He decides to cut it along a diagonal to get two congruent triangles. To the nearest inch, what is the length of the longest side of one of these triangles?

A. 17   **B.** 19   **C.** 22   **D.** 23   **E.** 24

Let's start by drawing a diagram:

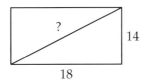

We have two congruent right triangles. The longest side of either one is the hypotenuse. Using the pythagorean theorem to get the length,

$$18^2 + 14^2 = h^2$$

$$520 = h^2$$

$$h = \sqrt{520} \approx 23$$

Answer $\boxed{(D)}$.

If you take enough ACT practice tests, what you'll find is that certain right triangles come up repeatedly. For example, the $3 - 4 - 5$ triangle:

A set of three whole numbers that satisfy the pythagorean theorem is called a pythagorean triple. Though not necessary, it'll save you quite a bit of time and improve your accuracy if you learn to recognize the common triples that show up:

$$3, 4, 5 \qquad 6, 8, 10 \qquad 5, 12, 13 \qquad 7, 24, 25 \qquad 8, 15, 17$$

Note that the $6 - 8 - 10$ triangle is just a multiple of the $3 - 4 - 5$ triangle.

Special Right Triangles

You will have to memorize two special right triangle relationships. The first is the $45° - 45° - 90°$:

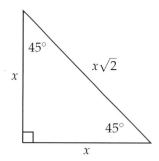

The best way to think about this triangle is that it's isosceles—the two legs are equal. We let their lengths be x. The hypotenuse, which is always the biggest side of a right triangle, turns out to be $\sqrt{2}$ times x.

We can prove this relationship using the pythagorean theorem, where h is the hypotenuse.

$$x^2 + x^2 = h^2$$

$$2x^2 = h^2$$

$$\sqrt{2x^2} = \sqrt{h^2}$$

$$x\sqrt{2} = h$$

I show you these proofs not because they will be tested on the ACT, but because they illustrate certain problem-solving concepts that you may have to use on tough ACT questions.

The second is the $30° - 60° - 90°$:

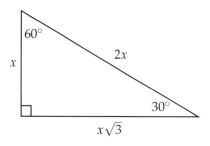

Because $30°$ is the smallest angle, the side opposite from it is the shortest. Let that side be x. The hypotenuse, the largest side, turns out to be twice x, and the side opposite $60°$ turns out to be $\sqrt{3}$ times x.

One common mistake students make is to think that because $60°$ is twice $30°$, the side opposite $60°$ must be twice as big as the side opposite $30°$. That relationship is NOT true. You cannot extrapolate the ratio of the sides from the ratio of the angles Yes, the side opposite $60°$ is bigger than the side opposite $30°$, but it isn't twice as long.

We can prove the $30 - 60 - 90$ relationship by using an equilateral triangle. Let each side be $2x$ (we could use x but you'll see why $2x$ makes things easier in a bit):

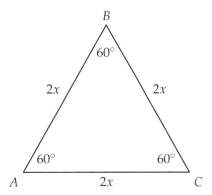

Drawing a line down the middle from B to $\overline{AC}$ creates two $30 - 60 - 90$ triangles. Because an equilateral triangle is symmetrical, AD is half of $2x$, or just x. That's why $2x$ was used—it avoids any fractions.

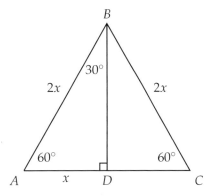

To find BD, we use the pythagorean theorem:

$$AD^2 + BD^2 = AB^2$$

$$x^2 + BD^2 = (2x)^2$$

$$BD^2 = (2x)^2 - x^2$$

$$BD^2 = 4x^2 - x^2$$

$$BD^2 = 3x^2$$

$$\sqrt{BD^2} = \sqrt{3x^2}$$

$$BD = x\sqrt{3}$$

Looking at the side lengths of triangle ABD, we can now see proof of the $30 - 60 - 90$ relationship.

EXAMPLE 4: In the figure below, $\angle C$ is a right angle and $\overline{AB}$ has a length of 4 inches. What is the area, in square inches, of $\triangle ABC$?

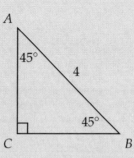

A. $\sqrt{2}$ **B.** $2\sqrt{2}$ **C.** 4   **D.** 8   **E.**

Using the $45 - 45 - 90$ triangle relationship, $AC = BC = \dfrac{4}{\sqrt{2}}$ (the hypotenuse is $\sqrt{2}$ times longer than each

leg). The area is then $\dfrac{1}{2}bh = \dfrac{1}{2}\left(\dfrac{4}{\sqrt{2}}\right)\left(\dfrac{4}{\sqrt{2}}\right) = \dfrac{1}{2}\left(\dfrac{16}{2}\right) = 4.$

Answer $\boxed{(C)}$.

EXAMPLE 5: In trapezoid $ABCD$ shown below, $\angle D$ measures $30°$ and $\angle A$ and $\angle B$ are both right angles. The given side lengths are in inches. Which of the following is closest to the area, in square inches, of $ABCD$?

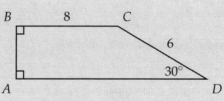

A. 8   **B.** 32   **C.** 40   **D.** 48   **E.** 56

The area of a trapezoid is given by $\dfrac{1}{2}(b_1 + b_2)h$, where b_1 and b_2 are the lengths of the parallel sides. To use this formula, we need to find the bottom side b_2 and the height h. We can do so by drawing a line from point C down to the base, forming a $30 - 60 - 90$ triangle.

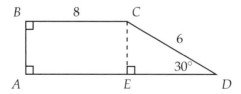

Using the $30 - 60 - 90$ triangle relationship, $CE = 3$ (half the hypotenuse of 6) and $ED = 3\sqrt{3}$. The base b_2 is then $AE + ED = 8 + 3\sqrt{3}$ and the height h is 3. Putting everything together,

$$\frac{1}{2}(b_1 + b_2)h = \frac{1}{2}(8 + (8 + 3\sqrt{3}))(3) \approx 32$$

Answer $\boxed{(B)}$.

Similar Triangles

When two triangles have the same angle measures, their sides are proportional:

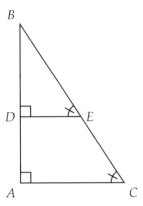

Because $\overline{DE}$ is parallel to $\overline{AC}$ in the figure above, $\angle BED$ is equal to $\angle BCA$. That makes $\triangle DBE$ similar to $\triangle ABC$. In other words, $\triangle DBE$ is just a smaller version of $\triangle ABC$. If we draw the two triangles separate from each other and give their sides some arbitrary lengths, we can see this more clearly.

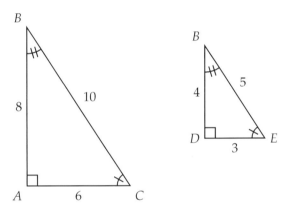

Given the numbers that we made up, the sides of $\triangle ABC$ are twice as long as the sides of $\triangle BDE$. Keep in mind this is just one possibility. Regardless of what the actual side lengths are, the ratios of the corresponding side lengths are always equivalent because these triangles are similar:

$$\frac{AB}{BD} = \frac{AC}{DE} = \frac{BC}{BE}$$

Not only does this ratio hold for the side lengths, but it also holds for the perimeters of the two triangles. Notice that the perimeter of $\triangle ABC$ is twice the perimeter of $\triangle BDE$ in the same way that $\overline{AB}$ is twice as long as $\overline{BD}$. This makes sense. If the sides are proportional, then the perimeters must also be proportional. To summarize,

$$\frac{AB}{BD} = \frac{AC}{DE} = \frac{BC}{BE} = \frac{\text{Perimeter of } \triangle ABC}{\text{Perimeter of } \triangle BDE}$$

EXAMPLE 6: In the figure below, $\triangle ABC$ is similar to $\triangle DEF$ and the lengths are given in inches. What is the perimeter, in inches, of $\triangle DEF$?

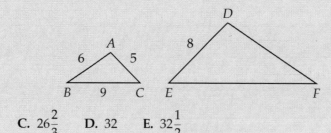

A. $24\dfrac{1}{3}$ **B.** 26 **C.** $26\dfrac{2}{3}$ **D.** 32 **E.** $32\dfrac{1}{2}$

For the sake of learning, we'll do this question the long way (see the next example for the faster solution). Given that the triangles are similar, $\overline{AB}$ corresponds to $\overline{DE}$, $\overline{AC}$ corresponds to $\overline{DF}$, and $\overline{BC}$ corresponds to $\overline{EF}$. Setting up the ratios,

$$\frac{AB}{DE} = \frac{AC}{DF} = \frac{BC}{EF}$$

$$\frac{6}{8} = \frac{5}{DF} = \frac{9}{EF}$$

We can cross multiply to solve for DF and EF.

$$6(DF) = (8)(5)$$

$$DF = \frac{40}{6} = \frac{20}{3} = 6\frac{2}{3}$$

$$6(EF) = (8)(9)$$

$$EF = 12$$

Finally, $DE + DF + EF = 8 + 6\dfrac{2}{3} + 12 = 26\dfrac{2}{3}$. Answer $\boxed{(C)}$.

EXAMPLE 7: The ratio of the corresponding side lengths of 2 similar triangles is 3:4. The perimeter of the smaller triangle is 24 centimeters. What is the perimeter of the larger triangle, in centimeters?

A. 18   **B.** 28   **C.** 32   **D.** 36   **E.** 40

For two similar triangles, the ratio of the side lengths is equal to the ratio of the perimeters. Therefore, the ratio of the perimeter of the smaller triangle to the perimeter of the larger triangle is also 3:4. Letting the perimeter of the larger triangle be x,

$$\frac{3}{4} = \frac{24}{x}$$

$$3x = 4(24)$$

$$x - 32$$

Answer $\boxed{(C)}$.

110

CHAPTER EXERCISE: Answers for this chapter start on page 233.

1. In △ABC, the length of $\overline{AC}$ is 8 inches, ∠B is a right angle, and ∠A measures 60°. What is the length, in inches, of $\overline{BC}$?

    A. 4
    B. $4\sqrt{2}$
    C. $4\sqrt{3}$
    D. $\dfrac{4}{3}$
    E. $\dfrac{8}{\sqrt{3}}$

2. In △ABC, the measure of ∠C is 90°. Which of the following statements could be true about △ABC ?

    A. $\overline{BC}$ is the hypotenuse.
    B. $\overline{AB} \cong \overline{AC}$
    C. ∠A is a right angle.
    D. ∠$BAC \cong$ ∠ABC
    E. The 3 sides of △ABC are congruent.

3. In the figure below, $\overline{AC}$ is congruent to $\overline{BC}$, and C is a point on $\overline{AD}$. What is the measure of ∠A ?

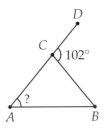

    A. 39°
    B. 49°
    C. 51°
    D. 64°
    E. 78°

4. The sides of one rectangle are twice as long as the sides of another rectangle. What is the ratio of the length of the diagonal of the smaller rectangle to the length of the diagonal of the larger rectangle?

    A. 1:2
    B. 1:$\sqrt{2}$
    C. 1:$2\sqrt{2}$
    D. 1:4
    E. 1:$4\sqrt{2}$

5. For the 2 similar right triangles shown below, A corresponds to F and the given dimensions are in inches. What is the length, in inches, of $\overline{DE}$?

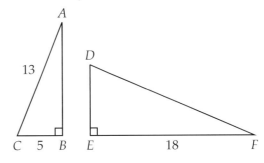

    A. 7.5
    B. 8
    C. 8.5
    D. 9
    E. 10

6. In the standard (x, y) coordinate plane, △ABC is a triangle with vertex B at $(-2, 2)$ and vertex C at $(4, 2)$. If $\overline{AB}$ is congruent to $\overline{AC}$, which of the following points could be the coordinates of vertex A ?

    A. $(1, 6)$
    B. $(2, 5)$
    C. $(3, 4)$
    D. $(4, 7)$
    E. $(10, 2)$

7. In the standard (x, y) coordinate plane, a rectangle has vertices at $(3, 2)$, $(3, -5)$, $(-2, 2)$, and $(-2, -5)$. Which of the following is closest to the length, in coordinate units, of a diagonal of this rectangle?

    A. 8
    B. 9
    C. 10
    D. 11
    E. 12

8. In the diagram below, $\triangle ABC$ is isosceles and $DECA$ is a rectangle. The measure of $\angle ABC$ is 4 times the measure of $\angle CAB$. What is the measure of $\angle BCE$?

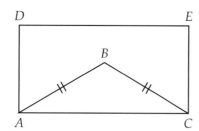

   A. 55°
   B. 60°
   C. 65°
   D. 70°
   E. 75°

9. Isosceles trapezoid $ABCD$ shown below has a height of 3 feet and parallel sides of 5 feet and 11 feet, respectively. What is the length, in feet, of $\overline{AB}$?

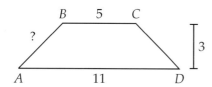

   A. 4
   B. $\dfrac{7}{2}$
   C. $3\sqrt{2}$
   D. $3\sqrt{3}$
   E. $3\sqrt{5}$

10. In $\triangle ABC$, the length of $\overline{AB}$ is 8 meters and the length of $\overline{BC}$ is 5 meters. Which of the following statements about the angles of $\triangle ABC$ must be true?

   A. The measure of $\angle A$ is greater than the measure of $\angle B$.
   B. The measure of $\angle A$ is greater than the measure of $\angle C$.
   C. The measure of $\angle B$ is greater than the measure of $\angle C$.
   D. The measure of $\angle C$ is greater than the measure of $\angle A$.
   E. The measure of $\angle C$ is greater than the measure of $\angle B$.

11. In the figure below, $\overline{AB}$ is parallel to $\overline{DE}$ and C is the intersection of $\overline{BE}$ and $\overline{AD}$. The given lengths are in meters. What is the length, in meters, of $\overline{DE}$?

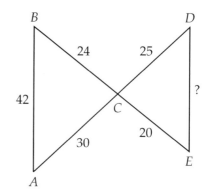

   A. 28
   B. $31\dfrac{2}{5}$
   C. 32
   D. 35
   E. $36\dfrac{4}{5}$

12. In trapezoid $KLMN$ below, O is the intersection of $\overline{KM}$ and $\overline{LN}$. The given lengths are in centimeters. To the nearest tenth of a centimeter, what is the length of $\overline{MO}$?

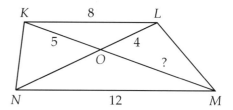

   A. 4.8
   B. 6.0
   C. 6.5
   D. 7.5
   E. 9.0

112

13. In the figure below, the measure of $\angle ABC$ is $60°$, the measure of $\angle ADC$ is $30°$, and $\overline{AB}$ is 2 inches long. What is the length, in inches, of $\overline{AD}$?

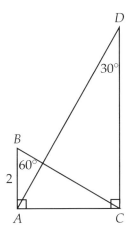

A. 6
B. 12
C. $2\sqrt{3}$
D. $4\sqrt{3}$
E. $6\sqrt{3}$

14. In the figure below, $\angle BDC$ is a right angle, D lies on $\overline{AC}$, and the measures of $\angle BAD$ and $\angle BCD$ are given. The length of $\overline{AC}$ is 12 meters. What is the approximate length, in meters, of $\overline{BD}$?

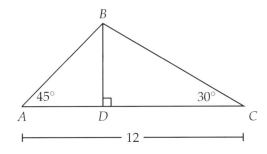

A. 4.4
B. 4.8
C. 5.2
D. 6.3
E. 7.4

15. In the figure below, trapezoid $ABCD$ has an area of 44 square feet and $\overline{CD}$ is $4\sqrt{2}$ feet long. What is the length, in feet, of $\overline{AD}$?

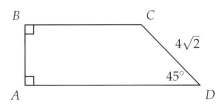

A. $9\sqrt{2}$
B. 13
C. 14
D. $14\sqrt{2}$
E. 15

16. In the figure below, D lies on $\overline{AC}$, E lies on $\overline{BC}$, and the given lengths are in inches. What is the area, in square inches, of $\triangle CDE$?

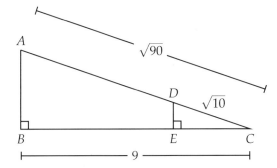

A. $\dfrac{1}{6}$
B. $1\dfrac{1}{2}$
C. 3
D. $4\dfrac{1}{2}$
E. 9

17. The side length of an equilateral triangle is n inches longer than the side length of a second equilateral triangle. The height of the first triangle is how many inches longer than the height of the second triangle?

A. $\dfrac{n}{2}$
B. n
C. $n\sqrt{3}$
D. $2n$
E. $\dfrac{n\sqrt{3}}{2}$

17 Circles

Circle Facts You Should Know:

Area of a circle: πr^2

Circumference of a circle: $2\pi r$

Arc Length: $\dfrac{\theta}{360} \times 2\pi r$ OR θr if θ is in radians

Area of a Sector: $\dfrac{\theta}{360} \times \pi r^2$ OR $\dfrac{1}{2}r^2\theta$ if θ is in radians

Central angles have the same measure as the arcs they "carve out."

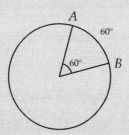

Many students confuse arc length with arc measure. Arc length is the actual distance one would travel along the circle from A to B. Arc measure is the number of degrees one turns through from A to B. Think of it as a rotation along the circle from A to B. A full rotation is $360°$.

Inscribed angles are half the measure of the arcs they "carve out."

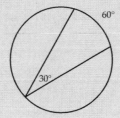

Angles inscribed in a semicircle are always 90°. This is just an extension of the previous fact. An angle inscribed in a semicircle carves out half a circle, or 180°, which means the angle itself is half that, or 90°.

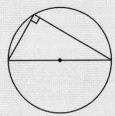

A radius drawn to a line tangent to the circle is perpendicular to that line:

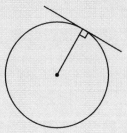

A radius drawn through the midpoint of a chord is perpendicular to that chord:

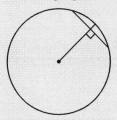

General equation of a circle in the xy-plane:

$$(x - h)^2 + (y - k)^2 = r^2$$

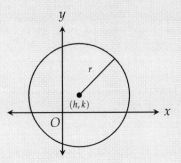

where (h, k) is the center of the circle and r is its radius.

EXAMPLE 1: In the figure below, a square with side length 2 inches is inscribed in a circle. What is the area, in square inches, of the circle?

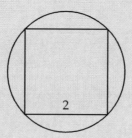

A. $\dfrac{\pi}{2}$ **B.** π **C.** 2π **D.** 3π **E.** 4π

Draw a diagonal of the square to get a $45 - 45 - 90$ triangle, whose side relationships we can use to get the length of the diagonal:

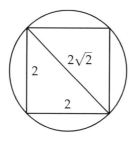

Because the diagonal of the square is also a diameter of the circle, the length of the diameter is $2\sqrt{2}$ inches, which means the radius is $\sqrt{2}$ inches. The area of the circle is then $\pi r^2 = \pi(\sqrt{2})^2 = 2\pi$. Answer $\boxed{(C)}$.

EXAMPLE 2: As shown in the figure below, C is the center of the circle, radius $\overline{BC}$ has a length of 2 inches, and $\angle ACB$ has a measure of $45°$. What is the area, in square inches, of the shaded region bounded by $\overline{AB}$ and minor arc $\overparen{AB}$?

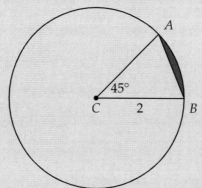

A. $\dfrac{\pi}{2} + \sqrt{2}$ **B.** $\dfrac{\pi}{2} - \dfrac{\sqrt{2}}{2}$ **C.** $\dfrac{\pi}{2} - \sqrt{2}$ **D.** $\pi - \sqrt{2}$ **E.** $\pi - 2$

To get the shaded area, we must subtract the area of the triangle from the area of the sector.

$$\text{Area of sector} = \frac{45°}{360°}\pi r^2 = \frac{1}{8}\pi(2^2) = \frac{\pi}{2}$$

To get the area of the triangle, draw the height from point A to base $\overline{BC}$. This makes a $45-45-90$ triangle. Because $\overline{AC}$ is also a radius, its length is 2 inches. Using the $45-45-90$ triangle relationship, the height is then $\frac{2}{\sqrt{2}} = \frac{2}{\sqrt{2}}\left(\frac{\sqrt{2}}{\sqrt{2}}\right) = \frac{2\sqrt{2}}{2} = \sqrt{2}.$

$$\text{Area of triangle} = \frac{1}{2}bh = \frac{1}{2}(2)(\sqrt{2}) = \sqrt{2}$$

$$\text{Area of shaded region} = \frac{\pi}{2} - \sqrt{2}$$

Answer (C).

EXAMPLE 3: In the figure below, which is not drawn to scale, a sector is shown shaded in a circle with radius 8 inches. The length of the arc of the unshaded sector is 15π inches. What is the measure of the central angle of the shaded sector?

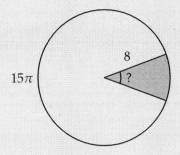

A. 20°   **B.** 22.5°   **C.** 30°   **D.** 32.5°   **E.** 45°

The circumference of the circle is $2\pi r = 2\pi(8) = 16\pi$, so the length of the arc of the shaded sector must be $16\pi - 15\pi = \pi$. Note that this is $\frac{\pi}{16\pi} = \frac{1}{16}$ of the entire circle. Therefore, the central angle is also $\frac{1}{16}$ of the circle:

$$\frac{1}{16} \times 360° = 22.5°$$

Answer (B).

EXAMPLE 4: The measure of an angle inscribed in a circle is $\frac{1}{2}$ the measure of the intercepted arc. Points $X, Y,$ and Z are on the circle shown below. What is the measure of $\angle XYZ$?

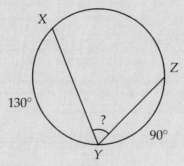

A. $60°$ **B.** $70°$ **C.** $80°$ **D.** $140°$ **E.** $160°$

The measure of minor arc $\overset{\frown}{XZ}$ is $360 - 130 - 90 = 140°$. Since $\angle XYZ$ is an inscribed angle, its measure is half the measure of its intercepted arc, $\overset{\frown}{XZ}$: $\frac{1}{2} \times 140 = 70°$. Answer $\boxed{(B)}$.

EXAMPLE 5: A diameter of a circle in the standard (x, y) coordinate plane has endpoints at $(1, 2)$ and $(7, 10)$. Which of the following is an equation of the circle?

A. $(x-4)^2 + (y-4)^2 = 5$ **B.** $(x-4)^2 + (y-6)^2 = 10$ **C.** $(x-5)^2 + (y-4)^2 = 10$

D. $(x-5)^2 + (y-4)^2 = 25$ **E.** $(x-4)^2 + (y-6)^2 = 25$

The center of the circle is just the midpoint of the two given endpoints:

$$\left(\frac{x_1 + x_2}{2}, \frac{y_1 + y_2}{2} \right) = \left(\frac{1+7}{2}, \frac{2+10}{2} \right) = (4, 6)$$

The diameter of the circle is the distance between the two endpoints:

$$\sqrt{(y_2 - y_1)^2 + (x_2 - x_1)^2} = \sqrt{(10-2)^2 + (7-1)^2} = \sqrt{8^2 + 6^2} = \sqrt{64 + 36} = 10$$

The radius is then $10 \div 2 = 5$.

Putting everything together, the equation of the circle is

$$(x-4)^2 + (y-6)^2 = 25$$

Answer $\boxed{(E)}$.

EXAMPLE 6: In the standard (x, y) coordinate plane, what are the coordinates of the center of the circle whose equation is $x^2 + 4x + y^2 - 8y - 16 = 0$?

A. $(-2, -4)$ **B.** $(-2, 4)$ **C.** $(2, -4)$ **D.** $(4, -2)$ **E.** $(4, 2)$

This question requires you to find the standard equation of the circle by completing the square twice, once for x and once for y. If you forgot how to complete the square, review the relevant section in the chapter on quadratics.

Completing the square for x,

$$x^2 + 4x + y^2 - 8y - 16 = 0$$

$$[(x + 2)^2 - 4] + y^2 - 8y - 16 = 0$$

Completing the square for y,

$$[(x + 2)^2 - 4] + [(y - 4)^2 - 16] - 16 = 0$$

Combining the constants,

$$(x + 2)^2 + (y - 4)^2 - 36 = 0$$

$$(x + 2)^2 + (y - 4)^2 = 36$$

Therefore, the coordinates of the center are $(-2, 4)$. Answer $\boxed{(B)}$.

CHAPTER EXERCISE: Answers for this chapter start on page 237.

1. The diameter of a circle is 30 inches. What is the circumference of the circle, in inches?

   A. 15π
   B. 30π
   C. 60π
   D. 225π
   E. 900π

2. A circle fits inside a rectangle 7 centimeters long and 5 centimeters wide and is tangent to 3 sides of the rectangle. What is the circumference, in centimeters, of the circle?

   A. 5π
   B. 7π
   C. 10π
   D. 14π
   E. 25π

3. Two chords of a circle are shown in the figure below, which is not drawn to scale. The given lengths are in inches. What is the value of x ?

   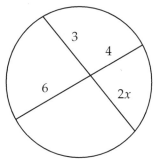

   (Note: When 2 chords of a circle intersect inside the circle, the product of the lengths of the 2 segments of one chord is equal to the product of the lengths of the 2 segments of the other chord.)

   A. 3
   B. 3.5
   C. 4
   D. 4.5
   E. 5

4. In the circle shown below, central angle $\angle AOB$ measures $30°$, and arc $\overset{\frown}{AB}$ is $\dfrac{\pi}{2}$ inches long. How many inches long is the circle's radius?

   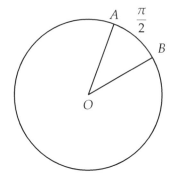

   A. 3
   B. $3\sqrt{3}$
   C. 4
   D. 6
   E. 12

5. A particular circle in the standard (x, y) coordinate plane has an equation of $x^2 + (y + 3)^2 = 29$. What are the radius of the circle, in coordinate units, and the coordinates of the center of the circle?

   A. Radius: 29, Center: $(0, -3)$
   B. Radius: $\sqrt{29}$, Center: $(0, 3)$
   C. Radius: $\sqrt{29}$, Center: $(0, -3)$
   D. Radius: 14.5, Center: $(0, 3)$
   E. Radius: 14.5, Center: $(0, -3)$

6. When two chords of a circle intersect, the product of the lengths of the segments of one chord equals the product of the lengths of the segments of the other chord. In the figure below, chords $\overline{AD}$ and $\overline{BC}$ intersect at X. The length of $\overline{AX}$ is 8 inches, the length of $\overline{DX}$ is 3 inches, and the length of $\overline{BC}$ is 10 inches. The length of $\overline{CX}$ is less than the length of $\overline{BX}$. What is the length, in inches, of $\overline{CX}$?

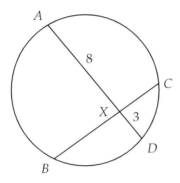

A. 3
B. 4
C. 5
D. 6
E. 7

7. The measure of an angle inscribed in a circle is $\frac{1}{2}$ the measure of the intercepted arc. The circle shown below has diameter $\overline{BC}$ and points A and D lie on the circle. The measure of $\angle CBD$ is $40°$. What is the measure of minor arc $\overset{\frown}{BD}$?

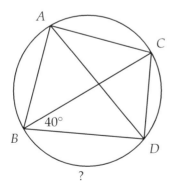

A. $90°$
B. $100°$
C. $110°$
D. $120°$
E. $130°$

8. A circle with a radius of 1 inch rolls along the inside of a rectangle with a length of 5 inches and a width of 9 inches, as shown in the diagram below. While it rolls, the circle always touches at least one side of the rectangle. It stops when it gets back to its starting point. How far, in inches, does the center of the circle travel?

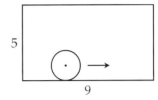

A. 14
B. 16
C. 18
D. 20
E. 22

9. Which of the following equations represents the circle with center $(1, 2)$ shown in the standard (x, y) coordinate plane below?

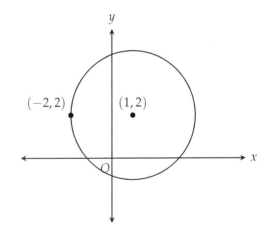

A. $(x - 1)^2 + (y - 2)^2 = 3$
B. $(x - 1)^2 + (y - 2)^2 = 9$
C. $(x - 1)^2 + (y + 2)^2 = 9$
D. $(x + 1)^2 + (y + 2)^2 = 3$
E. $(x + 1)^2 + (y + 2)^2 = 9$

10. To carve out slices, a pizza restaurant makes cuts every 4 inches along the edge of a circular pizza, as shown in the figure below. If the radius of the pizza is 10 inches long, what is the maximum number of full slices that the restaurant can carve out from this pizza?

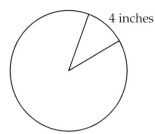

4 inches

   A. 7
   B. 8
   C. 14
   D. 15
   E. 16

11. In the figure below, $\overset{\frown}{AB}$ is an arc of the circle with center O. If the area of sector OAB is 96π square inches, what is the length of arc $\overset{\frown}{AB}$, in inches?

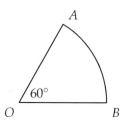

   A. 6π
   B. 8π
   C. 10π
   D. 12π
   E. 14π

12. A circle in the standard (x, y) coordinate plane intersects the y-axis at $(0, -2)$ and $(0, 4)$. The radius of the circle is 5 coordinate units. Which of the following could be the center of the circle?

   I. $(-4, 1)$
   II. $(0, 1)$
   III. $(4, 1)$

   A. I only
   B. II only
   C. III only
   D. I and III only
   E. I, II, and III

13. In the standard (x, y) coordinate plane, what is an equation of a circle that has center $(5, 3)$ and is tangent to the y-axis?

   A. $(x - 5)^2 + (y - 3)^2 = 9$
   B. $(x - 5)^2 + (y - 3)^2 = 25$
   C. $(x + 5)^2 + (y + 3)^2 = 5$
   D. $(x + 5)^2 + (y + 3)^2 = 9$
   E. $(x + 5)^2 + (y + 3)^2 = 25$

14. In the standard (x, y) coordinate plane, a circle determined by $x^2 - 6x + y^2 + 8 = 0$ is translated 2 units to the right and 1 unit down. Which of the following gives an equation of the translated circle?

   A. $(x - 5)^2 + (y + 1)^2 = 1$
   B. $(x - 5)^2 + (y - 1)^2 = 1$
   C. $(x - 3)^2 + y^2 = 1$
   D. $(x - 1)^2 + (y + 1)^2 = 1$
   E. $(x - 1)^2 + (y - 1)^2 = 1$

18

Area & Perimeter

Here are the area formulas you need to know:

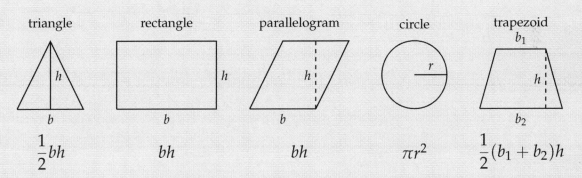

triangle	rectangle	parallelogram	circle	trapezoid
$\frac{1}{2}bh$	bh	bh	πr^2	$\frac{1}{2}(b_1 + b_2)h$

Don't make the common mistake of using the slant height for the parallelogram. Always calculate the area with the height perpendicular to the base.

Another thing to know is a special property of the rhombus (a parallelogram with sides of equal length). This property can come in handy when solving area problems:

The diagonals of a rhombus are perpendicular.

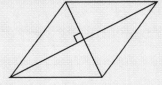

Because a square is also a rhombus, this property also applies to squares.

Onto the examples!

EXAMPLE 1: For trapezoid $ABCD$ shown below, $AB = 6$, $BC = 8$, and $DC = 10$. What is the area of the trapezoid?

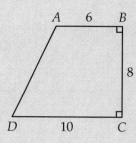

A. 54   **B.** 56   **C.** 64   **D.** 68   **E.** 72

Solution 1: Use the formula for the area of a trapezoid.

$$\text{Area} = \frac{1}{2}(b_1 + b_2)h = \frac{1}{2}(6 + 10)(8) = \frac{1}{2}(16)(8) = 64$$

Answer $\boxed{(C)}$.

Solution 2: Draw a line from A down to $\overline{DC}$ to form a triangle and a rectangle:

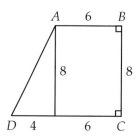

The area of the triangle is $\frac{1}{2}(4)(8) = 16$ and the area of the rectangle is $(6)(8) = 48$. The area of $ABCD$ is $16 + 48 = 64$. Answer $\boxed{(C)}$.

This second solution took a bit longer than the first, so why did I bother showing it? Because on the tougher questions, you won't have a formula to rely on. Instead, you'll have to figure out a strategy like the one we just used.

Don't be afraid of drawing extra lines in order to make a problem more approachable.

EXAMPLE 2: A triangular board with a base of 4 feet and a height of 5 feet is to be made from oak. The oak has a price of $25 for every 4 square feet of top surface area. What is the price of the oak needed to make this board?

A. $50.00   **B.** $62.50   **C.** $75.00   **D.** $87.50   **E.** $100.00

The board has an area of $\frac{1}{2} \times 4 \times 5 = 10$ square feet. 10 square feet $\times \dfrac{\$25}{4 \text{ square feet}} = \$62.50$.

Answer $\boxed{(B)}$.

EXAMPLE 3: In the figure below, $AB = 16$, $CF = 10$, and $DF = 20$. What is the area of the shaded region?

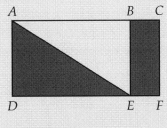

A. 110   **B.** 120   **C.** 130   **D.** 140   **E.** 150

The area of triangle ABE is $\frac{1}{2}(AB)(BE) = \frac{1}{2}(16)(10) = 80$. The area of rectangle $ACFD$ is $(20)(10) = 200$. We can get the area of the shaded region by subtracting the area of the triangle from the area of the rectangle: $200 - 80 = 120$. Answer $\boxed{(B)}$.

Example 3 exemplifies a very valuable strategy. Instead of trying to calculate what you want, try getting what you don't want, and then subtracting that out from the whole.

EXAMPLE 4: Joanna plans to completely line the inside of her garden with tiles 3 feet by 3 feet as shown by the shaded region below. Her garden is 60 feet by 45 feet. What is the minimum number of tiles she must use?

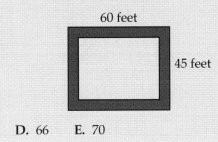

A. 54   **B.** 58   **C.** 62   **D.** 66   **E.** 70

Because she needs to cover 45 feet on the left and right sides and each tile is 3 feet long, she'll need $45 \div 3 = 15$ tiles on each side. For the top and bottom, she'll need $60 \div 3 = 20$ tiles each.

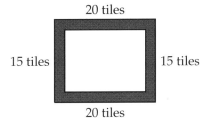

Now we have to be careful. The tiles in the corners each count towards two sides of the rectangle. For example, the tile in the top right corner would count towards the 20 tiles needed on top and also the 15 tiles needed on the right. So after we tile the left and right sides, we only need 18 additional tiles for the top and 18 tiles for the bottom.

$$15 + 15 + 18 + 18 = 66$$

Answer $\boxed{(D)}$.

EXAMPLE 5: In the figure below, the larger semicircle has a radius that is equal in length to the diameter of the smaller semicircle. If the radius of the larger semicircle has a length of b inches, what is the area of the shaded region in terms of b ?

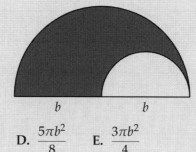

b b

A. $\dfrac{\pi b^2}{4}$ **B.** $\dfrac{3\pi b^2}{8}$ **C.** $\dfrac{\pi b^2}{2}$ **D.** $\dfrac{5\pi b^2}{8}$ **E.** $\dfrac{3\pi b^2}{4}$

Let's come up with an overall game plan before we do any calculations. To get the area of the shaded region, we need to subtract the area of the small semicircle from the area of the big semicircle.

$$\text{Area of big semicircle} = \frac{1}{2}\pi b^2$$

$$\text{Area of small semicircle} = \frac{1}{2}\pi \left(\frac{b}{2}\right)^2$$

$$\frac{1}{2}\pi b^2 - \frac{1}{2}\pi \left(\frac{b}{2}\right)^2 = \frac{1}{2}\pi b^2 - \frac{1}{8}\pi b^2 = \frac{3}{8}\pi b^2$$

Answer $\boxed{(B)}$. Note that $\frac{3}{8}\pi b^2$ is the same as $\frac{3\pi b^2}{8}$. A lot of students seem to forget that both forms are equivalent.

EXAMPLE 6: A rectangle has a perimeter of 36. Its width is twice its length. What is the area of the rectangle?

A. 36   **B.** 44   **C.** 60   **D.** 64   **E.** 72

This is more of an algebra problem than an area problem. Let w be the width and l be the length. We can make two equations:

$$2l + 2w = 36$$

$$w = 2l$$

Substituting the second equation into the first,

$$2l + 2(2l) = 36$$

$$6l = 36$$

$$l = 6$$

Since the length is 6, the width is $2l = 12$. The area is then $6 \times 12 = 72$. Answer $\boxed{(E)}$.

CHAPTER EXERCISE: Answers for this chapter start on page 240.

1. A rectangle with a length of 6 centimeters has the same area as a square with side length 18 centimeters. What is the perimeter, in centimeters, of the rectangle?

    A. 54
    B. 72
    C. 90
    D. 108
    E. 120

2. A circle shown below is inscribed in a square with a side length of 4 feet. What is the area of the shaded region, in square feet?

    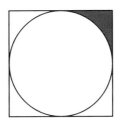

    A. $4 - 4\pi$
    B. $4 - 2\pi$
    C. $4 - \pi$
    D. $8 - 2\pi$
    E. $16 - 4\pi$

3. Trapezoid ABCD is shown in the standard (x, y) coordinate plane below. What is the area, in square coordinate units, of the trapezoid?

    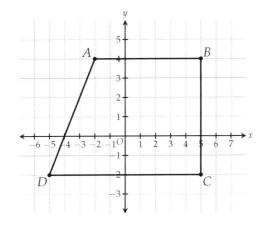

    A. 32
    B. 37
    C. 42
    D. 51
    E. 60

4. A grid composed of equally sized squares is shown in the figure below. If the area of the shaded region is 28 square feet, what is the area, in square feet, of outer square *ABCD* ?

    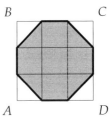

    A. 30
    B. 32
    C. 36
    D. 40
    E. 42

5. In the figure below, all the adjacent line segments intersect in right angles, and all segments have the same length. If the perimeter of the figure is 60 units long, what is the area, in square units, of the entire figure?

    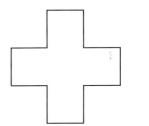

    A. 50
    B. 60
    C. 75
    D. 100
    E. 125

6. The perimeter of a rectangle is 94 inches. The length of the rectangle is 3 inches shorter than the width. What is the length of the rectangle, in inches?

    A. 19
    B. 22
    C. 25
    D. 28
    E. 31

7. What is the area of the triangle bounded by the lines $y = x$, $y = -x$, and $y = 5$ in the standard (x, y) coordinate plane?

    A. 12.5
    B. 25
    C. 50
    D. 62.5
    E. 75

8. The width of a rectangle is increased by 10% but its height is decreased by 10%. The area of the new rectangle is

    A. 10% greater than the area of the original
    B. 1% greater than the area of the original
    C. equal to the area of the original
    D. 1% less than the area of the original
    E. 10% less than the area of the original

9. The vertices of a triangle have the (x, y) coordinates indicated in the figure below. What is the area, in square coordinate units, of the triangle?

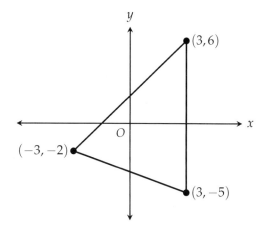

    A. 22
    B. 33
    C. 44
    D. 66
    E. 88

10. The outer square in the figure below contains square A and square B. If square A has an area of 16 square inches and square B has an area of 25 square inches, what is the perimeter, in inches, of the shaded region?

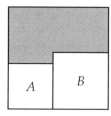

    A. 19
    B. 23
    C. 27
    D. 28
    E. 30

Use the following information to answer questions 11–12.

The dimensions of a pool, shown below, are 15 yards by 20 yards. The pool is bounded by a walking area with a width of 2 yards, as represented by the shaded region.

11. During the winter, the pool is enclosed by a fence. What is the perimeter, in yards, of the pool?

    A. 20
    B. 35
    C. 50
    D. 70
    E. 86

12. What is the area, in square yards, of the walking area?

    A. 74
    B. 108
    C. 118
    D. 156
    E. 168

13. Triangle ABC is inscribed in a rectangle as shown below. If $AB = 5$ m, $BC = 12$ m, and $AC = 13$ m, what is the area, in square meters, of the rectangle?

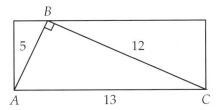

   A. 30
   B. 40
   C. 50
   D. 60
   E. 80

14. In the figure shown below, a square contains four congruent circles that are tangent to each other. If the area of the outer square is 64 square inches, what is the area, in square inches, of the shaded region?

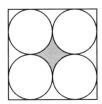

   A. $16 - 4\pi$
   B. $16 - \pi$
   C. $36 - 6\pi$
   D. $64 - 16\pi$
   E. $64 - 4\pi$

15. The total area of the figure shown below is 80 square feet. If the area of rectangle A is four times the area of square B, what is the perimeter, in feet, of the figure?

   A. 40
   B. 48
   C. 64
   D. 72
   E. 80

16. Let P denote the perimeter, in inches, of a rectangle with an area of 64 square inches. Which of the following must be true?

   A. $P \geq 8$
   B. $P \geq 32$
   C. $P \geq 64$
   D. $P \geq 128$
   E. $P \geq 256$

17. The design of a tile consists of five congruent rectangles as shown in the figure below. If the perimeter of each of the rectangles is 30 inches, what is the area, in square inches, of the tile?

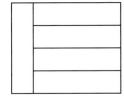

   A. 36
   B. 72
   C. 108
   D. 144
   E. 180

18. In the figure below, a rectangle has a width of 16 units and a height of 6 units. The left and right sides are each divided into 6 congruent segments. The top and bottom sides are each divided into 8 congruent segments. Triangles M and N are joined at the center of the rectangle. What is the ratio of the area of triangle M to the area of triangle N?

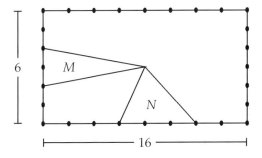

   A. $3 : 8$
   B. $2 : 3$
   C. $3 : 4$
   D. $7 : 9$
   E. $8 : 9$

19. In the figure below, a large square consists of four congruent rectangles and a smaller square. The perimeter of each of the congruent rectangles is 20 inches. What is the area, in square inches, of the large square?

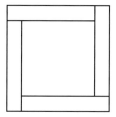

A. 36
B. 49
C. 64
D. 81
E. 100

20. The side lengths of the flat, trapezoidal wall of a living room are given in the figure below. James will paint the entire wall with 1 coat of paint, using paint that is sold only in 3-quart containers. Each quart of paint covers an area of 50 square feet with 1 coat of paint. What is the minimum number of containers of paint that James needs to buy?

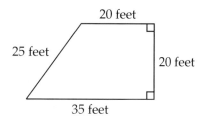

A. 3
B. 4
C. 5
D. 6
E. 7

21. An isosceles triangle is divided into 4 smaller congruent isosceles triangles as shown in the figure below. What is the ratio of the perimeter of one of the smaller triangles to the perimeter of the original triangle?

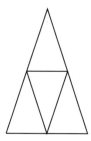

A. 1:2
B. 1:3
C. 1:4
D. 2:3
E. 2:5

22. In rhombus $CADB$ below, $\overline{AB}$ is 24 inches long and $\overline{CD}$ is 18 inches long. What is the area, in square inches, of $CADB$?

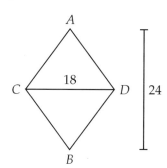

A. 108
B. 196
C. 216
D. 312
E. 432

130

23. A circle and a rectangle overlap as shown below. The area of the circle is 4 times the area of the rectangle. If the overlapping region is removed, the area of the remainder of the circle would be 30 square centimeters more than the area of the remainder of the rectangle. What is the area of the full rectangle, in square centimeters?

   A. 10
   B. 20
   C. 30
   D. 40
   E. 50

24. An artist has 30 triangular strips of cardboard, each a right triangle with dimensions in inches, as shown below. What is the maximum height, in inches, of a rectangular poster 15 inches wide that can be completely covered with these 30 strips of cardboard?

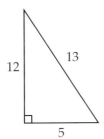

   A. 24
   B. 30
   C. 36
   D. 48
   E. 60

19 Volume

The volumes of each of the following three solids can be found by using the formula

$$\text{Volume} = \text{Area of base} \times \text{height}$$

That's why the volume of a cube is $V = s^3$ (the area of the base is s^2 and the height is s)

$$s$$

The volume of a rectangular box/prism is $V = lwh$ (the area of the base is lw and the height is h)

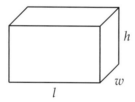

The volume of a cylinder is $V = \pi r^2 h$ (the area of the base is πr^2 and the height is h)

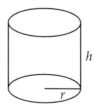

Now when it comes to cones and spheres, the general formula above doesn't apply. Instead, just memorize the following:

The volume of a cone is $V = \dfrac{1}{3}\pi r^2 h$

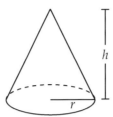

The volume of a sphere is $V = \dfrac{4}{3}\pi r^3$

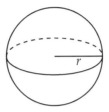

Even though the ACT may give you these formulas in the questions themselves, you should really memorize them.

EXAMPLE 1: A cube has a volume of 125 cubic inches. What is the total surface area, in square inches, of the cube?

A. 25   **B.** 30   **C.** 125   **D.** 150   **E.** 200

If we let the side of the cube be s, then

$$s^3 = 125$$

$$s = \sqrt[3]{125} = 5$$

Because a cube has 6 faces and each face is a square with area s^2, the total surface area is $6s^2 = 6(5)^2 = 150$. Answer $\boxed{(D)}$.

EXAMPLE 2: A water tank in the shape of a rectangular prism is 18 feet wide and 15 feet long. The volume of the water in the tank is 3,510 cubic feet. To the nearest foot, how deep is the water in the tank?

A. 13   **B.** 15   **C.** 18   **D.** 21   **E.** 23

Imagine the water in the tank as its own rectangular prism (the surface of the water is the "top" of the prism). This prism would then be 18 feet wide, 15 feet long, and d feet tall, where d is the depth.

$$18 \times 15 \times d = 3,510$$

$$270d = 3,510$$

$$d = 13$$

Answer $\boxed{(A)}$.

EXAMPLE 3: The radius of a right circular cylinder is 3 times the radius of a second right circular cylinder. The volume of the first cylinder is how many times the volume of the second cylinder?
(Note: $V_{cylinder} = \pi r^2 h$)

A. 3   B. 6   C. 9   D. 16   E. 27

If we let r be the radius of the second cylinder, then the radius of the first cylinder is $3r$. The volume of the second cylinder is then $\pi r^2 h$ and the volume of the first cylinder is $\pi(3r)^2 h = 9\pi r^2 h$, which is 9 times the volume of the second cylinder. Answer $\boxed{(C)}$.

If you have trouble working with variables in problems like this one, try making up numbers instead (e.g. let the radius and height of the second cylinder each be 1).

EXAMPLE 4: How many cubes of side length 0.5 inches are needed to form a rectangular solid that is 3 inches long, 4 inches wide, and 5 inches tall?

A. 30   B. 60   C. 120   D. 240   E. 480

The rectangular solid has a volume of $3 \times 4 \times 5 = 60\text{in}^3$. Each cube has a volume of $(0.5)^3 = 0.125\text{in}^3$. Therefore, $\dfrac{60}{0.125} = 480$ cubes are needed. Answer $\boxed{(E)}$.

CHAPTER EXERCISE: Answers for this chapter start on page 245.

1. Each edge of a cube has a length of 4 meters. What is the volume, in cubic meters, of the cube?

   A. 16
   B. 64
   C. 80
   D. 96
   E. 384

2. An empty cylindrical aquarium has a radius of 6 feet and a height of 5 feet. The aquarium will be filled with 20 cubic feet of water per minute. About how many minutes will it take to completely fill the aquarium?
   (Note: The volume of a cylinder with radius r and height h is $\pi r^2 h$.)

   A. 5
   B. 9
   C. 24
   D. 28
   E. 32

3. A snack company puts 6 granola bars in rectangular packages that are 4 inches wide, 5 inches long, and 2 inches tall. The packages are then delivered in rectangular shipping boxes that each have inside dimensions measuring 12 inches wide, 15 inches long, and 6 inches tall. What is the maximum number of granola bars that can be delivered in 1 shipping box?

   A. 9
   B. 18
   C. 27
   D. 54
   E. 162

4. The top surface of a rectangular tabletop made of marble has an area of 36 square feet. If the tabletop is 3 *inches* thick, how many cubic *feet* of marble does the tabletop consist of?

   A. 6
   B. 9
   C. 12
   D. 18
   E. 24

5. The radius of a sphere is 3 centimeters long. The radius of a second sphere is double the length of the radius of the first sphere. The volume of the second sphere is how many times greater than the volume of the first sphere?
   (Note: The volume of a sphere with radius r is $\frac{4}{3}\pi r^3$.)

   A. 2
   B. 3
   C. 8
   D. 9
   E. 27

6. A rectangular prism has a width that is twice the length and a height that is twice the width. The volume of the prism is 2,744 cubic feet. What is the width, in feet, of the prism?

   A. 7
   B. 9
   C. 14
   D. 18
   E. 21

7. A right circular cone is generated by rotating right triangle $\triangle ABC$ shown below $360°$ around $\overline{AB}$. What is the volume, in cubic feet, of this cone?
   (Note: The volume of a cone with radius r and height h is $\frac{1}{3}\pi r^2 h$.)

   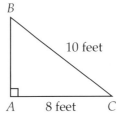

   A. $\dfrac{160}{3}\pi$
   B. 72π
   C. 96π
   D. 128π
   E. $\dfrac{640}{3}\pi$

8. Michelle cuts 2 inch by 2 inch squares from the four corners of a 16 inch by 12 inch rectangular piece of cardboard shown below. She then folds up the sides by 90° to form a rectangular box. How many cubes each having a side length of 1 inch can fit inside the resulting box?

   A. 96
   B. 176
   C. 192
   D. 280
   E. 384

9. The right triangular solid shown below is 4 feet thick. The hypotenuse of the base measures 15 feet and one of the legs measures 9 feet. What is the volume of this solid, in cubic feet?

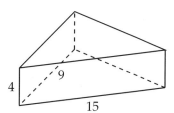

   A. 108
   B. 216
   C. 270
   D. 432
   E. 540

10. There are 80 cubic inches of water in the rectangular container shown below with dimensions given in inches. If 50 cubic inches of water are added to the container, by how many inches will the water level in the container rise?

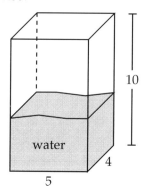

   A. 1
   B. 1.5
   C. 2
   D. 2.5
   E. 3

20

Systems of Equations

A system of equations refers to 2 or more equations that deal with the same set of variables.

$$-5x + y = -7$$
$$-3x - 2y = -12$$

There are two main ways of solving systems of 2 equations: substitution and elimination.

Substitution

Substitution is all about isolating one variable, either x or y, in the fastest way possible.

Taking the example above, we can see that it's easiest to isolate y in the first equation because it has no coefficient. Adding $5x$ to both sides, we get

$$y = 5x - 7$$

We can now substitute the y in the second equation with $5x - 7$ and solve from there.

$$-3x - 2(5x - 7) = -12$$
$$-3x - 10x + 14 = -12$$
$$-13x = -26$$
$$x = 2$$

Plugging $x = 2$ back into $y = 5x - 7$, $y = 5(2) - 7 = 3$.

The solution is $x = 2, y = 3$, which can be denoted as $(2, 3)$.

Elimination

Elimination is about getting the same coefficients for one variable across the two equations so that you can add or subtract the equations, thereby eliminating that variable.

Using the same example, we can multiply the first equation by 2 so that the y's have the same coefficient (we don't worry about the sign because we can add or subtract the equations).

$$-10x + 2y = -14$$
$$-3x - 2y = -12$$

To eliminate y, we add the equations.

$$-10x + 2y = -14$$
$$\underline{-3x - 2y = -12}$$
$$-13x = -26$$

Now we can see that $x = 2$. We can plug this value into either of the original equations to solve for y. We'll pick the first equation.

$$-10(2) + 2y = -14$$
$$-20 + 2y = -14$$
$$2y = 6$$
$$y = 3$$

And finally, we get the same solution as we got using substitution: $x = 2, y = 3$.

When solving systems of equations, you can use either method, but one of them will be faster than the other depending on the system. If you see a variable with no coefficient, like in $-5x + y = -7$ above, substitution is likely the best route. If you see matching coefficients or you see that it's easy to get matching coefficients, elimination is likely the best route. The example above was simple enough for both methods to work well (though substitution was slightly faster). In these cases, it comes down to your personal preference.

No solutions

A system of equations has no solutions when the same equation is set to a different constant:

$$3x + 2y = 5$$
$$3x + 2y = -4$$

The equations above contradict each other. There is no x and y that will make both of them true at the same time, so the system has no solution. Note that

$$3x + 2y = 5$$
$$6x + 4y = -8$$

also has no solution. Why? Because the second equation can be divided by 2 to again contradict the first equation.

EXAMPLE 1: For what value of a would the following system of equations have no solution?

$$-ax - 12y = 15$$
$$4x + 3y = -2$$

A. -16 **B.** -8 **C.** -2 **D.** 8   **E.** 16

We must get the coefficients to match so that we can compare the two equations. To do that, we multiply the second equation by -4:

$$-ax - 12y = 15$$
$$-16x - 12y = 8$$

See how the -12's match now? Now let's compare. If $a = 16$, then we get our two contradicting equations with no solution: the first is equal to 15 while the second is equal to 8. Answer $\boxed{(E)}$.

Though it's important for your understanding, the ACT typically won't ask you about systems of equations with no solution. The test is much more likely to ask you about systems with infinite solutions, which, by the way, are handled almost exactly the same way as systems with no solution.

Infinite solutions

A system of equations has infinite solutions when both equations are essentially the same:

$$3x + 2y = 5$$
$$3x + 2y = 5$$

$(1,1), (3, -2), (5, -5)$ are all solutions to the system above, to name just a few. Note that

$$6x + 4y = 10$$
$$3x + 2y = 5$$

also has an infinite number of solutions. The first equation can be divided by 2 to get the second equation.

EXAMPLE 2: The solution set of the system of equations below consists of all (x, y) such that $3x - 2y = 5$. What is the value of n ?

$$9x - 6y = 15$$
$$12nx - 24y = 20n$$

A. 2   **B.** 3   **C.** 4   **D.** 5   **E.** 6

Don't be thrown off by the initial wording in the question. When it states that the solution set consists of all (x, y) such that $3x - 2y = 5$, what it's really saying is that there are infinitely many solutions. After all, there are an infinite number of combinations of x and y that will make $3x - 2y = 5$ true. The second thing it's saying is that each equation in the system must be a multiple of $3x - 2y = 5$. In other words, each equation in the system must essentially be the same as $3x - 2y = 5$. That's the only way the system can produce the specified solution set.

To get the value of n, we go through the same process as before; we try to match the coefficients that we have actual values for, namely the coefficients of y. Since $-24 \div -6 = 4$, we multiply the first equation by 4.

$$36x - 24y = 60$$
$$12nx - 24y = 20n$$

Now the coefficients of y match and we can compare the other terms. The coefficients of x give $12n = 36$ and the constants give $20n = 60$. Either way, $n = 3$. Answer $\boxed{(B)}$.

Word problems

You will most definitely run into a question that requires you to translate a "real life" scenario into a system of equations. Here's a classic example:

EXAMPLE 3: Erin was put in charge of buying medals and trophies for a club award ceremony. She bought 50 items and spent a total of $1,400 (excluding tax). Medals cost $25 each and trophies cost $35 each. How many medals did Erin buy for the award ceremony?

   A. 10   **B.** 15   **C.** 20   **D.** 30   **E.** 35

Let x be the number of medals she bought and y be the number of trophies. We can then create the following system of equations:

$$x + y = 50$$
$$25x + 35y = 1400$$

Make sure you understand how we came up with these equations.

Now to solve this system, we'll use elimination. Multiply the first equation by 35 and subtract:

$$35x + 35y = 1750$$
$$25x + 35y = 1400$$
$$\overline{}$$
$$10x = 350$$
$$x = 35$$

Erin bought 35 medals. Answer $\boxed{(E)}$.

CHAPTER EXERCISE: Answers for this chapter start on page 247.

1. Which of the following (x, y) pairs is the solution for the system of equations $-3x + y = 7$ and $x - 2y = 6$?

   A. $(-4, -5)$
   B. $(-1, 4)$
   C. $(4, -1)$
   D. $(6, 0)$
   E. $(16, 5)$

2. If the system of equations below has infinitely many solutions, what is the value of k ?

$$3x - 2y = 12$$
$$9x - 6y = 4k$$

   A. 3
   B. 4
   C. 9
   D. 12
   E. 36

3. At Betty's Bakery, Oleg buys 3 bagels and 2 cups of coffee for $13.50 (before tax). The price of each cup of coffee is c dollars. The price of each bagel is 2 dollars more than the price of a cup of coffee. Which of the following systems, when solved, gives the price, b dollars, of a bagel and the price, c dollars, of a cup of coffee at Betty's Bakery?

   A. $2b + 3c = 13.50$
      $b = 2 + c$

   B. $2b + 3c = 13.50$
      $c = 2 + b$

   C. $3b + c = 13.50$
      $b = 2 + 2c$

   D. $3b + 2c = 13.50$
      $b = 2 + c$

   E. $3b + 2c = 13.50$
      $c = 2 + b$

4. If (x, y) is the solution to the system of equations below, then $y = ?$

$$3x = -4$$
$$2x - 3y = -1$$

   A. -5
   B. $-\dfrac{5}{2}$
   C. $-\dfrac{4}{3}$
   D. $-\dfrac{5}{9}$
   E. $\dfrac{11}{3}$

5. The solution of the system of equations below is the set of all (x, y) that satisfy the equation $y = -\dfrac{2}{3}x + \dfrac{5}{3}$. If it can be determined, what is the value of c ?

$$6x + 9y = 15$$
$$10x + cy = 25$$

   A. 9
   B. 12
   C. 13
   D. 15
   E. Cannot be determined from the given information

6. Given that $4x + 5y = 9$ and $3x - 4y = -32$, what is the value of $x - y$?

   A. -9
   B. -1
   C. 1
   D. 5
   E. 7

7. The value of y is half the value of x. The sum of x and y is 12. What is the value of xy ?

   A. 8
   B. 16
   C. 32
   D. 64
   E. 162

141

8. Yisel will order small and medium buckets of paint for the renovation of her house. The table below gives the number of gallons of paint in each bucket and the price per bucket.

Size	Gallons in each bucket	Price per bucket
Small	1	$20
Medium	3	$50

Yisel will order 40 buckets of paint containing a total of 100 gallons. Which of the following systems of equations correctly expresses the relationship between the number of small buckets s and the number of medium buckets m that Yisel will order?

A. $s + m = 40$
      $s + 3m = 100$

B. $s + m = 40$
      $20s + 50m = 100$

C. $s + m = 100$
      $s + 3m = 40$

D. $s + 3m = 40$
      $20s + 50m = 100$

E. $s + 3m = 100$
      $20s + 50m = 40$

9. What is the value of x in the solution of the system of equations below?

$$4x + y = a$$
$$x - 2y = 4a$$

A. $-\dfrac{2}{7}a$

B. $\dfrac{2}{3}a$

C. $\dfrac{5}{9}a$

D. $2a$

E. $6a$

Use the following information to answer questions 10–11.

The table below gives the prices for local and express train passes in the city of Stonebrid

	Local	Express
1-day	$4	$5
7-day	$18	$24

10. A group of tourists arrived at a Stonebridge train station and paid $432 for twenty 7-day passes. How many express passes did they purchase?

A.   8
B.   10
C.   12
D.   14
E.   15

11. When the Department of Transportation in Stonebridge decreases the price of 1-day local passes, the number of 1-day local passes sold per hour increases. The expression $rx + s$ represents the number of 1-day local passes sold in one hour when the price is x dollars per pass. When the price in the table was in effect, the number of 1-day local passes sold per hour was 40. When the price was decreased to $2, the number of 1-day local passes sold per hour was 50. What are the values of r and s ?

A. $r = -10, s = 80$
B. $r = -5, s = 60$
C. $r = 5, s = 40$
D. $r = 10, s = 30$
E. $r = 20, s = 10$

12. The solution to $a + x = b$ is $x = 2$. The solution to $ax = 2b$ is $x = 5$. What is the value of a ?

A. $\dfrac{1}{2}$

B. $\dfrac{3}{4}$

C.   1

D. $\dfrac{4}{3}$

E. $\dfrac{3}{2}$

21
Inequalities

Just as we can have equations and systems of equations, we can have inequalities and systems of inequalities.

The only difference is that you must reverse the inequality sign every time you multiply or divide both sides by a negative number.

For example,

$$2x + 3 < 9$$

In isolating x, do we have to reverse the inequality sign at any point? Well, we can subtract both sides by 3 to get $2x < 6$ and then divide both sides by 2 to get $x < 3$. Yes, we did a subtraction but at no point did we multiply or divide by a negative number. Therefore, the sign stays the same.

Let's look at another example:

$$3x + 5 < 4x + 4$$

The first step is to combine like terms. We subtract both sides by $4x$ to get the x's on the left hand side. We then subtract both sides by 5 to get the constants on the right hand side:

$$3x - 4x < 4 - 5$$
$$-x < -1$$

Notice that the sign hasn't changed yet. But to get rid of the negative in front of the x, we need to **multiply** both sides by -1. Now this operation does require a sign change.

$$x > 1$$

This concept is the cause of so many silly mistakes that it's important to reiterate it. Just working with negative numbers does NOT mean you need to change the sign. Some students see that they're dividing a negative number and impulsively reverse the sign. Don't do that. Only reverse the sign when you multiply or divide both sides **by** a negative number.

EXAMPLE 1: The inequality $7(x - 3) > 2(4x - 5)$ is equivalent to which of the following?

A. $x < -31$ B. $x > -12$ C. $x < -11$ D. $x > -6$ E. $x < 12$

Expanding both sides,

$$7x - 21 > 8x - 10$$
$$-x - 21 > -10$$
$$-x > 11$$
$$x < -11$$

Since we multipled both sides by -1 in the last step, we had to reverse the sign. Answer $\boxed{(C)}$.

For a visual representation of this answer, we can graph $x < -11$ on a number line:

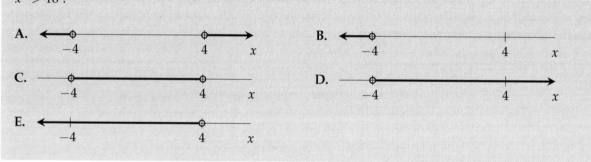

Notice that the circle is "hollow," which means $x = -11$ is not included in the solution set. If it were, the circle would be filled in.

Number lines show up regularly on the ACT, so let's walk through some additional question variations.

EXAMPLE 2: Which of the following number line graphs illustrates the solution set for the inequality $x^2 > 16$?

A.

$-4 \qquad 4 \qquad x$

B.

$-4 \qquad 4 \qquad x$

C.

$-4 \qquad 4 \qquad x$

D.

$-4 \qquad 4 \qquad x$

E.

$-4 \qquad 4 \qquad x$

Since $\sqrt{16} = 4$, we know $x > 4$. Now, your intuition about even exponents should tell you that there are probably going to be some negative solutions as well. After all, squaring a negative number results in a positive one. And indeed, if we start testing out some negative values, we quickly realize that $x < -4$ is also a possibility. Therefore, $x > 4$ or $x < -4$. Answer $\boxed{(A)}$. Notice that there wasn't a formal mathematical process we followed here. Sometimes, it's better to use your intuition and some efficient guessing and checking.

An important concept to glean from this question is the difference between **and** and **or**. The solution set was $x > 4$ OR $x < -4$. That means a number x has to satisfy only one of those conditions to be a solution. If the solution set had been $x > 4$ AND $x < -4$, then x would have to satisfy both conditions to be a solution, which, by the way, would be impossible since a number can't be greater than 4 and less than -4 at the same time. When there are no solutions, we say that the solution set is **empty**.

Taking a look back at the answer choices, we can see that choice (C) illustrates an "and": $x > -4$ AND $x < 4$.

EXAMPLE 3: The solution set of which of the following statements is shown in the graph below?

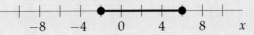

A. $x \geq -1$ or $x \leq 5$ B. $x \geq -1$ and $x \leq 5$ C. $x \leq -2$ or $x \geq 6$

D. $x \geq -2$ or $x \leq 6$ E. $x \geq -2$ and $x \leq 6$

Based on what we just learned, this one should be pretty easy. The line segment in the graph covers the values between -2 and 6 (inclusive). Therefore, it illustrates the solution set of $x \geq -2$ <u>and</u> $x \leq 6$. Answer $\boxed{(E)}$.

Notice that answer D is wrong because it has an "or". The solution set of D would look like this:

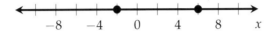

That's all real numbers. Make sure you understand why answers D and E result in different graphs.

When we're looking at inequalities with only one variable, it's easy enough to understand them using number line graphs. But what if we have two variables x and y in an inequality? For example, $y > -x - 1$. How would we represent that? In these cases, we use the standard (x, y) coordinate plane:

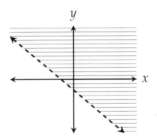

As shown by the shaded region above, the inequality $y > -x - 1$ represents all the points above the line $y = -x - 1$. If you have a hard time keeping track of what's above a line and what's below, just look at the y-axis. The line cuts the y-axis into two parts. The top part of the y-axis is always in the "above" region. The bottom part of the y-axis is always in the "below" region. If the graph doesn't show the intersection with the y-axis, you can always just draw your own vertical line through the graph to determine the "above" and "below" regions.

Also note that the line is dashed. Because $y > -x - 1$ and NOT $y = -x - 1$, the points on the line itself do not satisfy the inequality. If the equation were instead $y \geq -x - 1$, then the points on the line would satisfy the inequality and the line would be shown as solid.

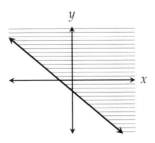

But what about a system of inequalities?

$$y \leq -x + 4$$

$$y \geq \frac{1}{2}x - 3$$

When it comes to graphing, the goal is to find the region with the points that satisfy the system. In this case, we want all the points below $y = -x + 4$ but above $y = \frac{1}{2}x - 3$. We can shade the regions below $y = -x + 4$ and above $y = \frac{1}{2}x - 3$ to see where the shaded regions overlap. The overlapping region will contain all the points that satisfy both inequalities.

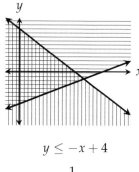

$$y \leq -x + 4$$

$$y \geq \frac{1}{2}x - 3$$

The overlapping region on the left represents all the solutions to the system.

EXAMPLE 4: A parabola and a line are graphed in the standard (x, y) coordinate plane below such that the shaded portion between them represents the solution set of one of the following systems of inequalities. Which one?

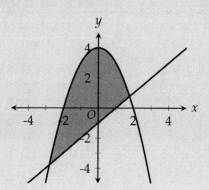

A. $y \geq x - 1$
     $y \leq 4 - x^2$

B. $y \leq x - 1$
     $y \geq 4 - x^2$

C. $y \geq x - 1$
     $y \geq 4 - x^2$

D. $y \geq x - 1$
     $y \leq x^2 + 4$

E. $y \leq x + 1$
     $y \geq x^2 + 4$

Since the parabola is an upside-down "U", we can infer from the answer choices that the equation of the parabola is $y = 4 - x^2$. The line has a slope of 1 and a y-intercept of -1, so its equation is $y = x - 1$.

The shaded region lies above the line and below the parabola. Therefore, $y \geq x - 1$ and $y \leq 4 - x^2$.

Answer $\boxed{(A)}$.

EXAMPLE 5: Which of the following graphs in the standard (x, y) coordinate plane represents the solution set of $|x| > 2$?

A.

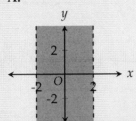

B.

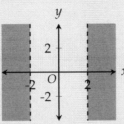

C.

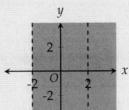

D.

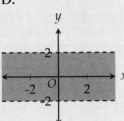

E.

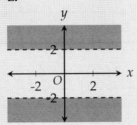

There are always two cases when dealing with absolute value: when the expression inside the absolute value is positive and when it's negative.

When x is positive, $|x| = x$, and $|x| > 2$ becomes $x > 2$.

When x is negative, $|x| = -x$, and $|x| > 2$ becomes $-x > 2$. Multiplying both sides by -1 (and reversing the sign), we get $x < -2$.

Therefore, $x > 2$ **or** $x < -2$. Graphically, this includes all points to the right of the vertical line $x = 2$ and all points to the left of the vertical line $x = -2$. Answer $\boxed{(B)}$.

EXAMPLE 6: Which of the following statements is equivalent to $|x + 3| > k$?

A. $x > -k - 3$ or $x < k - 3$ **B.** $x > -k - 3$ and $x < k - 3$ **C.** $x > k - 3$ or $x < -k - 3$

D. $x > k - 3$ and $x < -k - 3$ **E.** $x > k - 3$ and $x > -k - 3$

When $x + 3$ is positive, $|x + 3| = x + 3$.

$$|x + 3| > k$$
$$x + 3 > k$$
$$x > k - 3$$

When $x + 3$ is negative, $|x + 3| = -(x + 3)$.

$$|x + 3| > k$$
$$-(x + 3) > k$$
$$-x - 3 > k$$
$$-x > k + 3$$
$$x < -k - 3$$

147

To summarize, $x > k - 3$ or $x < -k - 3$. Answer $\boxed{(C)}$. This solution set can be graphed on the number line like so:

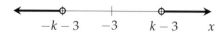

$$-k-3 \qquad -3 \qquad k-3 \qquad x$$

Notice that the graph illustrates an "or."

You may find it helpful to remember that inequalities of the form $|x| > a$ always result in an "or," whereas inequalities of the form $|x| < a$ always result in an "and."

CHAPTER EXERCISE: Answers for this chapter start on page 250.

1. The inequality $2(1 - 2x) < -3(x - 5)$ is equivalent to which of the following inequalities?

   A. $x > -17$
   B. $x > -13$
   C. $x > 17$
   D. $x < -7$
   E. $x < 13$

2. For what values of y is the inequality $\dfrac{3y - 5}{2} > y$ true?

   A. Only values less than -5
   B. Only values between -1 and 0
   C. Only values between 0 and 1
   D. Only values between 1 and 5
   E. Only values greater than 5

3. Jacob is given a budget of $200 to buy candles for a party. He will buy them from a store that sells candles for $4.25 each. Which of the following inequalities is true if and only if Jacob does not exceed his budget in buying c candles, where c is a whole number?

   A. $4.25 - c > 200$
   B. $4.25 + c \le 200$
   C. $4.25c \le 200$
   D. $4.25c > 200$
   E. $\dfrac{c}{4.25} > 200$

4. The number line graph below shows the solution set to which of the following statements?

   A. $x < 4$ and $x > -3$
   B. $x < 4$ or $x > -3$
   C. $x > 4$ and $x < -3$
   D. $x > 4$ or $x < -3$
   E. $x \ne 4$ and $x \ne -3$

5. Which of the following inequalities is a solution statement for $5x + 12 \ge 10x - 18$?

   A. $x \ge -2$
   B. $x \ge -\dfrac{2}{5}$
   C. $x \le -\dfrac{1}{6}$
   D. $x \le \dfrac{6}{5}$
   E. $x \le 6$

6. Which of the following graphs is that of the solution set of the inequality $-\dfrac{1}{2}x + 1 \ge 4$?

   A.
   B.
   C.
   D.
   E.

7. Given that $y \le 5$ and $x - y \le 9$, what is the greatest value that x can have?

   A. -14
   B. -4
   C. 0
   D. 4
   E. 14

8. For all real numbers $a, b, c,$ and d such that $a - b = c$ and $b > d$, which of the following statements is true?

   A. $a - d > c$
   B. $a - d < c$
   C. $b + d > c$
   D. $d - b > c$
   E. $d - b < c$

9. One of the following graphs shows the solution set for the system of inequalities $2x + 9 < 5$ and $-3x > 12$. Which one?

A.   empty set

B.

C.

D.

E.

10. The graph in the standard (x, y) coordinate plane below illustrates which of the following inequalities?

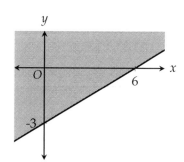

A. $y \geq -2x$

B. $y \geq -\frac{1}{2}x - 3$

C. $y \geq \frac{1}{2}x - 3$

D. $y \leq \frac{1}{2}x - 3$

E. $y \geq 2x - 3$

11. Whenever $(x - 5)(x + 2) < 0$, which of the following expressions *always* has a positive value?

A. $-x$

B. $x - 2$

C. $x + 1$

D. $x + 3$

E. $x^2 - 1$

12. One of the following graphs in the standard (x, y) coordinate plane represents the solution set of $|y| \geq |x|$. Which graph?

A.

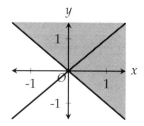

B.

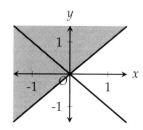

C.

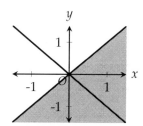

D.

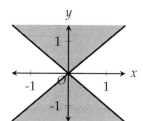

E.

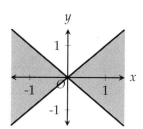

13. Given $m > n$ and $m^2 - n^2 > 2(m - n)^2$, then m must be:

   A. less than n.
   B. less than $3n$.
   C. greater than 0.
   D. greater than n.
   E. greater than $3n$.

14. The shaded region in the standard (x, y) coordinate plane below represents the solution set of which of the following systems of inequalities?

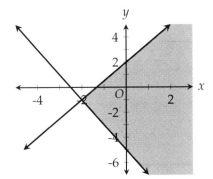

   A. $y \le \dfrac{2}{3}x + 2$ and $y \ge -\dfrac{1}{2}x - 5$

   B. $y \ge \dfrac{2}{3}x + 2$ and $y \le -\dfrac{1}{2}x - 5$

   C. $y \le \dfrac{3}{2}x + 2$ and $y \ge -2x - 5$

   D. $y \ge \dfrac{3}{2}x + 2$ and $y \le -2x - 5$

   E. $y \ge \dfrac{3}{2}x + 2$ and $y \ge -2x - 5$

15. One of the following graphs illustrates the solution set to the inequality $|x - a| \le 3$ for some positive a. Which one?

   A.

   $-a - 3 \quad\quad a - 3 \quad a + 3 \quad\quad x$

   B.

   $-a - 3 \quad\quad a - 3 \quad a + 3 \quad\quad x$

   C.

   $-a - 3 \quad\quad a - 3 \quad a + 3 \quad\quad x$

   D.

   $-a - 3 \quad\quad a - 3 \quad a + 3 \quad\quad x$

   E.

   $-a - 3 \quad\quad a - 3 \quad a + 3 \quad\quad x$

22
Trigonometry

Trigonometry is used to solve for a triangle's missing sides and angles. Let's illustrate the three essential trigonometric functions you need to know with a $5 - 12 - 13$ right triangle.

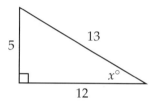

$$\sin x = \frac{\text{opposite}}{\text{hypotenuse}} = \frac{5}{13} \qquad \cos x = \frac{\text{adjacent}}{\text{hypotenuse}} = \frac{12}{13} \qquad \tan x = \frac{\text{opposite}}{\text{adjacent}} = \frac{5}{12}$$

It's important to see these trigonometric functions as ordinary numbers. After all, they're just ratios. For example, $\sin 30°$ is always equal to $\frac{1}{2}$. Why? Because all right triangles with a $30°$ angle are similar, which means the ratios of the sides stay the same.

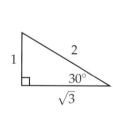
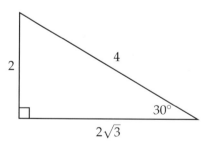

Many students over-complicate trigonometry by forgetting that $\sin x, \cos x,$ and $\tan x$ are just ratios. Perhaps because of the notation, students make mistakes like the following:

$$\frac{\sin 2x}{x} = \sin 2$$

The above is not possible because $\sin 2x$ represents a number, a single "entity." You cannot separate sin and $2x$ and treat them independently, just like you can't separate $f(x)$ into f and x.

The definitions of sine, cosine, and tangent are best memorized through the acronym **SOH-CAH-TOA**, S for sine (opposite over hypotenuse), C for cosine (adjacent over hypotenuse), and T for tangent (opposite over adjacent).

EXAMPLE 1: For right triangle $\triangle FGH$ shown below, which of the following expressions represents $\cos H$?

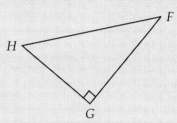

A. $\dfrac{FG}{FH}$ B. $\dfrac{FG}{GH}$ C. $\dfrac{FH}{GH}$ D. $\dfrac{GH}{FH}$ E. $\dfrac{GH}{FG}$

The side adjacent to $\angle H$ is $\overline{GH}$. The hypotenuse is $\overline{FH}$. Therefore, $\cos H = \dfrac{\text{adjacent}}{\text{hypotenuse}} = \dfrac{GH}{FH}$. Answer $\boxed{(D)}$.

Even though the hypotenuse is also "adjacent" to $\angle H$ ("adjacent" technically means "next to"), we never treat the hypotenuse as the adjacent side in trig functions.

EXAMPLE 2: Given that $\cos \angle E = \dfrac{1}{3}$ for right triangle $\triangle DEF$, what is the value of $\sin \angle E$?

A. $-\dfrac{1}{3}$ B. $\dfrac{2}{3}$ C. $\dfrac{\sqrt{8}}{3}$ D. $\dfrac{\sqrt{10}}{3}$ E. 3

First, draw it out.

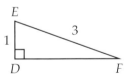

Because $\cos \angle E = \dfrac{1}{3}$, we can let adjacent side DE be 1 and hypotenuse EF be 3. Using the pythagorean theorem, $DF = \sqrt{3^2 - 1^2} = \sqrt{8}$. Therefore, $\sin \angle E = \dfrac{\text{opposite}}{\text{hypotenuse}} = \dfrac{\sqrt{8}}{3}$. Answer $\boxed{(C)}$.

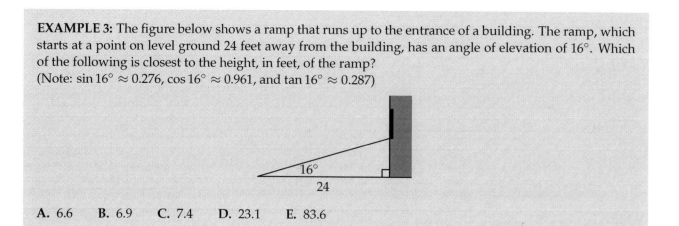

EXAMPLE 3: The figure below shows a ramp that runs up to the entrance of a building. The ramp, which starts at a point on level ground 24 feet away from the building, has an angle of elevation of 16°. Which of the following is closest to the height, in feet, of the ramp?
(Note: $\sin 16° \approx 0.276$, $\cos 16° \approx 0.961$, and $\tan 16° \approx 0.287$)

A. 6.6   **B.** 6.9   **C.** 7.4   **D.** 23.1   **E.** 83.6

Relative to the known angle of 16°, we have the adjacent side and we're looking for the opposite side. Which trig function relates the adjacent and the opposite? Tangent. With this in mind, we can set up an equation:

$$\tan 16° = \frac{\text{opposite}}{\text{adjacent}}$$

$$\tan 16° = \frac{h}{24}$$

$$h = 24 \tan 16° = 24(0.287) \approx 6.9$$

Answer $\boxed{(B)}$.

Law of Sines

The law of sines states that for a triangle $\triangle ABC$, where $\angle A$ is opposite side length a, $\angle B$ is opposite side length b, and $\angle C$ is opposite side length c,

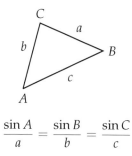

$$\frac{\sin A}{a} = \frac{\sin B}{b} = \frac{\sin C}{c}$$

which can also be represented as

$$\frac{a}{\sin A} = \frac{b}{\sin B} = \frac{c}{\sin C}$$

The law of sines comes in handy when you're working with a non-right triangle. You don't need to worry about when to apply it, however. Any ACT question requiring the law of sines will not only tell you that you need to use it but also remind you of what the formula is.

EXAMPLE 4: In $\triangle FGH$, the length of $\overline{FG}$ is 16 inches, the measure of $\angle G$ is 41°, and the measure of $\angle H$ is 72°. Which of the following expressions represents the length, in inches, of $\overline{FH}$?
(Note: According to the law of sines, the lengths of the sides of a triangle are proportional to the sines of the angles opposite those sides.)

A. $\dfrac{\sin 41°}{16 \sin 72°}$ B. $\dfrac{\sin 72°}{16 \sin 41°}$ C. $\dfrac{16 \sin 41°}{\sin 72°}$ D. $\dfrac{16 \sin 72°}{\sin 41°}$ E. $\dfrac{16}{(\sin 41°)(\sin 72°)}$

Drawing the triangle,

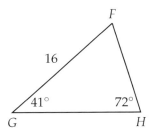

Using the law of sines,

$$\frac{FH}{\sin G} = \frac{FG}{\sin H}$$

$$\frac{FH}{\sin 41°} = \frac{16}{\sin 72°}$$

$$FH = \frac{16 \sin 41°}{\sin 72°}$$

Answer $\boxed{(C)}$.

Law of Cosines

The law of cosines states that for a triangle $\triangle ABC$, where $\angle A$ is opposite side length a, $\angle B$ is opposite side length b, and $\angle C$ is opposite side length c,

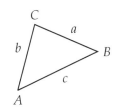

$$a^2 = b^2 + c^2 - 2bc \cos A$$

$$b^2 = a^2 + c^2 - 2ac \cos B$$

$$c^2 = a^2 + b^2 - 2ab \cos C$$

Note that these are all just different versions of the same formula. In each case, a pair of sides and the cosine of the angle between them can be used to find the side opposite that angle.

Again, it's more important that you know *how* to use the law of cosines rather than *when*; ACT questions requiring the law of cosines will tell you that you need to use it.

EXAMPLE 5: The law of cosines states that for any triangle, $c^2 = a^2 + b^2 - 2ab\cos C$, where a, b, and c are the lengths of the sides and C is the measure of the angle opposite the side of length c. A car travels 14 miles west, turns $52°$ toward the south, and then travels another 22 miles, as shown below. Which of the following is closest to the straight-line distance, in miles, between the car's initial position and final position?
(Note: $\cos 52° \approx 0.616$ and $\cos 128° \approx -0.616$.)

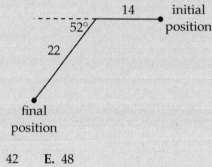

A. 28   **B.** 33   **C.** 36   **D.** 42   **E.** 48

We have one side of length 22 and one side of length 14. The angle between them measures $180 - 52 = 128°$. Using the law of cosines,

$$c^2 = a^2 + b^2 - 2ab\cos C$$

$$c^2 = 22^2 + 14^2 - 2(22)(14)\cos 128°$$

$$c^2 = 680 - 616(-0.616)$$

$$c^2 \approx 1059$$

$$c \approx \sqrt{1059} \approx 33$$

Answer (B).

Inverse Trig Functions

So far, we've only used trigonometry to find a triangle's missing side. Sometimes, we need to find a missing angle instead. To do so, we need to use the inverses of sine, cosine, and tangent. There are two ways of denoting these inverses:

- $\arcsin x$, $\arccos x$, and $\arctan x$
- $\sin^{-1} x$, $\cos^{-1} x$, and $\tan^{-1} x$

You'll see both notations on the ACT. Note that $\sin^{-1} x$ is NOT equivalent to $\dfrac{1}{\sin x}$. The definition of $\sin^{-1} x$ is always $\arcsin x$, not the reciprocal, which we'll talk about later in this chapter. The same applies to $\cos^{-1} x$ and $\tan^{-1} x$.

Now when we say $\arcsin x$, what is x? It's no longer the measure of an angle but a ratio of two sides. Remember that $\sin x$ takes an angle x and gives you the corresponding ratio. For example, $\sin 30° = \dfrac{1}{2}$. Now $\arcsin x$ does just the opposite. It takes a ratio and gives you back the corresponding angle. For example, $\arcsin \dfrac{1}{2} = 30°$. Let's dive into an example to fully illustrate.

EXAMPLE 6: For the right triangle shown in the figure below, the value of θ is given by which of the following expressions?

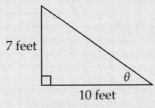

A. $\tan^{-1}\left(\dfrac{7}{10}\right)$ **B.** $\sin^{-1}\left(\dfrac{7}{10}\right)$ **C.** $\cos^{-1}\left(\dfrac{7}{10}\right)$ **D.** $\tan^{-1}\left(\dfrac{10}{7}\right)$ **E.** $\sin^{-1}\left(\dfrac{10}{7}\right)$

Relative to θ, we're given the opposite side and the adjacent side. Now what trig function relates the opposite and the adjacent? Tangent. Except this time, we want an angle, not a side. So the appropriate function is $\arctan x$, or $\tan^{-1} x$, where x is the ratio of opposite to adjacent.

$$\theta = \tan^{-1}\left(\frac{\text{opposite}}{\text{adjacent}}\right) = \tan^{-1}\left(\frac{7}{10}\right)$$

Answer $\boxed{(A)}$.

Radians

In trigonometry, sometimes radians are used instead of degrees. A radian is simply another unit used to measure angles. Just as we have feet and meters, pounds and kilograms, we have degrees and radians.

$$\pi \text{ radians} = 180°$$

If you've never used radians before, don't be put off by the π. After all, it's just a number. We could've written

$$3.14 \text{ radians} \approx 180°$$

instead, but we typically keep things in terms of π when we're working with radians. Furthermore, 3.14 is only an approximation. So, given the conversion factor above, how would we convert 45° to radians?

$$45° \times \frac{\pi \text{ radians}}{180°} = \frac{\pi}{4} \text{ radians}$$

Notice that the degree units (represented by the little circles) cancel out just as they should in any conversion problem. Now how would we convert $\dfrac{3\pi}{2}$ radians to degrees? Easy—flip the conversion factor.

$$\frac{3\pi}{2} \text{ radians} \times \frac{180°}{\pi \text{ radians}} = 270°$$

You might be wondering why we even need radians. Why not just stick with degrees? Is this another difference between the U.S. and the rest of the world, like it is with feet and meters? Nope. As it turns out, some calculations are much easier when the angles are expressed in radians (see the formulas in the chapter on circles).

EXAMPLE 7: Angle X measures $\dfrac{37}{6}\pi$ radians from its initial side to its terminal side. Angle X and Angle Y are coterminal. Which of the following could be the degree measure of Angle Y?

A. $20°$ **B.** $30°$ **C.** $45°$ **D.** $60°$ **E.** $90°$

Converting the radian measure of Angle X to degrees,

$$\frac{37}{6}\pi \text{ radians} \times \frac{180°}{\pi \text{ radians}} = 1110°$$

Now coterminal angles are angles that have the same initial and terminal sides. They're always a multiple of $360°$ apart, so we can continue to subtract 360 from 1110 until we get one of the answer choices: $1110 - 360 - 360 - 360 = 30°$. Answer $\boxed{(B)}$.

Trigonometry in the Coordinate Plane

When we're dealing with trig functions in the (x, y) coordinate plane, the sign of each one can vary depending on the quadrant in which the angle terminates.

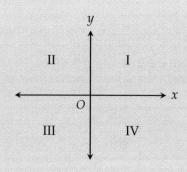

- Sine, cosine, and tangent are all positive in the first quadrant.
- Only sine is positive in the second quadrant.
- Only tangent is positive in the third quadrant.
- Only cosine is positive in the fourth quadrant.

These are best memorized through the acronym **ASTC** (All Students Take Calculus). All the functions are positive in the first quadrant, only sine is positive in the second, and so on.

So if somebody asked you for the tangent of $125°$, you probably wouldn't know the answer off the top of your head, but at least you'd be able to say that it's negative because $125°$ is in quadrant II.

To find the value of a trig function without a calculator,

1. Determine what the sign of the result should be (positive or negative).

2. Find the reference angle (the acute angle you get by drawing a straight line to the *x*-axis). If the angle is 225°, for example, the reference angle is $225° - 180° = 45°$:

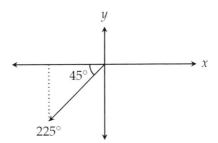

Don't memorize any formulas for finding the reference angle. Just draw a line to the *x*-axis and figure it out yourself!

3. Get the trig value for the reference angle by using the $45 - 45 - 90$ or $30 - 60 - 90$ special right triangle. Unfortunately, a calculator is necessary for reference angles outside these special right triangles. At this point, you might be wondering why I'm teaching you this process when you can just use your calculator on the ACT. I'll get to that in a minute. Bear with me.

4. Apply the sign from step 1 to the result from step 3. That's the answer.

Let's do a simple example: What is the value of $\sin 330°$?

Since 330° is in the fourth quadrant and sine is negative in the fourth quadrant, the result should be negative. Now let's find the reference angle with the help of a diagram:

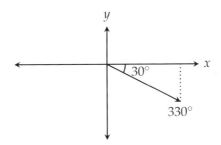

The reference angle is $360° - 330° = 30°$. Now step 3 requires us to find the value of $\sin 30°$. Using the $30 - 60 - 90$ triangle,

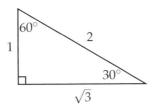

$$\sin 30° = \frac{\text{opp}}{\text{hyp}} = \frac{1}{2}$$

Since the result should be negative, $\sin 330° = \boxed{-\frac{1}{2}}$.

I show this example not because you'll be asked for the sine of 330° on the ACT (you'll have a calculator), but because it illustrates important concepts that carry over to other questions. Reference angles allow us to calculate trigonometric values for angles that don't fit in a right triangle.

EXAMPLE 8: In the standard (x, y) coordinate plane below, an angle with measure β has the positive x-axis as its initial side. Its terminal side starts at the origin and passes through $(-1, \sqrt{3})$. What is the value of $\cos \beta$?

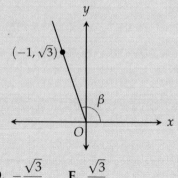

A. $-\dfrac{1}{2}$ B. $\dfrac{1}{2}$ C. $-\dfrac{\sqrt{3}}{3}$ D. $-\dfrac{\sqrt{3}}{2}$ E. $\dfrac{\sqrt{3}}{2}$

Because β is an angle in the second quadrant, $\cos \beta$ must be negative. This eliminates choices B and E.

Now, draw a vertical line from $(-1, \sqrt{3})$ down to the x-axis to get a right triangle with reference angle α.

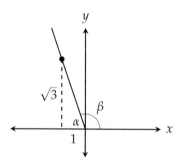

Just as we found $\sin 330°$ earlier by using $\sin 30°$, we can find $\cos \beta$ by using the cosine of the reference angle, $\cos \alpha$. So what is $\cos \alpha$? Well, we need to get the hypotenuse first. Using the pythagorean theorem, we find that the hypotenuse is $\sqrt{1^2 + (\sqrt{3})^2} = \sqrt{4} = 2$ (it's a $30 - 60 - 90$ triangle). So, $\cos \alpha = \dfrac{\text{adjacent}}{\text{hypotenuse}} = \dfrac{1}{2}$, but

because we've already established that $\cos \beta$ must be negative, $\cos \beta = -\dfrac{1}{2}$. Answer $\boxed{(A)}$. Could we have

done it another way by using $\arctan(\sqrt{3})$ to calculate α? Sure. But it's important that you understand how reference angles work.

Graphs of Trig Functions

Because trig functions take an input (an angle) and return an output (a ratio), we can graph them as functions in the (x, y) coordinate plane. For the ACT, it's worth knowing what the graphs of $\sin x$, $\cos x$, and $\tan x$ look like. Note that they're typically graphed with the x-axis in radians.

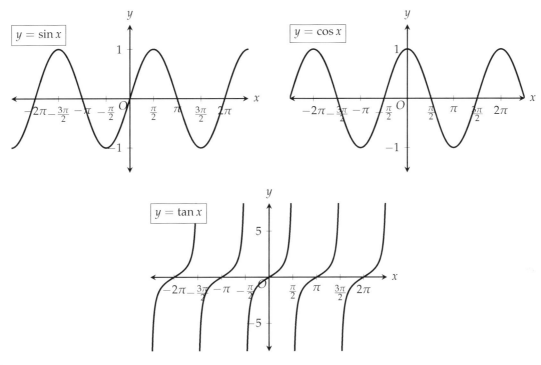

Domain

- The domain of $y = \sin x$ is all real numbers. In other words, x can be any number.

- The domain of $y = \cos x$ is also all real numbers.

- The domain of $y = \tan x$ is all real numbers except every other multiple of $90°$ ($\frac{\pi}{2}$ radians). If you look at the graph of $y = \tan x$ above, there are vertical asymptotes at each "odd" multiple of $\frac{\pi}{2}$ along the x-axis, which means $\tan x$ is undefined for those values of x.

Range

- The range of $y = \sin x$ is $-1 \leq y \leq 1$. The minimum is -1 and the maximum is 1.

- The range of $y = \cos x$ is $-1 \leq y \leq 1$. The minimum is -1 and the maximum is 1.

- The range of $y = \tan x$ is all real numbers.

Period

Period refers to the interval over which a graph repeats. For example, the period of $\sin x$ is 2π because the graph repeats every 2π units along the x-axis; the graph from -2π to 0 looks the same as the graph from 0 to 2π.

- The period of $y = \sin x$ is 2π.

- The period of $y = \cos x$ is 2π.

- The period of $y = \tan x$ is π.

Amplitude

Amplitude refers to half the distance between the maximum and the minimum. For example, the amplitude of $\sin x$ is 1 because the distance between the maximum of 1 and the minimum of -1 is 2. Half of 2 is equal to 1. Amplitude applies only to sine and cosine since tangent doesn't have a minimum or a maximum.

- The amplitude of $y = \sin x$ is 1.
- The amplitude of $y = \cos x$ is 1.

Transformations

We can change the properties of a graph by modifying certain constants. So for

$$y = a \sin b(x + c) + d$$

- $|a|$ is the new amplitude.
- b changes the period (calculating the new period is beyond the scope of the ACT).
- c shifts the graph horizontally.
- d shifts the graph vertically.

The same applies to graphs of cosine and tangent. When it comes to horizontal and vertical shifts, the concepts aren't any different from what we learned previously in the chapter on functions.

EXAMPLE 9: The graph of $y = a \sin x + 1$ is shown in the (x, y) coordinate plane below. What is the value of a ?

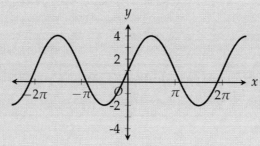

A. $\dfrac{1}{3}$ B. $\dfrac{1}{2}$ C. 2   D. 3   E. 4

Solution 1: $|a|$ is the amplitude, which we can calculate from the graph. The maximum is 4 and the minimum is -2. The distance between them is $4 - (-2) = 6$, and half of 6 is 3. Therefore, $|a| = 3$, which means $a = 3$ or $a = -3$. Because the graph isn't "flipped" over the x-axis compared to $y = \sin x$, a must be positive. Answer $\boxed{(D)}$.

Solution 2: The maximum possible value of $\sin x$, according to its range, is 1. So when $\sin x = 1$, the value of y must be equal to the maximum of the graph, which is 4.

$$a \sin x + 1 = 4$$
$$a(1) + 1 = 4$$
$$a + 1 = 4$$
$$a = 3$$

Again, the answer is $\boxed{(D)}$.

Trigonometric Identities

For the ACT, you need to know the two most important trig identities:

$$\tan x = \frac{\sin x}{\cos x} \qquad \sin^2 x + \cos^2 x = 1$$

and 3 reciprocal identities:

$$\csc x = \frac{1}{\sin x} \qquad \sec x = \frac{1}{\cos x} \qquad \cot x = \frac{1}{\tan x}$$

Note that $\sin^2 x$ is shorthand for $(\sin x)^2$, which is not the same as $\sin x^2$.

EXAMPLE 10: For all x such that $\sin x \neq 0$ and $\cos x \neq 0$, the expression $\sec^2 x - \tan^2 x$ is equivalent to:

A. $\cos x$ **B.** $\cos^2 x$ **C.** $\sin^2 x$ **D.** -1 **E.** 1

$$\sec^2 x - \tan^2 x = (\sec x)^2 - (\tan x)^2 = \left(\frac{1}{\cos x}\right)^2 - \left(\frac{\sin x}{\cos x}\right)^2 = \frac{1}{\cos^2 x} - \frac{\sin^2 x}{\cos^2 x} = \frac{1 - \sin^2 x}{\cos^2 x} = \frac{\cos^2 x}{\cos^2 x} = 1$$

Answer $\boxed{(E)}$.

CHAPTER EXERCISE: Answers for this chapter start on page 253.

1. A water slide starts at the top of a ladder and extends to the ground, as shown in the figure below. The slide is 30 feet long and the ladder is 12 feet high. The measure of the angle from the ground to the slide is θ. Which of the following equations *must* be true?

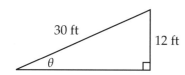

A. $\sin \theta = \dfrac{12}{30}$

B. $\sin \theta = \dfrac{30}{12}$

C. $\cos \theta = \dfrac{12}{30}$

D. $\cos \theta = \dfrac{30}{12}$

E. $\tan \theta = \dfrac{12}{30}$

2. In $\triangle ABC$ below, $\angle A$ is a right angle. Which of the following is an equivalent expression for $\dfrac{BC}{AC}$ in terms of $\angle C$?

A. $\dfrac{1}{\sin \angle C}$

B. $\dfrac{1}{\cos \angle C}$

C. $\dfrac{1}{\tan \angle C}$

D. $\sin \angle C$

E. $\cos \angle C$

3. In right triangle $\triangle JKL$ shown below, $\sin J = \dfrac{4}{9}$. What is the value of $\sin K$?

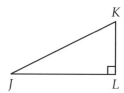

A. $\dfrac{9}{4}$

B. $\dfrac{\sqrt{65}}{4}$

C. $\dfrac{\sqrt{97}}{4}$

D. $\dfrac{\sqrt{65}}{9}$

E. $\dfrac{\sqrt{97}}{9}$

4. The graph of $y = \cos 2x$ is shown in the standard (x, y) coordinate plane below. What is the period of $\cos 2x$?

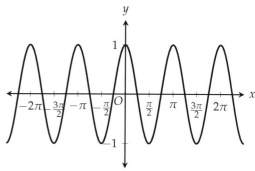

A. $\dfrac{\pi}{2}$

B. π

C. $\dfrac{3\pi}{2}$

D. 2π

E. 1

5. Which of the following is equivalent to
$3 - \sin^2 \theta - \cos^2 \theta$?

A. -2

B. -1

C. 1

D. 2

E. 3

6. Given that $\tan \alpha = \dfrac{9}{12}$, which of the following could be the value of $\sin \alpha$?

A. $\dfrac{3}{15}$

B. $\dfrac{9}{15}$

C. $\dfrac{12}{15}$

D. $\dfrac{9}{18}$

E. $\dfrac{12}{18}$

7. In right triangle $\triangle CDE$ shown below, the length of $\overline{CD}$ is 120 meters and the measure of $\angle E$ is $40°$. How long, in meters, is $\overline{DE}$?

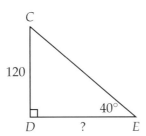

A. $120 \sin 40°$

B. $120 \tan 40°$

C. $\dfrac{120}{\sin 40°}$

D. $\dfrac{120}{\cos 40°}$

E. $\dfrac{120}{\tan 40°}$

8. In the circle below, the shaded sector has a central angle with measure $\dfrac{2\pi}{5}$ radians. What is the ratio of the area of the shaded sector to the area of the circle?

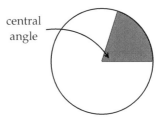

A. $\dfrac{1}{5}$

B. $\dfrac{2}{5}$

C. $\dfrac{1}{6}$

D. $\dfrac{2}{9}$

E. $\dfrac{5}{36}$

9. In a right triangle, one of the angle measures is θ. If $\cos \theta = \dfrac{12}{37}$ and $\tan \theta = \dfrac{35}{12}$, what is the value of $\sin \theta$?

A. $\dfrac{12}{35}$

B. $\dfrac{35}{37}$

C. $\dfrac{37}{35}$

D. $\dfrac{35}{\sqrt{1,081}}$

E. $\dfrac{12}{\sqrt{2,594}}$

10. What is the amplitude of the function defined by $y = \dfrac{1}{3} \sin(2x + 1)$?

A. $\dfrac{1}{3}$

B. $\dfrac{1}{2}$

C. $\dfrac{2}{3}$

D. 2

E. π

11. James wants to approximate the height of a utility pole. He stands 150 ft away from the pole at point C and finds that the angle of elevation from C to the top of the pole measures $26°$, as shown in the figure below.

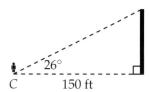

Given the trigonometric approximations in the tables below, which of the following is closest to the height, in feet, of the utility pole?

$\sin 26°$	0.438	$\sin 64°$	0.899
$\cos 26°$	0.899	$\cos 64°$	0.438
$\tan 26°$	0.488	$\tan 64°$	2.050

A. 66
B. 73
C. 135
D. 308
E. 342

12. In the circle with center A shown below, the length of radius $\overline{AB}$ is 2 inches and $\overline{BC}$ is perpendicular to radius $\overline{AD}$ at C. In terms of α, which of the following expressions gives the length, in inches, of $\overline{CD}$?

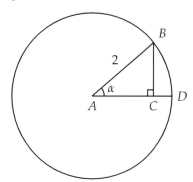

A. $2\sin\alpha$
B. $2\cos\alpha$
C. $2 - \sin\alpha$
D. $2 - 2\sin\alpha$
E. $2 - 2\cos\alpha$

13. Ruth wants to cut out a triangular flag from a rectangular piece of cloth. As shown in the figure below, the height of the cloth is h meters and the three vertices of the flag are marked as points R, S, and T. Ruth uses a protractor to find the angles measures for $\angle RST$, $\angle SRT$, and $\angle T$. She does not have a ruler to determine any unknown lengths. Which of the following expressions can Ruth use to find the length, in meters, of $\overline{ST}$? (Note: The law of sines states that for a triangle $\triangle ABC$ with sides of lengths a, b, and c opposite their respective angles,

$$\frac{\sin\angle A}{a} = \frac{\sin\angle B}{b} = \frac{\sin\angle C}{c}.)$$

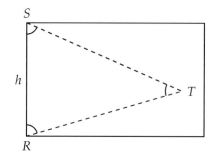

A. $\dfrac{h\sin\angle SRT}{\sin\angle T}$

B. $\dfrac{h\sin\angle RST}{\sin\angle T}$

C. $\dfrac{h\sin\angle T}{\sin\angle SRT}$

D. $\dfrac{\sin\angle T}{h\sin\angle SRT}$

E. $\dfrac{\sin\angle T}{h\sin\angle RST}$

14. What is the range of the function defined by $y = 3\cos(\pi x)$ in the standard (x, y) coordinate plane?

A. $-6\pi \le y \le 6\pi$
B. $-3\pi \le y \le 3\pi$
C. $-\pi \le y \le \pi$
D. $-2 \le y \le 2$
E. $-3 \le y \le 3$

15. In the figure below, points B and C lie on a circle with center A and a radius of 6 inches. If the area of $\triangle ABC$ is 12 square inches, which of the following expressions gives the measure of $\angle BAC$?

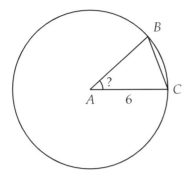

A. $\sin^{-1}\left(\dfrac{1}{3}\right)$

B. $\cos^{-1}\left(\dfrac{1}{3}\right)$

C. $\sin^{-1}\left(\dfrac{2}{3}\right)$

D. $\cos^{-1}\left(\dfrac{2}{3}\right)$

E. $\tan^{-1}\left(\dfrac{2}{3}\right)$

16. Which of the following is equal to $\dfrac{\tan\theta}{\sin\theta}$ when $\cos\theta = \dfrac{3}{4}$ and $0 < \theta < \dfrac{\pi}{2}$?

A. $\dfrac{\sqrt{7}}{4}$

B. $\dfrac{\sqrt{7}}{3}$

C. $\dfrac{3}{4}$

D. $\dfrac{4}{3}$

E. $\dfrac{12}{7}$

17. In $\triangle PQR$ below, $\angle Q$ measures $34°$, $\angle R$ measures $68°$, and the length of $\overline{PR}$ is 40 inches. To the nearest inch, what is the length of $\overline{PQ}$?

(Note: The law of sines gives the equation $\dfrac{a}{\sin A} = \dfrac{b}{\sin B} = \dfrac{c}{\sin C}$ for a triangle with angles $\angle A$, $\angle B$, and $\angle C$ opposite sides of length a, b, and c, respectively. Note also that $\sin 68° \approx 0.927$ and $\sin 34° \approx 0.559$.)

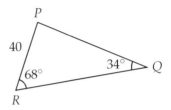

A. 24
B. 43
C. 66
D. 71
E. 77

18. Triangle ABC has vertices at $A(1,3)$, $B(4,7)$, and $C(9,3)$, as shown in the standard (x,y) coordinate plane below. What is the value of $\tan\angle C$?

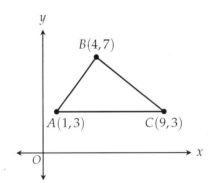

A. $\dfrac{1}{2}$

B. $\dfrac{4}{3}$

C. $\dfrac{4}{5}$

D. $\dfrac{4}{\sqrt{41}}$

E. $\dfrac{5}{8}$

19. Which of the following is equivalent to the expression $\sec x - \sin x \tan x$?

    (Note: $\sec x = \dfrac{1}{\cos x}$ and $\tan x = \dfrac{\sin x}{\cos x}$)

    A. $\cos x$
    B. $\sin x$
    C. $\sec x$
    D.   0
    E.   1

20. In $\triangle PQR$ shown below, the length of $\overline{PQ}$ is 15 inches, the length of $\overline{PR}$ is 21 inches, and the measure of $\angle P$ is 39°. Which of the following is closest to the length, in inches, of $\overline{QR}$? (Note: The law of cosines states that for any triangle, $c^2 = a^2 + b^2 - 2ab \cos C$, where a, b, and c are the lengths of the sides and C is the measure of the angle opposite the side of length c. Note also that $\cos 39° \approx 0.78$.)

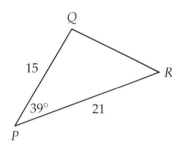

    A.   9.8
    B.   12.6
    C.   13.2
    D.   18.5
    E.   34.0

21. Given that α is measured in radians and $2\cos^2 \alpha - 5\cos \alpha = -2$ for $0 < \alpha < \dfrac{\pi}{2}$, what is the value of $\sin \alpha$?

    A. $\dfrac{1}{4}$
    B. $\dfrac{1}{2}$
    C. $\dfrac{\sqrt{2}}{2}$
    D. $\dfrac{\sqrt{3}}{4}$
    E. $\dfrac{\sqrt{3}}{2}$

22. The functions $f(x) = \sin x$ and $g(x) = \sin\left(x + \dfrac{\pi}{2}\right) - 2$ are graphed in the standard (x, y) coordinate plane below. Which of the following sequences of transformations could be applied to $f(x)$ such that the image of the graph of $f(x)$ is the graph of $g(x)$?

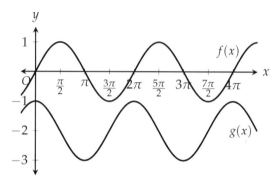

    A.   Shift $f(x)$ 2 units right and $\dfrac{\pi}{2}$ units down.
    B.   Shift $f(x)$ 2 units left and $\dfrac{\pi}{2}$ units down.
    C.   Shift $f(x)$ $\dfrac{\pi}{2}$ units right and 2 units up.
    D.   Shift $f(x)$ $\dfrac{\pi}{2}$ units right and 2 units down.
    E.   Shift $f(x)$ $\dfrac{\pi}{2}$ units left and 2 units down.

23

Permutations & Probability

Permutation questions deal with the number of arrangements. If your math teacher covered permutations in school, then you probably came across a formula like $_nP_k = \dfrac{n!}{(n-k)!}$. For the ACT, you can forget all that stuff. All you need to know is one simple strategy:

Multiply the number of CHOICES you have at each step.

EXAMPLE 1: How many different ways can Carol choose 1 sandwich and 1 bag of chips from a selection of 5 different sandwiches and 10 different bags of chips?

A. 5   **B.** 15   **C.** 25   **D.** 30   **E.** 50

Carol has 5 choices for the sandwich and 10 choices for the chips, giving a total of $5 \times 10 = 50$ possibilities. Answer $\boxed{(E)}$.

EXAMPLE 2: In how many distinct orders can 4 books be placed on a shelf?

A. 4   **B.** 12   **C.** 16   **D.** 24   **E.** 120

Let's draw 5 slots to visualize the order of the books on the shelf.

For the first slot, we have 4 choices for the book we put there. Once we fill that slot, we have 3 remaining choices for the second slot. Once the second slot is filled, we have 2 choices for the third slot. And finally, once the first 3 slots are filled, there is only 1 remaining choice for the last slot.

Multiplying the number of choices we have at each step, we get $4 \times 3 \times 2 \times 1 = 24$ distinct orders. Answer $\boxed{(D)}$.

Let's move on to probability.

Probability can be defined as

$$\frac{\text{number of target outcomes}}{\text{total number of possible outcomes}}$$

If there are 5 answer choices to a question, for instance, the probability of picking the correct answer at random is $\frac{1}{5}$. That's 1 target outcome out of a total of 5 possible outcomes.

On the ACT, probability questions typically involve **events**, such as a flipping a coin and getting "tails", rolling a dice and getting a "5", or randomly picking a jellybean from a jar and getting a red one.

If the probability of an event happening is x, then the probability of that event not happening is $1 - x$. The reverse is also true. If the probability of an event not happening is x, then the probability of that event happening is $1 - x$.

Two events are **independent** if the outcome of one event does not affect the outcome of the other. The probability of two independent events happening is equal to the product of the probabilities of each one happening on its own.

For example, the outcome of a dice roll does not affect the outcome of a coin flip. Therefore, the probability of flipping "tails" AND rolling a "3" is

$$\frac{1}{2} \times \frac{1}{6} = \frac{1}{12}$$

However, drawing a card from a deck and then drawing a second one without replacing the first card are NOT independent. So for a deck with 10 red cards and 10 black cards, the probability of drawing two red cards is NOT

$$\frac{10}{20} \times \frac{10}{20} = \frac{1}{4}$$

Instead you have to consider how the first event affects the probability of the second event. In this case, drawing the initial red card reduces the number of red cards in the deck to 9 and the total number of cards in the deck to 19. Therefore, the probability of drawing two red cards is actually

$$\frac{10}{20} \times \frac{9}{19} = \frac{9}{38}$$

EXAMPLE 3: A coin is flipped 3 times. What is the probability of the coin landing heads up all 3 times?

A. $\frac{1}{16}$ **B.** $\frac{1}{8}$ **C.** $\frac{3}{8}$ **D.** $\frac{1}{4}$ **E.** $\frac{1}{2}$

The probability of each flip coming up heads is $\frac{1}{2}$. Because each flip is independent, the probability of getting 3 heads is

$$\left(\frac{1}{2}\right)\left(\frac{1}{2}\right)\left(\frac{1}{2}\right) = \frac{1}{8}$$

Answer $\boxed{(B)}$.

EXAMPLE 4: In a bag containing marbles, 12 are green and the rest are blue. The probability of drawing a blue marble from the bag is $\dfrac{3}{4}$. How many blue marbles are in the bag?

A. 18   B. 24   C. 30   D. 36   E. 42

If the probability of drawing a blue marble is $\dfrac{3}{4}$, then the probability of drawing a green marble is $1 - \dfrac{3}{4} = \dfrac{1}{4}$. That means one-fourth of the marbles in the bag are green. Since there are 12 green marbles, there must be a total of $12 \times 4 = 48$ marbles in the bag. The number of blue marbles is then $48 - 12 = 36$. Answer $\boxed{(D)}$.

EXAMPLE 5: A number is randomly chosen from the set $\{-3, -2, -1, 0, 1\}$ and another number is randomly chosen from the set $\{-1, 2, 5\}$. What is the probability that the product of the two chosen numbers is negative?

A. $\dfrac{2}{3}$ B. $\dfrac{2}{5}$ C. $\dfrac{3}{5}$ D. $\dfrac{7}{15}$ E. $\dfrac{8}{15}$

First, find the total number of possible outcomes. There are 5 choices in the first set and 3 choices in the second set, giving a total of $5 \times 3 = 15$ possible products. Now how many of these products are negative?

Well, if we start with the -1 in the second set and multiply that with each element in the first set, we get 1 negative product (when we multiply -1 and 1). Moving on to the 2 in the second set, we get 3 more negative products (2 and -3, 2 and -2, 2 and -1). Finally, multiplying the 5 in the second set gives us yet another 3 negative products (5 and -3, 5 and -2, 5 and -1). Altogether, there are $1 + 3 + 3 = 7$ negative outcomes.

$$\frac{\text{Negative Outcomes}}{\text{Total Outcomes}} = \frac{7}{15}$$

Answer $\boxed{(D)}$.

CHAPTER EXERCISE: Answers for this chapter start on page 257.

1. There are 18 jelly beans in a jar: 6 are red, 7 are green, and 5 are purple. What is the probability that a jelly bean chosen at random from the jar is red or purple?

   A. $\dfrac{1}{3}$

   B. $\dfrac{2}{3}$

   C. $\dfrac{5}{6}$

   D. $\dfrac{11}{18}$

   E. $\dfrac{13}{18}$

2. The circular region below has 8 sectors of equal area. Each sector is labeled with a symbol. If a pebble is dropped randomly onto the region, what is the probability that the pebble will land on a sector whose label is a star?

   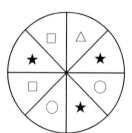

   A. $\dfrac{1}{8}$

   B. $\dfrac{1}{4}$

   C. $\dfrac{3}{8}$

   D. $\dfrac{1}{2}$

   E. $\dfrac{3}{4}$

3. If a number is chosen at random from the set $\{2, 4, 6, \ldots, 20\}$, what is the probability that the chosen number is divisible by 3?

   A. $\dfrac{1}{3}$

   B. $\dfrac{1}{5}$

   C. $\dfrac{1}{6}$

   D. $\dfrac{3}{5}$

   E. $\dfrac{3}{10}$

4. Alec has 2 stacks of cards. The first stack contains 5 red cards and 5 black cards. The second stack contains 3 red cards, 4 black cards, and 5 blue cards. Alec draws one card at random from each stack. What is the probability that both cards drawn are black?

   A. $\dfrac{1}{8}$

   B. $\dfrac{1}{6}$

   C. $\dfrac{1}{4}$

   D. $\dfrac{1}{3}$

   E. $\dfrac{5}{6}$

5. Debbie chooses her outfit for the day from 6 shirts, 3 pairs of jeans, 2 jackets, and 3 pairs of sneakers. How many different outfits are possible if she chooses exactly 1 shirt, 1 pair of jeans, 1 jacket, and 1 pair of sneakers?

   A. 4

   B. 5

   C. 14

   D. 54

   E. 108

6. An exam contains 4 questions. Each question has 5 answer choices. Which of the following expressions gives the total number of possible answer combinations for this exam?

    A. 4^5
    B. 5^4
    C. $4(3)(2)$
    D. $5(4)$
    E. $5(4)(3)(2)$

7. A pastry shop gives each customer a ticket with a 3-digit order number. Each digit must be between 1 and 7, inclusive, and cannot be repeated in the same order number. How many different order numbers are possible?

    A. 60
    B. 120
    C. 210
    D. 216
    E. 343

8. A box contains b blue marbles and w white marbles. If the probability of randomly drawing a white marble from the box is $\frac{3}{7}$, what is the value of $\frac{w}{b}$?

    A. $\frac{1}{4}$
    B. $\frac{1}{2}$
    C. $\frac{2}{3}$
    D. $\frac{3}{4}$
    E. $\frac{4}{3}$

9. In a jar filled with gumballs, 42 are red, 33 are purple, and the rest are orange. The probability of randomly selecting an orange gumball from the jar is $\frac{1}{6}$. How many orange gumballs does the jar contain?

    A. 10
    B. 15
    C. 20
    D. 30
    E. 35

10. A bag contains 36 cookies: 16 chocolate chip, 8 oatmeal, and 12 peanut butter. How many additional oatmeal cookies must be added to the bag so that the probability of randomly selecting an oatmeal cookie is $\frac{1}{3}$?

    A. 4
    B. 5
    C. 6
    D. 9
    E. 12

11. Syed is playing a game that involves rolling a standard six-sided dice 6 times. If he rolls each number exactly once, he will win a prize. He has already rolled a "2" and a "5". What is the probability that he will win a prize? (Note: The faces of a standard six-sided dice are numbered from 1 to 6.)

    A. $\frac{1}{24}$
    B. $\frac{1}{54}$
    C. $\frac{1}{120}$
    D. $\frac{1}{720}$
    E. $\frac{3}{32}$

Data & Statistics

Data questions require you to interpret tables and graphs.

EXAMPLE 1: Josephine surveyed a random sample of 150 juniors and seniors at her school. They were asked whether they regularly bring their own lunch to school or buy lunch from the cafeteria. The results are organized in the table below. The number of juniors who regularly buy lunch from the cafeteria is not shown.

	Bring Lunch	Buy Lunch	
Juniors	34	?	82
Seniors	40	28	68
	74	76	150

PART 1: How many juniors in the sample regularly buy lunch from the cafeteria?

A. 14   **B.** 28   **C.** 34   **D.** 48   **E.** 54

PART 2: Which of the following is closest to the percent of students in the sample who are seniors and regularly bring lunch to school?

A. 23%   **B.** 27%   **C.** 45%   **D.** 54%   **E.** 59%

Part 1 Solution: Subtract the number of juniors who bring lunch from the total number of juniors: $82 - 34 = 48$. Answer $\boxed{(D)}$.

Part 2 Solution: The number of seniors who regularly bring lunch to school is 40. The total number of students in the sample is 150. $\frac{40}{150} \times 100\% \approx 27\%$. Answer $\boxed{(B)}$.

EXAMPLE 2: Cliff took a walk on Sunday to get some fresh air. The graph below plots Cliff's distance from home along the y-axis and the elapsed time during the walk along the x-axis. Which of the following accurately describes Cliff's walk?

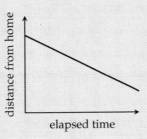

A. He walked at a constant speed toward home.
B. He walked at a constant speed away from home.
C. He walked in a circle around his home.
D. He walked slower and slower toward home.
E. He walked faster and faster away from home.

The slope of the graph does not change, which means Cliff walked the same distance for every equivalent unit of time. Therefore, he walked at a constant speed. Cliff's distance from home at the start is greater than his distance from home towards the end. Therefore, he walked toward home instead of away from it. Answer (A).

Whereas data questions are typically broader in scope, statistics questions require you to analyze data with specific measurements such as the mean and the median. Before we get into any examples, let's run through the key terms by using a simple list of numbers:

$$5, 6, 2, 2, 2, 7$$

The **mean** of the list is the average:

$$\frac{5 + 6 + 2 + 2 + 2 + 7}{6} = \boxed{4}$$

The **median** is the number in the middle when the list is in order. For example, the median for $1, 2, 3, 4, 5$ is 3. For our particular list, which, when ordered, looks like

$$2, 2, 2, 5, 6, 7$$

there is no single middle number we can consider the median. When that happens, the median is the average of the two middle numbers:

$$\frac{2 + 5}{2} = \boxed{3.5}$$

Now what if the list were 100 numbers long? How would you determine the median? Take half to get 50. The 50th and 51st numbers would be the ones in the middle you would average.

For an ordered list of 101 numbers, take half to get 50.5. Round up. The 51st number is the median.

Seems a little counterintuitive, right? If you find this hard to memorize, just keep the smallest case in your back pocket. For a list of 3 numbers, the second one is obviously the median. How would we get this mathematically? Take half of 3 to get 1.5. Then round up to 2.

For a list of 4 numbers, the median is the average of the second and third numbers. To get this mathematically, take half of 4 to get 2 and remember to include the next number, 3.

In both cases, we "rounded up." When there was an odd number of numbers, we rounded 1.5 up to 2. When there was an even number of numbers, we rounded 2 up to 3, which indicated that two numbers would contribute to the median. This technique may seem a bit odd, but many students have found it helpful in quickly finding the median of a large batch of numbers.

The **mode** is the number that shows up most often. In our particular list, it's $\boxed{2}$.

The **range** is the difference between the biggest number in the list and the smallest number:

$$7 - 2 = \boxed{5}$$

The **standard deviation** is a measure of how spread out a list of numbers is. In other words, how much they "deviate" from the mean. The standard deviation is lower when more numbers are closer to the mean and higher when more numbers are spread out away from the mean. For example, our list

$$2, 2, 2, 5, 6, 7$$

would have a higher standard deviation than the following list

$$5, 5, 5, 5, 6, 7$$

because the second list is more tightly clustered around the mean. It turns out that the standard deviation of our list is 2.28 and the standard deviation of the second list is 0.83. Don't worry about how we got those values—you'll never be asked to calculate the standard deviation on the ACT. Just know what it is and you'll be fine.

EXAMPLE 3: A data set containing 4 elements has a mean of 12. Three of the elements are 11, 15, and 9. Which of the following is the fourth element?

A. 12   **B.** 13   **C.** 14   **D.** 15   **E.** 16

The sum of the 4 elements in the data set must be $4 \times 12 = 48$. To get the fourth element, we subtract the three known elements from the sum: $48 - 11 - 15 - 9 = 13$. Answer $\boxed{(B)}$.

EXAMPLE 4: The stem-and-leaf plot below shows the number of menu items at each of 18 restaurants in Stoneville. What is the median number of menu items?

Stem	Leaf
1	1 3 6 6 7 9
2	3 4 5 7 8 8 9
3	1 1 1 2 2

(Note: For example, 23 menu items would have a stem value of 2 and a leaf value of 3.)

A. 24   **B.** 25   **C.** 26   **D.** 27   **E.** 28

Because there are 18 data points, the median is the average of the 9th and 10th data points. From the stem-and-leaf plot, the 9th data point is 25 (9 "leaves" from the top). The 10th data point is 27. The average of 25 and 27 is 26. Answer $\boxed{(C)}$.

EXAMPLE 5: In a distribution of student test scores, 68% of the scores fall within 1 standard deviation from the mean, 82% of the scores fall within 2 standard deviations from the mean, and 94% of the scores fall within 3 standard deviations from the mean. What percentage of the test scores fall between 1 standard deviation and 3 standard deviations from the mean?

A. 12%   **B.** 14%   **C.** 26%   **D.** 81%   **E.** 82%

Remember that standard deviation is just a number. So if the standard deviation is 5, then 68% of the scores are within 5 of the mean. You'll never have to actually calculate the standard deviation on the ACT. For this question, the answer is simply $94\% - 68\% = 26\%$. Answer (C).

EXAMPLE 6: Each number in a list is halved, and each resulting number is then decreased by 4. If n is the mean of the final list, which of the following expressions gives the mean of the original list in terms of n ?

A. $\frac{1}{2}n - 4$ **B.** $\frac{1}{2}(n-4)$ **C.** $n+4$ **D.** $2n+4$ **E.** $2(n+4)$

When an operation is applied to every number in a list, it is also implicitly applied to both the mean and the median. For example, if every number in a list is increased by 10, then the mean and the median both increase by 10.

For this question, let x be the mean of the original list. Then

$$\frac{x}{2} - 4 = n$$
$$\frac{x}{2} = n + 4$$
$$x = 2(n + 4)$$

Answer (E). Working backwards is also fine: $n \to n+4 \to 2(n+4)$.

EXAMPLE 7: A list contains 7 integers. For this list, the mean and the mode are both equal to 0. What is the maximum number of positive integers the list can contain?

A. 1   **B.** 2   **C.** 3   **D.** 4   **E.** 5

For the mode to be 0, there must be at least two 0's in the list. For the mean to be 0, the sum of integers in the list must be 0. Since we want as many positive integers as possible, we need to minimize the number of 0's and the number of negative integers in the list. Therefore, the best case is two 0's, four positive integers, and 1 negative integer (negative enough to zero out the positive integers). Answer (D).

EXAMPLE 8: A scatterplot consisting of 10 data points is shown in the standard (x, y) coordinate plane below. Which of the following equations best fits the data in the scatterplot?

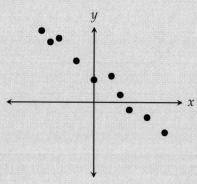

A. $y = -x - 4$ **B.** $y = -x + 4$ **C.** $y = x - 4$ **D.** $y = x + 4$ **E.** $y = 4$

Draw a line that you think best fits the data.

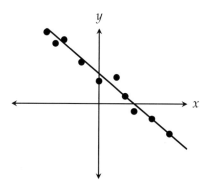

This line has a negative slope and a positive y-intercept. Of all the answer choices, only $\boxed{(B)}$ gives a line that meets these criteria. In statistics, a line that best models or approximates the given data is called the **line of best fit**. For the data in this example, the line of best fit is $y = -x + 4$.

CHAPTER EXERCISE: Answers for this chapter start on page 259.

1. Robert is training for a track and field competition. The finishing times, in minutes, for his practice runs last month are listed below. What is the median of Robert's finishing times for last month, in minutes?

   9.7, 8.4, 11.1, 9.3, 10.8, 8.1, 9.5

   A. 8.4
   B. 9.4
   C. 9.5
   D. 9.6
   E. 10.8

2. Nathan took 9 tests in history class. In the first 4 tests, he scored 89, 84, 92, and 97 points, respectively. The average of his last 5 test scores was 86 points. What was the average of all 9 of Nathan's test scores in history class?

   A. 85
   B. 86
   C. 87
   D. 88
   E. 89

   ┌─────────────────────────────────────┐
   │ Use the following information to answer │
   │ questions 3–4.   │
   └─────────────────────────────────────┘

Al's Airlines sells flight tickets weeks in advance. The table below gives the ticket prices from February 21 through February 24 for a certain flight offered by Al's Airlines.

Date	Price
Feb. 21	$240
Feb. 22	$230
Feb. 23	$242
Feb. 24	$225
Feb. 25	$235
Feb. 26	$244

3. What is the average daily ticket price of the flight from February 21 to February 26?

   A. $235
   B. $236
   C. $237
   D. $238
   E. $240

4. Between which of the following two consecutive days did the ticket price increase the most?

   A. February 21 and February 22
   B. February 22 and February 23
   C. February 23 and February 24
   D. February 24 and February 25
   E. February 25 and February 26

5. An employee at Amy's Apparel listed the prices of the tee-shirts in the store during an inventory check. The mean of the prices is 28 dollars and the standard deviation is 5 dollars. A tee-shirt that has a price of 16 dollars is how many standard deviations below the mean?

   A. 1.8
   B. 2.2
   C. 2.4
   D. 3.2
   E. 3.6

6. A list has 17 positive numbers. The 17 numbers in a second list are obtained by squaring each number in the first list. The 17 numbers in a third list are obtained by decreasing each number in the second list by 12. The median of the third list is 37. What is the median of the first list?

   A. 5
   B. 7
   C. 25
   D. 625
   E. 2,401

Use the following information to answer questions 7–11.

Jeff and Abigail left for work at the same time and traveled in opposite directions along the same straight highway. Jeff started in City A and drove towards City B while Abigail started in City B and drove towards City A. The graph below shows their respective commutes to work.

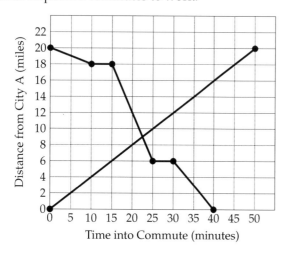

7. What is the distance, in miles, between City A and City B?

   A.   10
   B.   20
   C.   22
   D.   24
   E.   50

8. Jeff and Abigail passed each other on the highway after about how many minutes into the commute?

   A.   9
   B.   12.5
   C.   22.5
   D.   25
   E.   27.5

9. How many times did Abigail make a stop during her commute?

   A.   0
   B.   1
   C.   2
   D.   4
   E.   5

10. Jeff's commute took how many minutes longer than Abigail's commute?

    A.   10
    B.   15
    C.   20
    D.   25
    E.   30

11. During which of the following time intervals was Abigail driving faster than Jeff?

       I.   0 to 10 minutes
      II.   15 to 25 minutes
     III.   30 to 40 minutes

    A.   I only
    B.   II only
    C.   I and III only
    D.   II and III only
    E.   I, II, and III

Use the following information to answer questions 12–14.

The graph below shows the number of orders processed by a manufacturer on each day of a certain week. The model curve represents an equation that best fits the actual data.

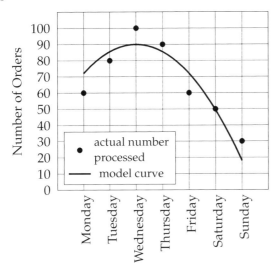

12. The model curve gives which of the following values for the number of orders processed on Wednesday?

    A. 60
    B. 70
    C. 80
    D. 90
    E. 100

13. For which day does the model curve come the closest to fitting the actual number of orders processed?

    A. Tuesday
    B. Wednesday
    C. Thursday
    D. Friday
    E. Saturday

14. For the week shown in the graph, what was the median number of orders processed per day?

    A. 50
    B. 60
    C. 70
    D. 80
    E. 90

Use the following information to answer questions 15–16.

The stem-and-leaf plot below shows the number of books owned by each of 14 students in a class.

Stem	Leaf
0	2 2 3 5
1	1 1 2 2 2 6
2	1 1 1 8

(Note: For example, 12 books would have a stem value of 1 and a leaf value of 2.)

15. If a student from the class is selected at random, what is the probability that the chosen student owns more than 15 books?

    A. $\dfrac{2}{7}$
    B. $\dfrac{3}{7}$
    C. $\dfrac{1}{14}$
    D. $\dfrac{3}{14}$
    E. $\dfrac{5}{14}$

16. The mean number of books owned increased to 13 after a new student joined the class. How many books does the new student own?

    A. 5
    B. 18
    C. 21
    D. 26
    E. 28

17. The median of a list of 7 numbers is x. Three of the numbers in the list are equal to x. If 4 numbers greater than x can be added to the list such that x is still the median, how many numbers in the list are less than x ?

    A. 0
    B. 1
    C. 2
    D. 3
    E. 4

181

18. The results of a survey are represented as points in the standard (x, y) coordinate plane below. If a is a real number chosen for best fit, which of the following equations most closely fits the survey data?

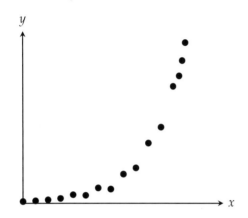

A. $y = a$
B. $y = ax$
C. $y = \dfrac{a}{x}$
D. $y = a\sqrt{x}$
E. $y = a^x$

19. A data set has a mean of 6, a median of 7, and an only mode of 8. If the data set contains 4 integers, which of the following statements *must* be true about the data set?

A. The smallest integer is 1.
B. The smallest integer is 2.
C. One of the integers is 7.
D. The sum of the 4 integers is 28.
E. The sum of the 4 integers is 32.

20. The members of a data set are listed below. A new data set is created from the original data set by adding integers a, b, and c, where $a \leq 19$, $b \leq a$, and $c \geq 35$. What is the median of the new data set?

$$15, \ 19, \ 25, \ 29, \ 33, \ 33, \ 41$$

A. 25
B. 27
C. 29
D. 31
E. 33

21. The table below gives the cost of buying printing paper by the box from a certain supplier. The cost per box depends on the number of boxes in the order.

Number of boxes (x)	Cost per box
$0 < x < 20$	$50.00
$20 \leq x < 40$	$46.00
$40 \leq x < 60$	$42.00
$60 \leq x < 80$	$38.00

Which of the following graph best illustrates this information?

A.

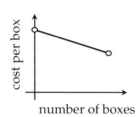

B.

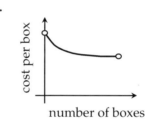

C.

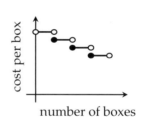

D.

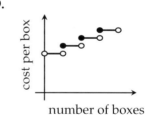

E.

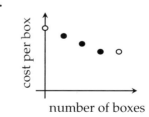

25
Logarithms

Warning: Logarithms rarely show up on the exam. This chapter is only for those who want to cover all their bases (haha!).

At this point, we know how to solve an equation like

$$x^3 = 8$$

We take the cube root of both sides to get $x = 2$. But what about

$$3^x = 8$$

Do we take the xth root of both sides? That doesn't really work. Instead, we have to use logs (short for logarithms).

Here's how they work. Given an equation like $3^x = 8$, we can isolate x like so:

$$x = \log_3 8$$

The little "3" is called the base. The "8" is called the argument or the power. Notice where those two numbers came from and where they were placed. It's important that you know how to go from one form to the other:

$$3^x = 8 \qquad\qquad x = \log_3 8$$

Now to evaluate $\log_3 8$, we need a calculator, which would give you

$$x = \log_3 8 \approx 1.89$$

As you can see, $\log_3 8$ is just a number. That's all it is. Don't be scared by it. Now we can state that

$$3^{1.89} = 8$$

We used a calculator for this one, but don't worry about any calculator steps. The ACT will never ask you to evaluate a logarithm that you can't do by hand.

Lastly, a log with a base of 10 is typically written without the base. For example, $\log 7 = \log_{10} 7$.

EXAMPLE 1: What is the value of $\log_2\left(\dfrac{1}{8}\right)$?

A. -3 **B.** $-\dfrac{1}{3}$ **C.** $\dfrac{1}{4}$ **D.** $\dfrac{1}{3}$ **E.** 3

Let $\log_2\left(\dfrac{1}{8}\right) = x$. Then by definition,

$$2^x = \frac{1}{8}$$

Since $2^{-3} = \dfrac{1}{2^3} = \dfrac{1}{8}$, $x = -3$. Answer $\boxed{(A)}$.

EXAMPLE 2: Given that $5^{2x} = 9$, which of the following gives the value of x ?

A. $\dfrac{\log_2 9}{5}$ **B.** $\dfrac{\log_5 9}{2}$ **C.** $2\log_5 9$ **D.** $5\log_2 9$ **E.** $9\log_2 5$

The equation $5^{2x} = 9$ is equivalent to

$$2x = \log_5 9$$
$$x = \frac{\log_5 9}{2}$$

Answer $\boxed{(B)}$.

Laws of Logarithms

There are several laws of logarithms you should know:

- $\log_a 1 = 0$
- $\log_a a = 1$
- $\log_a(xy) = \log_a x + \log_a y$
- $\log_a(x^y) = y\log_a x$
- $\log_a\left(\dfrac{x}{y}\right) = \log_a x - \log_a y$
- $\log_a b = \dfrac{\log_c b}{\log_c a}$

The first two don't really need to be memorized because they stem from the basic definition of a logarithm. You should memorize the rest.

The last one allows you to change the base of a logarithm. For example, if you wanted to convert $\log_2 5$ to a logarithm expression in base 10, which might be easier to input on your calculator, then $\log_2 5 = \dfrac{\log 5}{\log 2}$.

EXAMPLE 3: Which of the following is equivalent to $\log_3 5 + \log_3 7$?

A. $\log_3 12$ **B.** $\log_3 35$ **C.** $2\log_3 6$ **D.** 12^3 **E.** 3^{12}

$$\log_3 5 + \log_3 7 = \log_3(5 \cdot 7) = \log_3 35$$

Answer $\boxed{(B)}$.

EXAMPLE 4: If $p = \log_2 x$, what is the value of $\log_2(2x^3)$ in terms of p ?

A. $6p$ **B.** $2p^3$ **C.** $1 + 3p$ **D.** $3 + 3p$ **E.** $1 + p^3$

$$\log_2(2x^3) = \log_2 2 + \log_2 x^3 = 1 + 3\log_2 x = 1 + 3p$$

Answer $\boxed{(C)}$. Note that we cannot move the exponent "3" to the front first because it applies only to x, not the entire argument.

EXAMPLE 5: If $\log_3 b - \log_3 4 = 2$, then $b = ?$

A. 6   **B.** 8   **C.** 13   **D.** 24   **E.** 36

$$\log_3 b - \log_3 4 = 2$$
$$\log_3\left(\frac{b}{4}\right) = 2$$

By definition,

$$3^2 = \frac{b}{4}$$
$$b = 3^2 \cdot 4 = 36$$

Answer $\boxed{(E)}$.

CHAPTER EXERCISE: Answers for this chapter start on page 262.

1. What is the value of x if $\log_4 x = 3$?

   A. $\sqrt[4]{3}$
   B. $\sqrt[3]{4}$
   C. 12
   D. 64
   E. 81

2. If $a = \log_5 3$ and $b = \log_5 4$, which of the following expressions is equal to 12?

   A. ab
   B. $a + b$
   C. $5^a + 5^b$
   D. 5^{a+b}
   E. 25^{ab}

3. If c is a positive number such that $\log_c 9 = \dfrac{1}{2}$, then $c = ?$

   A. $\dfrac{1}{3}$
   B. $\sqrt{3}$
   C. 3
   D. 18
   E. 81

4. If $\log_5 4 = x$, what is the value of 5^{2-x} ?

   A. $\dfrac{1}{25}$
   B. $\dfrac{4}{25}$
   C. $\dfrac{25}{4}$
   D. 21
   E. 25

5. Given that $\log_3 x^2 = c$, what is the value of $\log_3 x$ in terms of c ?

   A. $\dfrac{c}{2}$
   B. $c - 2$
   C. $2c$
   D. c^2
   E. $\sqrt{c}$

6. If $\log_2 7 = p$ and $\log_2 3 = q$, what is the value of $\log_2 63$ in terms of p and q ?

   A. $3pq$
   B. $p + 2q$
   C. $p + 3q$
   D. $3p + 3q$
   E. $p + q^2$

7. For all $x > 0$, which of the following expressions is equivalent to $\log\left((3x)^2\right)$?

   A. $\log 3 + 2 \log x$
   B. $2 \log 3 + \log x$
   C. $2 \log 3 + 2 \log x$
   D. $2(\log 3)(\log x)$
   E. $\log 6 + \log 2x$

8. If a, b, and c are positive numbers such that $a^x = b$ and $a^y = c$, then $xy = ?$

   A. $\sqrt[a]{bc}$
   B. $\log_a(bc)$
   C. $\log_b a + \log_c a$
   D. $(\log_a b)(\log_a c)$
   E. $(\log_b a)(\log_c a)$

9. If $x > 0$ and $\log_4(x + 3) + \log_4(x - 3) = 2$, then $x = ?$

   A. 5
   B. $\sqrt{7}$
   C. 8
   D. $\sqrt{17}$
   E. 25

10. If $\log_b 40 - \log_b 5 = 3$, then $b = ?$

    A. 2
    B. 5
    C. 8
    D. 15
    E. 512

26

A Mix of Algebra Topics

Word Problems

For almost all word problems, the strategy will be to use a variable to translate the problem into math. What you choose to be the variable depends on whether it makes the algebra in the problem easier or harder. Obviously, you'll want to choose variables that make the algebra easier.

EXAMPLE 1: Jasper drove 78 miles this week, which is 12 less than twice the number of miles he drove last week. How many miles did Jasper drive last week?

A. 33   **B.** 37   **C.** 41   **D.** 45   **E.** 49

Let the number of miles Jasper drove last week be x. Then

$$78 = 2x - 12$$
$$90 = 2x$$
$$x = 45$$

Answer $\boxed{(D)}$.

EXAMPLE 2: Jackie bought a new case of blue and red pens. The case contains 72 pens with twice as many blue pens as red pens. How many blue pens does the case contain?

A. 24   **B.** 36   **C.** 48   **D.** 52   **E.** 56

If we let the number of red pens be x, then the number of blue pens is $2x$. Setting up an equation,

$$x + 2x = 72$$
$$3x = 72$$
$$x = 24$$

The number of blue pens is then $2x = 2(24) = 48$. Answer $\boxed{(C)}$.

Modeling Questions

A lot of questions on the ACT deal with equations that model real-life situations. There's nothing special about these questions. It's all just algebra.

EXAMPLE 3: After touchdown, the speed of a plane on the runway is given by $70 - \frac{1}{8}t^2$ meters per second, where t is the number of seconds after touchdown.

Part 1: What is the plane's speed, in meters per second, 4 seconds after touchdown?

A. 32   **B.** 54   **C.** 60   **D.** 64   **E.** 68

Part 2: Which of the following is closest to the number of seconds it takes for the plane to come to a complete stop after touchdown?

A. 16   **B.** 18   **C.** 20   **D.** 24   **E.** 28

Part 1 Solution: Plugging in $t = 4$,

$$70 - \frac{1}{8}t^2 = 70 - \frac{1}{8}(4)^2 = 70 - \frac{1}{8}(16) = 70 - 2 = 68$$

Answer $\boxed{(E)}$.

Part 2 Solution: The plane comes to a complete stop when its speed is 0. Setting up an equation to solve for t,

$$70 - \frac{1}{8}t^2 = 0$$
$$-\frac{1}{8}t^2 = -70$$
$$t^2 = 560$$
$$t = \sqrt{560} \approx 24$$

Answer $\boxed{(D)}$.

Linear Programming

Whenever you see a question asking for the maximum or minimum given a set of constraints (inequalities), **you only need to check the vertices of the shaded region**. The maximum or minimum always occurs at one of the vertices.

EXAMPLE 4: The solution set for a system of 3 linear inequalities is graphed in the standard (x, y) coordinate plane below. For values of x and y in this solution set, what is the maximum value of $5x + 4y$?

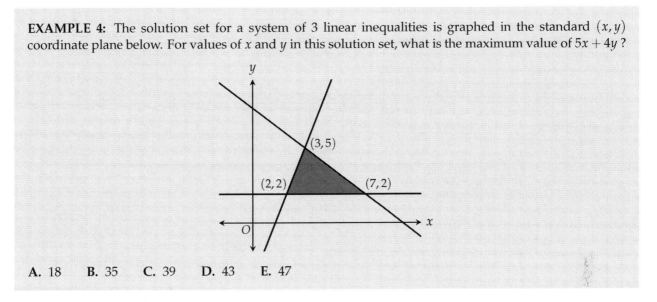

A. 18   **B.** 35   **C.** 39   **D.** 43   **E.** 47

To find the maximum, we only need to check the vertices of the shaded region: $(2, 2), (3, 5)$, and $(7, 2)$. Vertex $(2, 2)$ gives a value of $5(2) + 4(2) = 18$. Vertex $(3, 5)$ gives a value of $5(3) + 4(5) = 35$. Vertex $(7, 2)$ gives a value of $5(7) + 4(2) = 43$. Comparing these values, we can see that the maximum is 43. Answer $\boxed{(D)}$.

CHAPTER EXERCISE: Answers for this chapter start on page 263.

1. One number is 8 more than another. When the 2 numbers are added, their sum is 30. What is the larger number?

   A.   8
   B.   11
   C.   16
   D.   19
   E.   22

2. A city charges a fine of $50 for a driver's first parking violation and a fine of $80 for each parking violation thereafter. Which of the following equations represents the total amount in fines, d dollars, a driver must pay for n parking violations?

   A. $d = 30 + 50n$
   B. $d = -80 + 130n$
   C. $d = 130 - 80n$
   D. $d = 50 + 80n$
   E. $d = -30 + 80n$

3. Sportsmen's Tennis Club charges a court fee of $20.00 plus a fee of $8.00 per hour of court time. Midtown Tennis Club does not charge a court fee, only a fee of $12.00 per hour of court time. For which of the following number of hours of court time is the total fee equal for both clubs?

   A.   4
   B.   5
   C.   6
   D.   7
   E.   8

4. The time t, in minutes, a customer spends in a store can be modeled by the equation $t = 2n^{\frac{2}{3}} + 3$, where n is the number of items the customer purchases. According to this model, a customer who spends 21 minutes in the store purchases how many items?

   A.   4
   B.   6
   C.   9
   D.   27
   E.   64

5. In manufacturing, the maximum operating temperature refers to the highest temperature at which a device is able to operate effectively. An industrial grade device has a maximum operating temperature in degrees Celsius of 85°. Given that the equation $F = \frac{9}{5}C + 32$ gives the relationship between C and F, where F is the temperature in degrees Fahrenheit and C is the temperature in degrees Celsius, what is the maximum operating temperature of an industrial grade device in degrees Fahrenheit?

   A.   165°
   B.   170°
   C.   175°
   D.   180°
   E.   185°

6. Numbers a, b, and c are positive integers such that a is 3 less than b and c is 6 more than a. If $ac = 135$, then $b = ?$

   A.   8
   B.   10
   C.   12
   D.   15
   E.   18

7. The shelves of a bookcase hold a total of 126 books. The number of books on each shelf is 5 more than the number of shelves. How many shelves does the bookcase have?

   A.   4
   B.   8
   C.   9
   D.   13
   E.   14

8. The total resistance R_T of a parallel circuit with two resistors is given by the formula $\frac{1}{R_T} = \frac{1}{R_1} + \frac{1}{R_2}$, where R_1 and R_2 are the resistances of the first and second resistors, respectively. If the total resistance of the parallel circuit is 5 ohms, and $R_1 = 6$ ohms, what is the resistance, in ohms, of the second resistor?

   A. 11
   B. 18
   C. 20
   D. 24
   E. 30

9. The height of a falling object can be modeled by $h = 50 - 6t - 2t^2$, where h is the height, in feet, and t is the time, in seconds. Using this model, how many seconds will it take the object to fall to a height of 14 feet?

   A. 1
   B. 2
   C. 3
   D. 6
   E. 9

10. Jason has $546 in his bank account. Each day after the first day, he will withdraw $20 more than what he withdrew the previous day. How many dollars must Jason withdraw on the first day so that his bank account is empty by the end of the 7th day?

   A. $18
   B. $21
   C. $24
   D. $38
   E. $41

11. A farm uses a limited amount of land to produce potatoes and tomatoes. The coordinate plane below shows the constraints on the farm's weekly production. The shaded region represents the possible combinations of the number of potatoes and the number of tomatoes produced in 1 week. Each vertex of the shaded region has integer coordinates (thousands). The farm makes a profit of $0.10 per potato sold and $0.20 per tomato sold. Under the given constraints, what is the maximum possible profit, in dollars, the farm can make from 1 week of production?

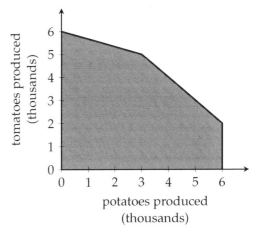

   A. $600
   B. $1,000
   C. $1,100
   D. $1,200
   E. $1,300

27

Miscellaneous Topics I

Sequences

Every **arithmetic sequence** has a **common difference**. Each term is found by adding the common difference to the previous term. For example, the arithmetic sequence below has a first term of -1 and a common difference of 2.

$$-1, 1, 3, 5, 7, \ldots$$

The nth term of an arithmetic sequence is $a_1 + (n-1)d$, where a_1 is the first term and d is the common difference.

For instance, the 10th term of the sequence above is $-1 + (10-1)(2) = 17$.

The sum of the first n terms of an arithmetic sequence is $\frac{n}{2}(a_1 + a_n)$.

The sum of the first 10 terms of the sequence above is $\frac{10}{2}(-1 + 17) = 80$.

> **EXAMPLE 1:** The third term of an arithmetic sequence is 10. The common difference of the sequence is 3. What is the sum of the first 18 terms of the sequence?
>
>   **A.** 504   **B.** 531   **C.** 558   **D.** 585   **E.** 612

Since the 3rd term is 10, the 2nd term must be $10 - 3 = 7$ and the 1st term must be $7 - 3 = 4$. The 18th term is then $a_1 + (n-1)d = 4 + (18-1)(3) = 55$. Finally, the sum of the first 18 terms is $\frac{18}{2}(4 + 55) = 9(59) = 531$.

Answer $\boxed{(B)}$.

Every **geometric sequence** has a **common ratio**. Each term is found by multiplying the previous term by the common ratio. For example, the geometric sequence below has a first term of 3 and a common ratio of 2.

$$3, 6, 12, 24, 48, \ldots$$

The nth term of a geometric sequence is $a_1(r)^{n-1}$, where a_1 is the first term and r is the common ratio.

For instance, the 10th term of the sequence above is $3(2)^{10-1} = 3(2)^9 = 1,536$.

For the ACT, you don't need to know the formula for summing up the first n terms of a geometric sequence.

EXAMPLE 2: The first term of a geometric sequence is 3. The common ratio of the sequence is -2. Of the first 9 terms of the sequence, how many have a value greater than 20?

A. 2   B. 3   C. 4   D. 5   E. 6

List out the first 9 terms:
$$3, -6, 12, -24, 48, -96, 192, -384, 768, \ldots$$

3 of these terms have a value greater than 20. Answer $\boxed{(B)}$.

Venn Diagrams

Venn diagrams are a way of organizing and keeping track of different groups. For example, the venn diagram below classifies 40 people in terms of whether they speak English or Spanish: 20 people speak only English, 10 people speak only Spanish, 8 people speak both English and Spanish, and 2 people speak neither.

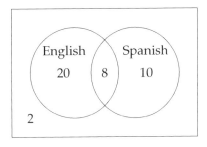

EXAMPLE 3: In a city neighborhood, 80 residents own a car and 125 residents own a bicycle. If a total of 180 residents live in the neighborhood and all of them own at least a car or a bike, how many own both a car and a bike?

A. 25   B. 30   C. 35   D. 40   E. 45

If x is the number of residents who own both a car and a bike, then the number of residents who own only a car is $80 - x$ and the number of residents who own only a bike is $125 - x$, giving the following venn diagram:

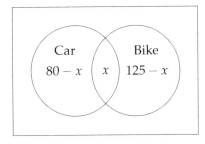

Since the total number of residents is 180,

$$(80 - x) + x + (125 - x) = 180$$
$$205 - x = 180$$
$$-x = -25$$
$$x = 25$$

Answer $\boxed{(A)}$.

EXAMPLE 4: In a survey of pet owners, some responded that they own only one type of pet and others responded that they own more than 1 type. The table below gives information about the owners who responded to the survey and the types of pets they own. According to the table, how many pet owners own dogs only?

Number of pet owners	Pet(s) owned
29	at least a dog
21	at least a cat
25	at least a bird
8	both dogs and birds but not cats
3	both cats and birds but not dogs
12	birds only
7	cats only

A. 5   B. 6   C. 10   D. 19   E. 21

Create a 3-circle venn diagram and fill it in with the numbers given.

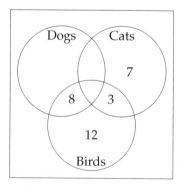

Since 35 own at least a bird, the number of people who own all three types is $25 - 8 - 3 - 12 = 2$. Since 21 own at least a cat, the number of people who own both dogs and cats but not birds is $21 - 3 - 7 - 2 = 9$. Finally, the number of people who own only dogs is $29 - 8 - 2 - 9 = 10$. Answer $\boxed{(C)}$.

Brute Force/Trial and Error

Not all questions can be solved with "pure" arithmetic and algebra. Sometimes, you have no choice but to get your hands dirty with a "non-mathematical" approach, whether it be listing things out or guessing and checking.

EXAMPLE 5: If Isabelle writes down every integer from 1 to 100, inclusive, how many times will she write the digit "4"?

A. 18   **B.** 19   **C.** 20   **D.** 21   **E.** 22

List out the numbers with a units digit of 4 and all the numbers in the 40's:

$$4, 14, 24, 34, 40, 41, 42, 43, 44, 45, 46, 47, 48, 49, 54, 64, 74, 84, 94$$

There are 19 numbers, but because 44 contains two 4's, Isabelle will write the digit "4" 20 times. Answer $\boxed{(C)}$.

EXAMPLE 6: A can of tennis balls contains at most 3 balls. If 12 cans contain a total of 28 tennis balls, what is the maximum number of these 12 cans that can contain exactly two tennis balls?

A. 6   **B.** 7   **C.** 8   **D.** 9   **E.** 10

This question requires some guessing and checking. Let's see if we can have 10 cans that each contain exactly two tennis balls. The 10 cans would account for $10 \times 2 = 20$ tennis balls and the 2 remaining cans would have to contain the $28 - 20 = 8$ remaining balls. Since each can contains at most 3 tennis balls, this is impossible.

How about 9 cans? The 9 cans would account for $9 \times 2 = 18$ tennis balls and the remaining 3 cans would have to contain the remaining $28 - 18 = 10$ tennis balls. This is still impossible since 3 cans would only be able to hold 9 tennis balls.

How about 8 cans? The 8 cans would account for $8 \times 2 = 16$ tennis balls and the remaining 4 cans would have to contain the remaining $28 - 16 = 12$ tennis balls. This is possible if each of the 4 cans contains 3 tennis balls. Answer $\boxed{(C)}$.

CHAPTER EXERCISE: Answers for this chapter start on page 266.

1. In a class of 31 students, 14 are on the math team, 19 are on the science team, and 6 are on both. How many students are on neither team?

   A. 1
   B. 2
   C. 3
   D. 4
   E. 5

2. The first 3 terms of an arithmetic sequence are $1\frac{1}{2}$, $2\frac{5}{8}$, and $3\frac{3}{4}$. What is the next term in the sequence?

   A. $4\frac{3}{8}$
   B. $4\frac{1}{2}$
   C. $4\frac{5}{8}$
   D. $4\frac{7}{8}$
   E. 5

3. When x is divided by 6, the remainder is 3. When x is divided by 7, the remainder is 4. What is the smallest possible value of x ?

   A. 33
   B. 39
   C. 45
   D. 51
   E. 57

4. At a gift shop, small candles sell for $2.00 each and large candles sell for $3.25 each. Freddie wants to buy at least 1 candle of each size and he must spend exactly $53.00. What is the maximum number of large candles Freddie can buy?

   A. 8
   B. 10
   C. 12
   D. 14
   E. 16

5. What is the 6th term of the geometric sequence below?

   $$-\frac{2}{3}, \frac{1}{3}, -\frac{1}{6}, \frac{1}{12}, \cdots$$

   A. $-\frac{1}{15}$
   B. $-\frac{1}{24}$
   C. $\frac{1}{18}$
   D. $\frac{1}{36}$
   E. $\frac{1}{48}$

6. If x is a real number such that $x^2 < -x$, which of the following statements must be true?

   A. $0 < x < 1$
   B. $x > 1$
   C. $-1 < x < 0$
   D. $x < -1$
   E. $x = -1$ or $x = 1$

7. The second term of an arithmetic sequence is -8, and the fourth term is 6. What is the first term?

   A. -22
   B. -15
   C. -7
   D. -1
   E. 7

8. How many terms in the arithmetic sequence below have a value less than 31?

   $$-5, -3, -1, 1, \ldots$$

   A. 15
   B. 16
   C. 17
   D. 18
   E. 19

9. The tourism department of a city created the Venn diagram below to show the transportation options used by 120 tourists. There are only 3 transportation options in the city: taxi, train, and bus. Of the 120 tourists, how many used at least 2 of these transportation options?

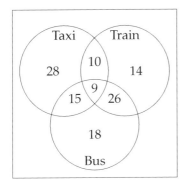

A. 9
B. 34
C. 45
D. 51
E. 60

10. In the arithmetic sequence below, how many terms are there between -15 and -43, exclusive of -15 and -43?

$$-3, -7, -11, -15, \ldots, -43$$

A. 5
B. 6
C. 7
D. 8
E. 25

11. The diagonals of a square, a pentagon, and a hexagon are drawn in the figure below. How many diagonals does a decagon have? (Note: A decagon has 10 sides.)

square   pentagon   hexagon

A. 27
B. 35
C. 37
D. 45
E. 90

12. During a trivia night, a group of 90 people was split up into 16 teams. Each of the 16 teams contained at least 1 person but no more than 7 people. At most how many teams contained exactly 4 people?

A. 6
B. 7
C. 8
D. 9
E. 10

13. In a certain geometric sequence, each term after the first is found by multiplying the previous term by a fixed positive integer. The sum of the first 2 terms of the sequence is 60. Which of the following values CANNOT be the first term of the geometric sequence?

A. 5
B. 6
C. 8
D. 12
E. 15

14. Every year, Savin High School gives out three types of student awards: leadership, community service, and academic excellence. Each awarded student can be given 1 type, 2 types, or all 3 types of these awards. The school gives out 20 leadership awards, 90 community service awards, and 60 academic excellence awards every year. For a year, what is the minimum number of students who can be given a community service award only?

A. 10
B. 30
C. 40
D. 50
E. 70

28

Miscellaneous Topics II

Matrices

A $m \times n$ matrix is a collection of mn elements arranged in m rows and n columns. For example, the following is a 2×3 matrix:

$$\begin{bmatrix} 1 & 2 & 3 \\ 4 & 5 & 6 \end{bmatrix}$$

Matrix addition/subtraction is only possible when the matrices have the same number of rows and columns. In other words, their *dimensions* must be the same. To add matrices, just sum their respective elements.

$$\begin{bmatrix} 2 & 3 \\ 4 & 5 \end{bmatrix} + \begin{bmatrix} 1 & -2 \\ -3 & 8 \end{bmatrix} = \begin{bmatrix} 2+1 & 3-2 \\ 4-3 & 5+8 \end{bmatrix} = \begin{bmatrix} 3 & 1 \\ 1 & 13 \end{bmatrix}$$

To subtract matrices, subtract their respective elements.

$$\begin{bmatrix} 2 & 3 \\ 4 & 5 \end{bmatrix} - \begin{bmatrix} 1 & -2 \\ -3 & 8 \end{bmatrix} = \begin{bmatrix} 2-1 & 3+2 \\ 4+3 & 5-8 \end{bmatrix} = \begin{bmatrix} 1 & 5 \\ 7 & -3 \end{bmatrix}$$

When multiplying matrices, you cannot just multiply their respective elements. It doesn't work that way. For multiplication to work, the dimensions have to line up in a certain way. Let's say we want to multiply a 2×3 matrix by a 3×4 matrix. Is this possible? Yes, because the number of columns of the first matrix is equal to the number of rows of the second matrix:

$$2 \times \boxed{3} \quad \boxed{3} \times 4$$

The result would be a 2×4 matrix (the number of rows of the first matrix and the number of columns of the second matrix):

$$\boxed{2} \times 3 \quad 3 \times \boxed{4}$$

See how this works? Would it be possible to multiply a 3×4 matrix by a 2×3 matrix? No, because the number of columns of the first matrix doesn't equal the number of rows of the second matrix. Order matters in matrix multiplication.

Don't worry about how to actually perform the multiplication. Matrix multiplication shows up so rarely that you're better off just learning how to do it on your calculator.

EXAMPLE 1: The matrix $A = \begin{bmatrix} 3 & 4 \\ 5 & 6 \end{bmatrix}$ and its *transpose*, A^t, is $\begin{bmatrix} 3 & 5 \\ 4 & 6 \end{bmatrix}$. What is $A + A^t$?

A. $\begin{bmatrix} 0 & 0 \\ 0 & 0 \end{bmatrix}$ B. $\begin{bmatrix} 3 & 4 \\ 5 & 6 \end{bmatrix}$ C. $\begin{bmatrix} 6 & 8 \\ 10 & 12 \end{bmatrix}$ D. $\begin{bmatrix} 6 & 9 \\ 9 & 12 \end{bmatrix}$ E. $\begin{bmatrix} 6 & 10 \\ 8 & 12 \end{bmatrix}$

$$\begin{bmatrix} 3 & 4 \\ 5 & 6 \end{bmatrix} + \begin{bmatrix} 3 & 5 \\ 4 & 6 \end{bmatrix} = \begin{bmatrix} 3+3 & 4+5 \\ 5+4 & 6+6 \end{bmatrix} = \begin{bmatrix} 6 & 9 \\ 9 & 12 \end{bmatrix}$$

Answer (D).

EXAMPLE 2: Matrices $X, Y,$ and Z are defined below.

$$X = \begin{bmatrix} 4 & 3 \\ -1 & 2 \end{bmatrix}, Y = \begin{bmatrix} 5 & 8 \\ 1 & 6 \end{bmatrix}, Z = \begin{bmatrix} 2 & 4 & 9 \\ 3 & 2 & 5 \end{bmatrix}$$

Which of the following matrix products is undefined?
A. XY B. XZ C. YX D. YZ E. ZX

Matrix X is a 2×2 matrix. Matrix Y is also a 2×2 matrix. Matrix Z is a 2×3 matrix. Remember that for matrix multiplication to be possible, the number of columns of the first matrix must be equal to the number of rows of the second matrix. Therefore,

- XY is defined: $2 \times \boxed{2}$ $\boxed{2} \times 2$
- XZ is defined: $2 \times \boxed{2}$ $\boxed{2} \times 3$
- YX is defined: $2 \times \boxed{2}$ $\boxed{2} \times 2$
- YZ is defined: $2 \times \boxed{2}$ $\boxed{2} \times 3$
- ZX is undefined: $2 \times \boxed{3}$ $\boxed{2} \times 2$

Answer (E).

Logic

Let's say we have the following statement:

If A, then B.

The only logically equivalent statement is the *contrapositive*, in which A and B are swapped and then negated:

If not B, then not A.

The following statements are NOT equivalent:

- If B, then A. (*converse*)
- If not A, then not B. (*inverse*)

In some cases, the converse and the inverse turn out to be true statements, but that does not mean they are logically equivalent to the original.

EXAMPLE 3: Isaac is shopping for clothes at a store and makes the following true statement: "If a shirt is on sale, then the shirt's size is large." Which of the following statements is logically equivalent to Isaac's statement?

A. "A shirt's size is large if and only if the shirt is on sale."
B. "If a shirt's size is large, then the shirt is on sale."
C. "If a shirt's size is large, then the shirt is NOT on sale."
D. "If a shirt is NOT on sale, then the shirt's size is NOT large."
E. "If a shirt's size is NOT large, then the shirt is NOT on sale."

The only logical equivalent is the contrapositive:

> If a shirt's size is NOT large, then the shirt is NOT on sale.

Answer (E).

Visualizations

Some visualization questions require you to construct and analyze a mental image while others require you to draw out different scenarios. Regardless, they typically aren't that hard as long as you take your time. The only way to improve on these questions is practice. Unfortunately, practice can be hard to come by because these questions don't show up very often. Hopefully, you'll have a good enough feel for them after doing the chapter exercise.

EXAMPLE 4: A right circular cone is intersected by a plane that is perpendicular to the base and does not intersect the center of the base, as shown below. Which of the following figures shows the shape of the intersection?

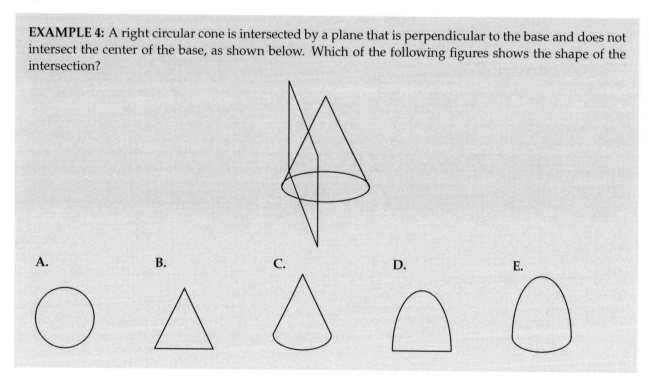

A.   B.   C.   D.   E.

Imagine taking a knife and vertically cutting off a piece of a cone. What would the shape of the cut look like? Well, the bottom of a cone is flat, so the shape's bottom would be straight. And unless we cut directly down from the tip of the cone, we wouldn't get a triangle. If the cut was made against a curved portion of the cone, then the resulting shape would be a "rounded triangle":

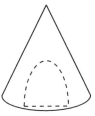

Answer (D) .

Ellipses

Ellipses are essentially ovals. The standard equation of an ellipse is

$$\frac{(x-h)^2}{a^2} + \frac{(y-k)^2}{b^2} = 1$$

where (h, k) is the center of the ellipse. If $a^2 > b^2$, then the ellipse is a "fat ellipse" (longer horizontally). Here's one way to remember this: a^2 is underneath the x in the equation, so if a^2 is larger, the ellipse is longer in the x-direction.

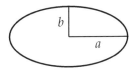

If $b^2 > a^2$, then the ellipse is "skinny" (longer vertically). We can use the same memorization strategy: b^2 is underneath the y in the equation, so if b^2 is larger, the ellipse is longer in the y-direction.

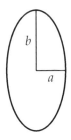

Note how a is like a "horizontal radius" and b is like a "vertical radius". The "long diameter" is always called the major axis. The "small diameter" is always called the minor axis.

EXAMPLE 5: Which of the following is an equation of the ellipse shown in the standard (x,y) coordinate plane below?

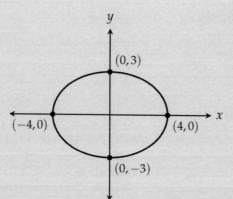

A. $\dfrac{x^2}{4}+\dfrac{y^2}{3}=0$ **B.** $\dfrac{x^2}{4}+\dfrac{y^2}{3}=1$ **C.** $\dfrac{x^2}{9}+\dfrac{y^2}{16}=1$ **D.** $\dfrac{x^2}{16}+\dfrac{y^2}{9}=0$ **E.** $\dfrac{x^2}{16}+\dfrac{y^2}{9}=1$

The ellipse has its center at $(0,0)$ and is longer horizontally. Therefore, the equation is of the form

$$\frac{x^2}{a^2}+\frac{y^2}{b^2}=1$$

where $a^2 > b^2$. Since the "horizontal radius" of the ellipse is 4 and the "vertical radius" is 3, $a=4$ and $b=3$. Plugging in these values, we get

$$\frac{x^2}{16}+\frac{y^2}{9}=1$$

Answer (E).

CHAPTER EXERCISE: Answers for this chapter start on page 269.

1. At The Southside Tennis Club, a player cannot become a member unless the player is invited by at least 3 members of the club. If Tony became a member of The Southside Tennis Club today, then which of the following statements *must* be FALSE?

   A. Exactly 3 members invited Tony to the tennis club.
   B. Every member invited Tony to the tennis club.
   C. Less than 3 members invited Tony to the tennis club.
   D. At most 3 members did not invite Tony to the tennis club.
   E. More than 3 members did not invite Tony to the tennis club.

2. Given the matrix equation shown below, what is the value of *a* ?

$$\begin{bmatrix} b \\ a \end{bmatrix} - \begin{bmatrix} 3 \\ b \end{bmatrix} = \begin{bmatrix} 5 \\ 2 \end{bmatrix}$$

   A. 0
   B. 4
   C. 6
   D. 8
   E. 10

3. The figure below shows a paper cut-out of a shape consisting of 6 squares, each labeled with a number. The paper cut-out is folded along the dotted lines to form a cube. In the resulting cube, what is the number of the face opposite the face numbered 2 ?

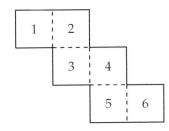

   A. 1
   B. 3
   C. 4
   D. 5
   E. 6

4. Right triangle *ABC*, shown below, is rotated 90° clockwise around *A* and then reflected over $\overline{AC}$. Which of the following shows the final orientation of *ABC* ?

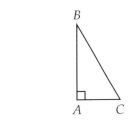

   A.

   B.

   C.

   D.

   E.
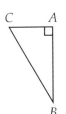

5. If $\det \begin{bmatrix} a & b \\ c & d \end{bmatrix} = ad - bc$, then $\det \begin{bmatrix} x & -w \\ z & 2y \end{bmatrix} =$?

   A. $-2xy - wz$
   B. $2xy - wz$
   C. $2xy + wz$
   D. $2yz - wz$
   E. $xz + 2wy$

6. The graph of f is shown in the standard (x, y) coordinate plane below. If a horizontal line, not shown, is graphed in the same plane, all of the following could be the number of points of intersection of the line and the graph of f EXCEPT:

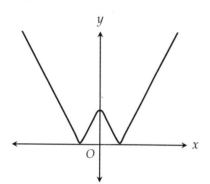

   A. 0
   B. 1
   C. 2
   D. 3
   E. 4

7. The *determinant* of a matrix $\begin{bmatrix} a & b \\ c & d \end{bmatrix}$ equals $ad - bc$. If the determinant of the matrix $\begin{bmatrix} y & y \\ 6 & y \end{bmatrix}$ is -9, what is the value of y ?

   A. -5
   B. -3
   C. $-\dfrac{3}{2}$
   D. 2
   E. 3

8. How many different circles in the same plane as the square below have at least one diameter whose endpoints are vertices of the square?

   A. 2
   B. 3
   C. 4
   D. 5
   E. 6

9. The graph of $\dfrac{x^2}{49} + \dfrac{y^2}{25} = 1$ has a y-intercept at which of the following points?

   A. $(0, 5)$
   B. $(0, 7)$
   C. $(0, 10)$
   D. $(0, 25)$
   E. $(0, 49)$

10. In the standard (x, y) coordinate plane, the line segment with endpoints $(-1, 8)$ and $(2, 5)$ can be represented by the matrix $\begin{bmatrix} -1 & 2 \\ 8 & 5 \end{bmatrix}$. The matrix $\begin{bmatrix} 3 & c \\ 3 & 0 \end{bmatrix}$ represents a certain translation of the line segment. What is the value of c ?

    A. -3
    B. 4
    C. 5
    D. 6
    E. 9

11. Jay makes the statement, "If you are learning algebra in school, then you have passed the 7th grade." Which of the following statements is logically equivalent to Jay's statement?

    A. You are learning algebra in school, and you have passed the 7th grade.
    B. If you have passed the 7th grade, then you are learning algebra in school.
    C. If you are not learning algebra in school, then you have not passed the 7th grade.
    D. If you have not passed the 7th grade, then you are not learning algebra in school.
    E. If you are not learning algebra in school, then you have passed the 7th grade.

12. In the figure below, 6 points are spaced 1 unit apart around a 2×1 rectangle (not shown). How many triangles can be formed by using 3 of the 6 points as vertices?

    • • •

    • • •

    A. 8
    B. 12
    C. 14
    D. 16
    E. 18

13. If $A = \begin{bmatrix} 1 & 2 \\ 3 & 4 \end{bmatrix}$ and the matrix product AB is a 2×3 matrix, which of the following could be matrix B ?

    A. $\begin{bmatrix} 2 \\ 5 \\ -1 \end{bmatrix}$

    B. $\begin{bmatrix} 3 & 6 \\ -1 & 4 \end{bmatrix}$

    C. $\begin{bmatrix} 5 & 2 & 1 \\ 9 & -2 & 3 \end{bmatrix}$

    D. $\begin{bmatrix} 5 & 0 \\ 4 & -2 \\ 6 & -3 \end{bmatrix}$

    E. $\begin{bmatrix} -1 & 2 & 1 \\ 3 & -5 & 4 \\ 1 & -2 & 7 \end{bmatrix}$

14. One of the following equations is that of the ellipse shown in the standard (x, y) coordinate plane below. Which one? (Note: The coordinate units on the x-axis are the same length as the coordinate units on the y-axis.)

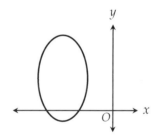

    A. $x^2 + y^2 = 16$

    B. $\dfrac{(x+4)^2}{16} + \dfrac{(y-3)^2}{4} = 1$

    C. $\dfrac{(x+4)^2}{4} + \dfrac{(y-3)^2}{16} = 1$

    D. $\dfrac{(x-4)^2}{16} + \dfrac{(y+3)^2}{4} = 1$

    E. $\dfrac{(x-4)^2}{4} + \dfrac{(y+3)^2}{16} = 1$

205

29
Answers to the Exercises

Chapter 1: Absolute Value

1. $\boxed{B}$ $|3-6| - |8-2| = |-3| - |6| = 3 - 6 = -3$.

2. $\boxed{B}$ $|-4(6) - (4)(-3)| = |-24 + 12| = |-12| = 12$.

3. $\boxed{A}$ This problem is best solved by trying out different numbers. If $x = 3$, for example, then $-|x| = -3$, which doesn't work. If $x = -3$, then $-|x| = -|-3| = -3$, which does work. The only answer choice that includes negative numbers is $x \leq 0$.

4. $\boxed{C}$ There are two cases. When $x - 7 = 18$, $x = 25$. When $x - 7 = -18$, $x = -11$.

5. $\boxed{D}$ We test each answer choice. Only answer choice D works: $|x||y| = |3||-2| = 3 \cdot 2 = 6$, which is equal to $-xy = -(3)(-2) = 6$.

6. $\boxed{E}$ Let's try out different numbers. If $x = 3$, then $|-x| + |x| = 6$. The only answer choices that give 6 when $x = 3$ are D and E. Let's try a negative number. If $x = -3$, then $|-x| + |x| = 6$. Between D and E, only E gives 6 when $x = -3$.

7. $\boxed{E}$ Since $b \geq 0$, $|-4b|^2 - |-b|^3 = (4b)^2 - (b)^3 = 16b^2 - b^3$. Another way is to make up a number for b and test each answer choice.

8. $\boxed{A}$ We try out different numbers. If $x = 3$, then $|-2x| - 2|x| = |-6| - 2(3) = 6 - 6 = 0$. The only answer choice that gives 0 when $x = 3$ is A. As it turns out, the expression is always equal to 0.

9. $\boxed{E}$ What are the numbers that are 3 units from -7? We have $-7 + 3 = -4$ and $-7 - 3 = -10$. Of the answer choices, only E gives an equation for which $x = -4$ and $x = -10$ are both solutions.

206

Chapter 2: Exponents & Radicals

1. **E** Multiply the coefficients and add the exponents: $-5a^2b^3 \cdot -3a^2b = 15a^4b^4$

2. **E** Multiply the coefficients and add the exponents: $(2ab^3)(3a^7b^2) = 6a^8b^5$

3. **A** $(x^4)^{-3} = \dfrac{1}{(x^4)^3} = \dfrac{1}{x^{12}}$

4. **C** For the decimal to come right after the leading "2," the decimal needs to move 7 digits to the left. Therefore, the answer is either 2.6×10^7 or 2.7×10^7. Between the two, 2.7×10^7 is the closer estimate.

5. **E** The result will be positive because the outer exponent is even. Note that it isn't because the inner exponent (the "6") is even. Once we know the sign of the result, we can multiply the exponents: $(-b^6)^{32} = b^{192}$

6. **A** Add the exponents: $x^4 \cdot x^4 \cdot x^4 \cdot x^4 = x^{16}$

7. **B** The most we can pull out from both terms is $6x^2y^2$: $6x^2y^2(x+y)$

8. **A** Trial and error should give $b = -2$ as the only answer: $\left(-\dfrac{1}{2}\right)^{-2} = 4$

9. **E** To find a relationship between m and n, we must get the bases to be the same. That way, we can equate the exponents. Fortunately, $\sqrt{2}$ is $2^{\frac{1}{2}}$ and 8 is 2^3.

$$(\sqrt{2})^m = 8^n$$
$$(2^{\frac{1}{2}})^m = (2^3)^n$$
$$2^{\frac{1}{2}m} = 2^{3n}$$
$$\frac{1}{2}m = 3n$$
$$m = 6n$$
$$\frac{m}{n} = 6$$

10. **B** $\sqrt{75} - \sqrt{12} = \sqrt{5 \cdot 5 \cdot 3} - \sqrt{2 \cdot 2 \cdot 3} = 5\sqrt{3} - 2\sqrt{3} = 3\sqrt{3}$

11. **A** Subtract the exponents: $\dfrac{a^6b^4c}{4a^3b^7c^3} = \dfrac{a^3b^{-3}c^{-2}}{4} = \dfrac{a^3}{4b^3c^2}$

12. **D** Factor out $\dfrac{1}{7^{30}}$ from both terms: $\dfrac{1}{7^{30}} - \dfrac{1}{7^{31}} = \dfrac{1}{7^{30}}\left(1 - \dfrac{1}{7}\right) = \dfrac{1}{7^{30}}\left(\dfrac{6}{7}\right) = \dfrac{6}{7^{31}}$

Chapter 3: Manipulating and Solving Equations

1. $\boxed{B}$ Since b^2 is never less than 0, the value of a is at its largest when $b^2 = 0$. When $b^2 = 0$, $b = 0$ and $a = \pm 8$. Since we want the largest value, $a = 8$.

2. $\boxed{E}$ The left side simplifies to $\dfrac{(x-1)(10-6)}{3(5)} = \dfrac{(x-1)(4)}{15} = \dfrac{4x-4}{15}$

$$\frac{4x-4}{15} = 2$$
$$4x - 4 = 30$$
$$4x = 34$$
$$x = \frac{34}{4} = \frac{17}{2} = 8\frac{1}{2}$$

3. $\boxed{D}$ Move c to the left and ax to the right. Then divide both sides by a.

$$b - ax = c$$
$$b - c = ax$$
$$\frac{b-c}{a} = x$$

4. $\boxed{B}$ The smallest possible positive values of x and y are 8 and 1, respectively. The value of xy is then $8 \cdot 1 = 8$.

5. $\boxed{A}$

$$7 + (x - 7) = 7 - (7 + y)$$
$$x = -y$$
$$\frac{x}{y} = -1$$

6. $\boxed{B}$

$$5.7x + 8.85 = 1.02 - 3.3x$$
$$9x + 8.85 = 1.02$$
$$9x = -7.83$$
$$x = -0.87$$

7. $\boxed{E}$ Cross multiply.

$$\frac{3-a}{4-a} = \frac{3}{5}$$
$$5(3-a) = 3(4-a)$$
$$15 - 5a = 12 - 3a$$
$$-2a = -3$$
$$a = \frac{3}{2}$$

8. $\boxed{D}$ Multiply the two equations. Notice that the b's cancel out.

$$\frac{a}{b} \times \frac{b}{c} = \frac{3}{4} \times \frac{8}{9}$$
$$\frac{a}{c} = \frac{24}{36} = \frac{2}{3}$$
$$\frac{c}{a} = \frac{3}{2}$$

9. $\boxed{D}$ We have to do some trial and error. When $y = 1$, $x = 48$. When $y = 2$, $x = 12$. When $y = 3$, there is no integer value of x that works. When $y = 4$, $x = 3$. When $y = 5$ or $y = 6$, there are no integer values of x that work. It's obvious at this point that we can stop, especially since $y = 7$ gives $y^2 = 49$, which is greater than the 48 on the right side. The possible values of x are $48, 12$, and 3.

10. $\boxed{A}$ Dividing the first equation by 2, $2.5x = y$. Multiplying the second equation by 6, $y = 4z$. From these two equations, we can see that y is clearly the largest. Between x and z, x is larger because it only takes 2.5 x's to get y, whereas it takes 4 z's to get y. Putting it all together, $z < x < y$. Keep in mind that all numbers are positive (the answer might be different if they were negative).

11. $\boxed{E}$ Cross multiply.

$$\frac{x+2y}{3x-y} = \frac{4}{3}$$
$$3(x+2y) = 4(3x-y)$$
$$3x + 6y = 12x - 4y$$
$$-9x = -10y$$
$$\frac{x}{y} = \frac{10}{9}$$

Chapter 4: Expressions

1. $\boxed{B}$ $x(3-x) - 4(x+2) = 3x - x^2 - 4x - 8 = -x^2 - x - 8$

2. $\boxed{C}$ The first term, the one with the highest power, is always the product of the highest power terms from each group. In this case, there are 5 groups and the highest power term in each is x. Their product is x^5. The last term is the constant term, which can be found by multiplying the constants in each group: $-1 \cdot 2 \cdot -3 \cdot 4 \cdot -5 = -120$.

3. $\boxed{E}$ $(4x^2 - 3x + 7) - (-2x^2 + 5x - 3) = 4x^2 - 3x + 7 + 2x^2 - 5x + 3 = 6x^2 - 8x + 10$

4. $\boxed{D}$ $\dfrac{2x^2 - 3x - 2}{x - 2} = \dfrac{(2x+1)(x-2)}{x-2} = 2x + 1$

5. $\boxed{A}$ If the total cost was d dollars, $d - 250$ dollars were spent on making hot dogs. Since the cost of each hot dog is \$1.25, the stand sold $(d - 250) \div 1.25$ hot dogs, which is equal to $\dfrac{d}{1.25} - \dfrac{250}{1.25} = 0.8d - 200$

6. $\boxed{D}$ Jane paid $R - D$ dollars, which represents $\dfrac{R-D}{R}$ of the retail price.

7. $\boxed{C}$ First, solve for N: $N = y - 4$. Now,
$$M - N = (3 - x) - (y - 4) = 3 - x - y + 4 = -x - y + 7$$

8. $\boxed{A}$ We can factor the negative out of the second term and distribute it to the first term.
$$(3x - 1)(-x - 4) = -(3x - 1)(x + 4) = (-3x + 1)(x + 4)$$
Remember that the negative can only be distributed to one term, not both.

9. $\boxed{D}$ $\dfrac{4x^2 + 4x - 8}{2x + 4} = \dfrac{4(x^2 + x - 2)}{2(x + 2)} = \dfrac{4(x + 2)(x - 1)}{2(x + 2)} = 2(x - 1)$

10. $\boxed{A}$ The number of regular tickets sold must have been $n - p$ for a total of $30(n - p)$ dollars. Premium tickets amounted to $80p$ dollars. Adding everything up, we get total sales of $30(n - p) + 80p = 30n - 30p + 80p = 30n + 50p$ dollars.

Chapter 5: Numbers and Operations

1. $\boxed{A}$ $\dfrac{16 - 2 \cdot 3}{1 + 4 \cdot \frac{1}{6}} = \dfrac{16 - 6}{1 + \frac{2}{3}} = \dfrac{10}{\frac{5}{3}} = 10 \times \dfrac{3}{5} = 6$

2. $\boxed{B}$ $22 - \dfrac{2}{3} - 1\dfrac{1}{6} = 22 - \dfrac{4}{6} - 1\dfrac{1}{6} = 22 - 1\dfrac{5}{6} = 21 - \dfrac{5}{6} = 20\dfrac{1}{6}$

3. $\boxed{D}$ Buying 4 watermelons separately would cost $4 \times 4.29 = \$17.16$. Buying them 4 at a time saves $17.16 - 14.80 = \$2.36$. That's a savings of $2.36 \div 4 = \$0.59$ on each watermelon.

4. $\boxed{E}$ $\dfrac{1}{1 + \dfrac{1}{1 + \frac{1}{3}}} = \dfrac{1}{1 + \dfrac{1}{\frac{4}{3}}} = \dfrac{1}{1 + \frac{3}{4}} = \dfrac{1}{\frac{7}{4}} = \dfrac{4}{7}$

5. $\boxed{D}$ On the first trip, he spent $50 - 12 = \$38$. On the second trip, he spent $30 - 8 = \$22$. If he had $\$45$ after these purchases, he must have started with $45 + 38 + 22 = \$105$.

6. $\boxed{D}$ There are a total of six breaks—one break after each of the first six sections, no break after the seventh since it's the last section. Therefore, the students spend a total of $6 \times 2 = 12$ minutes on break.

7. $\boxed{B}$ The 3 large-size boxes will fit $800 \times 3 = 2,400$ lightbulbs, leaving $6,000 - 2,400 = 3,600$ lightbulbs for the small-size boxes. The minimum number of small-size boxes needed is $3,600 \div 350 \approx 10.29$, but because we can't have a fraction of a box, we need to round up to 11.

8. $\boxed{A}$ Job A will pay $45 \times 10 = \$450$ for the first 10 hours worked. To get the next $1,350 - 450 = \$900$ to meet his goal, Mark will need to work $900 \div 60 = 15$ more hours. That's a total of $10 + 15 = 25$ hours at Job A. At Job B, Mark will need to work for $1,350 \div 50 = 27$ hours. Therefore, Job A allows Mark to work $27 - 25 = 2$ fewer hours.

9. $\boxed{E}$ The number of cupcakes is $15 \times 8 + 30 \times 12 = 480$. The number of cookies recorded in inventory so far is $15 \times 8 + 5 \times 12 = 180$. That's a difference of $480 - 180 = 300$, which means there must be $300 \div 6 = 50$ six-item boxes of cookies.

10. $\boxed{A}$ There are a total of $25 \times 6 = 150$ cans of soda in the six-item boxes. That's enough to fill $150 \div 8 = 18.75$ eight-item boxes. Since we only want whole boxes, we round down to 18.

11. $\boxed{B}$ If Sierra bought $\dfrac{1}{5}$ of the candy bars, she must have bought $45 \div 5 = 9$ eight-item boxes. The price of each eight-item box was then $\$93.60 \div 9 = \$10.40$.

Chapter 6: Properties of Numbers

1. $\boxed{B}$ Try to get the original number for each answer choice. First, divide each of them by 4. Then divide the result by 6. The only answer choice that gives an integer result after these steps is 552.

2. $\boxed{A}$ 10^{-80} means move the decimal point to the left 80 times. The first move puts the decimal point to the left of the "4". All 79 subsequent moves require zeros as placeholders. Therefore, the decimal representation is a decimal point, followed by 79 zeros, then the digits 4 and 6.

3. $\boxed{B}$ The denominators are 24, 9, and 4. Now how do we get the least common multiple (LCM) of these denominators? Well, the LCM of 9 and 4 is 36. The LCM of 36 and 24 is 72. Therefore, 72 is the LCM of all three numbers.

4. $\boxed{D}$ The easiest way to handle this question is to make up some numbers. Try to keep them as simple as possible. If we let $x = 10$ and $y = 15$, then $z = 150$. Of the answer choices, only 20 is not a factor of z.

5. $\boxed{E}$ Convert the fractions into decimals: $\frac{5}{9} \approx 0.5555$, $\frac{4}{7} \approx 0.5714$, $\frac{6}{11} \approx 0.5454$. Now it's easy to see that $\frac{6}{11} < \frac{5}{9} < \frac{4}{7}$.

6. $\boxed{C}$ The 3 alarm bells ring at the same time whenever the number of elapsed minutes is a multiple of 6, 8, and 10. The lowest common multiple of 6, 8, and 10 is 120.

7. $\boxed{C}$ For each number, list out a few more digits so that they're easier to compare:

$$0.\overline{423} = 0.423\underline{4}23\ldots$$

$$0.4\overline{23} = 0.4232\underline{3}\ldots$$

$$0.42\overline{3} = 0.4233\underline{3}\ldots$$

Comparing the respective ten-thousandths digits (underlined), we can see that $0.4\overline{23} < 0.42\overline{3} < 0.\overline{423}$.

8. $\boxed{D}$ The maximum value of $\frac{a}{b}$ is reached when a is at its largest and b is at its smallest. Therefore, we let $a = 18$ and $b = 3$, giving a maximum of $\frac{18}{3} = 6$.

9. $\boxed{C}$ 21.6 microseconds $\times$ $\dfrac{1 \text{ second}}{1,000,000 \text{ microseconds}}$ $= 21.6 \times 10^{-6}$ seconds $= 2.16 \times 10^{-5}$ seconds

10. $\boxed{A}$ Try out different numbers for x. When $x = 2$, the result is not an integer, so answer B is out. When $x = 5$, the result is not an integer, so answer C is out. When $x = -3$, the result is an integer, so x does not have to be positive. Answer D is out. When $x = 3$, the result is an integer, so x does not have to be negative. Answer E is out. However, x *must* be odd.

11. $\boxed{E}$ The greatest value is reached when the largest number is the numerator (top) and the smallest number is the denominator (bottom). However, integer a should not be used because it's negative. Therefore, the expression with the greatest value is $\frac{d}{b}$.

12. $\boxed{D}$ The quickest way to do this question is guess and check, starting with the larger answer choices. The LCM of 28 and 32 is not 96 since 28 does not go into 96. The LCM of 24 and 32 is 96 since both numbers go into 96 and there isn't a smaller common multiple. Therefore, the answer is 24.

13. $\boxed{A}$ Let's say $n = 10$. Then $\dfrac{n}{500} = \dfrac{10}{500} = \dfrac{2}{100} = 0.02$. In this case, there are 2 digits to the right of the decimal point. Is there a way to get just 1 digit to the right of the decimal point? Yes. When $n = 100$, $\dfrac{n}{500} = \dfrac{100}{500} = \dfrac{2}{10} = 0.2$. Therefore, the minimum is 1. Why did I pick 100? Because to get the minimum number of digits in a decimal, the fraction needs to be able to reduce to a denominator of 10. Note that numbers like 200 and 300 also work.

14. $\boxed{A}$ Every number that's divisible by 2, 3, 4, and 5 must be divisible by 60 (the LCM of 2, 3, 4, and 5). So how many multiples of 60 are there below 600? Dividing 600 by 60, we get 10, but because 600 doesn't count (it's not below itself), the answer is 9.

15. $\boxed{B}$ A rational number is one that can be expressed as a fraction of integers. Even though $\dfrac{1}{0}$ is a fraction of integers, the result is undefined and therefore neither rational nor irrational. $\dfrac{1}{\sqrt{5}}$ is irrational (cannot be expressed as a fraction of integers). Lastly, $\dfrac{1}{-1}$ is clearly a fraction of integers and therefore rational. Even though it simplifies to -1, what matters is that it can be expressed as a fraction of integers.

Chapter 7: Complex Numbers

1. $\boxed{C}$ We quickly evaluate each answer choice. For A, the absolute value is $\sqrt{0^2 + (-2)^2} = 2$. For B, it's $\sqrt{0^2 + 3^2} = 3$. For C, it's $\sqrt{(-1)^2 + (1)^2} = \sqrt{2}$. For D, it's $\sqrt{(1)^2 + (2)^2} = \sqrt{5}$. For E, it's $\sqrt{2^2 + (-1)^2} = \sqrt{5}$. Of these, answer C has the smallest absolute value.

2. $\boxed{D}$ The product of two complex numbers is a real number only if the two complex numbers are conjugates. The conjugate of $3 - 5i$ is $3 + 5i$. We can multiply them to confirm that the product is a real number: $(3 - 5i)(3 + 5i) = 9 + 15i - 15i - 25i^2 = 9 - 25i^2 = 9 + 25 = 34$.

3. $\boxed{E}$

$$(5 + 4i)(\sqrt{2} - 9i) = 5\sqrt{2} - 45i + 4i\sqrt{2} - 36i^2 = (5\sqrt{2} - 36i^2) + (4\sqrt{2} - 45)i$$
$$= (5\sqrt{2} + 36) + (4\sqrt{2} - 45)i$$

4. $\boxed{A}$ $\sqrt{-27} - \sqrt{-12} = (\sqrt{27} \cdot \sqrt{-1}) - (\sqrt{12} \cdot \sqrt{-1}) = 3\sqrt{3} \cdot i - 2\sqrt{3} \cdot i = 3i\sqrt{3} - 2i\sqrt{3} = i\sqrt{3}$

5. $\boxed{C}$ First, take the square root of both sides. Then isolate x.

$$(x - 2)^2 = -16$$
$$x - 2 = \pm\sqrt{-16}$$
$$x = 2 \pm \sqrt{-16} = 2 \pm \sqrt{16} \cdot \sqrt{-1} = 2 \pm 4i$$

6. $\boxed{D}$ The equation is true when either $x^2 + 3 = 0$ or $x - 3 = 0$. When $x^2 + 3 = 0$, $x^2 = -3$ and $x = \pm i\sqrt{3}$ (two imaginary solutions). When $x - 3 = 0$, then $x = 3$ (a positive real solution). All in all, there are 2 imaginary solutions and 1 positive real solution.

7. $\boxed{C}$ A root at $\frac{1}{3}$ tells us that the polynomial has a factor of $(3x - 1)$. Roots at $-3i$ and $3i$ tell us that the polynomial has a factor of $(x^2 + 9)$. To confirm this, we can plug in $x = -3i$ and see that $(-3i)^2 + 9 = 9i^2 + 9 = 0$. The result is also 0 when $x = 3i$. Therefore, the polynomial must be $(3x - 1)(x^2 + 9)$.

8. $\boxed{E}$ The complex number $3 - 2i$ is represented simply by the point $(3, -2)$ in the complex plane, 3 along the real axis and -2 along the imaginary axis.

9. $\boxed{A}$ We can plug in one of the solutions back into the equation to solve for b. Let's plug in $2 + 5i$.

$$(x - 2)^2 = ((2 + 5i) - 2)^2 = (5i)^2 = 25i^2 = -25$$

Therefore, $b = -25$.

10. $\boxed{A}$ Multiply both the top and the bottom by the conjugate of the denominator, which is $3 + 2i$.

$$\frac{(1 + i)}{(3 - 2i)} \cdot \frac{(3 + 2i)}{(3 + 2i)} = \frac{3 + 2i + 3i + 2i^2}{9 + 6i - 6i - 4i^2} = \frac{3 + 2i^2 + 5i}{9 - 4i^2} = \frac{1 + 5i}{13} = \frac{1}{13} + \frac{5}{13}i$$

Chapter 8: Rates

1. $\boxed{C}$ The squirrel has gathered a total $20 \times 6 = 120$ acorns. To make that last 24 days, it should eat $120 \div 24 = 5$ acorns per day.

2. $\boxed{A}$ At Shop A, the cost would be 30 staplers $\times \dfrac{\$10}{6 \text{ staplers}} = \$50$. At Shop B, the cost would be 30 staplers $\times$ $\dfrac{\$8}{5 \text{ staplers}} = \$48$. The difference is $50 - 48 = 2$ dollars.

3. $\boxed{E}$ The vegetable should be fermented for $18 \times 5 = 90$ hours. That's $90 \div 24 = 3$ days with a remainder of 18 hours.

4. $\boxed{D}$ The apprentice can only make $\dfrac{1}{3} \times 15 = 5$ suits in a week. If they alternate weeks, they will make $15 + 5 = 20$ suits every two weeks.

$$180 \text{ suits } \times \frac{2 \text{ weeks}}{20 \text{ suits}} = 18 \text{ weeks}$$

5. $\boxed{C}$ The 5 hoses will be able to pump $5 \times 3 = 15$ gallons of water per minute.

$$18,000 \text{ gallons} \times \frac{1 \text{ minute}}{15 \text{ gallons}} \times \frac{1 \text{ hour}}{60 \text{ minutes}} = 20 \text{ hours}$$

6. $\boxed{C}$ The difference in cost between a 4-day stay and a 6-day stay is $570 - 400 = \$170$. For that amount, you get an extra 2 days. Therefore, the daily rate must be $170 \div 2 = \$85$. Since the cost for a 4-day stay is $400, the fixed upfront fee must be $400 - 4 \times 85 = \$60$. Now that we know the fixed upfront fee and the daily rate, we can calculate the charge for a 10-day stay to be $60 + 10 \times 85 = \$910$.

7. $\boxed{D}$ 12 seconds is $\dfrac{12}{60} = \dfrac{1}{5} = 0.2$ minutes.

$$\frac{2.4 \text{ miles}}{7.2 \text{ minutes}} \times \frac{60 \text{ minutes}}{1 \text{ hour}} = 20 \frac{\text{miles}}{\text{hour}}$$

8. $\boxed{E}$ $(3 + m)$ minutes $\times \dfrac{10 \text{ bottles}}{3 \text{ minutes}} = \dfrac{30 + 10m}{3}$ bottles $= 10 + \dfrac{10m}{3}$ bottles

9. $\boxed{C}$ The current 15 employees can bake $15 \times 30 = 450$ cookies per hour. An employee assigned to packaging can pack 5 cookies every 12 minutes, or 25 cookies every hour. Therefore, $450 \div 25 = 18$ employees should be hired for packaging.

10. $\boxed{C}$ In the two hours that Megan grades alone, she finishes $5 \times 2 = 10$ essays. The remaining $65 - 10 = 55$ essays are graded during the time Megan and Kristie work together. They can finish $5 + 6 = 11$ essays per hour, so Kristie only needs to grade for $55 \div 11 = 5$ hours. By the time they finish, Kristie will have graded $5 \times 6 = 30$ essays.

Chapter 9: Ratio & Proportion

1. $\boxed{C}$ $\dfrac{36}{54} = \dfrac{4}{6} = \dfrac{2}{3} = 2{:}3$

2. $\boxed{A}$ Burgers per hour is just the number of burgers divided by the number of hours: $\dfrac{b}{t}$.

3. $\boxed{C}$ Since x and y are inversely proportional, they multiply to a constant k.

$$xy = k$$

Plugging in values to solve for k,

$$k = (4)(6) = 24$$

When $x = 8$,

$$xy = 24$$
$$(8)y = 24$$
$$y = 3$$

4. $\boxed{D}$ Let b be the total number of boys and g be the total number of girls at this school.

$$\frac{3}{7}b = \frac{6}{7}g$$
$$3b = 6g$$
$$b = 2g$$

There are twice as many boys as girls.

5. $\boxed{E}$ The room in the blueprint is 10 inches wide while the actual room is 25 feet wide, so 1 inch in the blueprint represents 2.5 feet in reality. Since the length of the room in the blueprint is 8 inches long, the length in reality is $8 \times 2.5 = 20$ feet. The perimeter is then $25 + 25 + 20 + 20 = 90$ feet.

6. $\boxed{B}$ $700 \text{ megabytes} \times \dfrac{50 \text{ seconds}}{280 \text{ megabytes}} = 125 \text{ seconds}$

7. $\boxed{A}$ If we let the length of AB be $4x$, then the lengths of BC, CD, and AD are $5x$, $4x$, and $5x$, respectively. Since the perimeter is 108,

$$4x + 5x + 4x + 5x = 108$$
$$18x = 108$$
$$x = 6$$

So, $AB = 4(6) = 24$ and $BC = 5(6) = 30$. The area is then $AB \times BC = 24 \times 30 = 720$.

8. $\boxed{C}$ The ratio of blue beads to red beads in a large necklace is $24{:}36 = 2{:}3$. Out of every 5 beads, 3 of them are red. Since the same is true of the small necklace, there must be $\dfrac{3}{5} \times 20 = 12$ red beads in the small necklace.

9. $\boxed{C}$ We can think of the ratio of water to calcium phosphate in the original recipe as a conversion factor.

$$5\frac{1}{4}\ \text{mL of water} \times \frac{1\frac{3}{4}\ \text{mL of calcium phosphate}}{3\frac{1}{2}\ \text{mL of water}} = 5.25 \times \frac{1.75}{3.5} = 2.625 = 2\frac{5}{8}$$

We can also setup an equation of proportions and solve it to get the same answer.

$$\frac{x}{5.25} = \frac{1.75}{3.5}$$

$$x = \frac{1.75}{3.5} \times 5.25 = 2.625 = 2\frac{5}{8}$$

10. $\boxed{D}$ Brianna has enough balsamic vinegar for $(20 \div 2) \times 5 = 50$ servings of salad dressing. She has enough sesame oil for $\left(6 \div \frac{2}{3}\right) \times 5 = 45$ servings of salad dressing. Since she has to maintain the same ratio of ingredients, sesame oil is the limiting ingredient (45 compared to 50). Therefore, the most she can make is 45 servings of salad dressing.

11. $\boxed{E}$ There are a total of $210 + 140 = 350$ students at the competition. At Salem High School, there are $\frac{3}{7} \times 210 = 90$ juniors and $\frac{4}{7} \times 210 = 120$ seniors. At Swampscott High School, there are $\frac{4}{7} \times 140 = 80$ juniors and $\frac{3}{7} \times 140 = 60$ seniors. Therefore, seniors account for $\frac{120 + 60}{350} = \frac{180}{350} = \frac{18}{35}$ of the attending students.

12. $\boxed{B}$ Let the number of one-bedroom apartments be 5 and the number of two-bedroom apartments be 3. Renovation costs were $3,200 \times 5 = \$16,000$ for the one-bedroom apartments and $4,000 \times 3 = \$12,000$ for the two-bedroom apartments, and so a total of $16,000 + 12,000 = \$28,000$ was paid to renovate 8 apartments. That's an average renovation cost of $28,000 \div 8 = \$3,500$ per apartment.

Chapter 10: Percent

1. $\boxed{D}$ $\dfrac{50-80}{80} \times 100 = -0.375 \times 100 = -37.5\%$

2. $\boxed{D}$ $30(1.70)(1.05) = \$53.55$

3. $\boxed{D}$ After the discount, the second toaster costs $0.8p$. The total for two toasters is then $p + 0.8p = 1.8p$.

4. $\boxed{E}$ 0.08 percent is equivalent to $\dfrac{8}{10,000}$. Setting up a proportion where x is the number of flowers grown,

$$\frac{8}{10,000} = \frac{6}{x}$$

Cross multiplying,
$$8x = 60,000$$
$$x = 7,500$$

5. $\boxed{D}$ Let x be the regular price for half a pound of beef. Setting up an equation to solve for x,

$$0.6x = 3$$
$$x = 5$$

The price for a *full* pound of beef is then $5 \times 2 = \$10$.

6. $\boxed{C}$ There are 4 choices for a drink and 3 choices for pizza, giving a total of $4 \times 3 = 12$ possible options. Of those options, 3 of them cost a total of $3.25 (water and vegetable, tea and pepperoni, coffee and cheese). Calculating the percentage, $\dfrac{3}{12} = \dfrac{1}{4} = 25\%$.

7. $\boxed{A}$ Green gumballs make up $100 - 30 - 25 = 45\%$ of the gumballs in the jar. Let the number of gumballs in the jar be x.

$$0.45x = 36$$
$$x = 80$$

Since there are 80 gumballs in the jar, the number of red gumballs must be $0.25 \times 80 = 20$.

8. $\boxed{D}$ Kendra answered $0.80 \times 35 = 28$ questions correctly in the first section. There were a total of $35 + 25 = 60$ questions on the test. She answered $0.75 \times 60 = 45$ of them correctly. Therefore, she must have answered $45 - 28 = 17$ questions correctly in the second section.

9. $\boxed{D}$ Let Max's initial weight be x.

$$1.15x = 46$$
$$x = 40$$

Max gained $46 - 40 = 6$ pounds while Boxer gained $\dfrac{1}{2} \times 6 = 3$. Since Boxer and Max weighed the same initially, Boxer's current weight must be $40 + 3 = 43$ pounds.

10. $\boxed{C}$ Let the original price of the computer be p. The discounted price during the sale was $0.6p$. The correct total was $(1.05)(0.6)p = 0.63p$ (tax on discounted price). The incorrect total that Walter paid was $0.6p + 0.05p = 0.65p$ (tax on original price). The amount by which Walter overpaid was $0.65p - 0.63p = 0.02p$, which represents 2% of the original price.

Chapter 11: Functions

1. $\boxed{E}$ $f(-2) = -3(-2)^3 = 24$

2. $\boxed{D}$ Start with what's inside the parentheses. $3\Phi(2\Phi4) = 3\Phi\dfrac{2}{4} = 3\Phi\dfrac{1}{2} = \dfrac{3}{\frac{1}{2}} = 6$

3. $\boxed{C}$ A graph intersects the x-axis when $y = 0$.

$$0 = x(x+1)(x-3)^2$$
$$x = 0, -1, 3$$

Therefore, the graph intersects the x-axis 3 times.

4. $\boxed{E}$ Because we can't divide by 0, f is undefined when $49 - x^2 = 0$, $x = \pm 7$. Therefore, the domain of f cannot contain -7 or 7.

5. $\boxed{C}$ First, $g(3) = -\sqrt{3+1} = -2$. Then, $f(g(3)) = f(-2) = (-2)^2 - 3 = 1$.

6. $\boxed{D}$

$$(2, n) \boxdot (-4, n) = 3$$
$$\frac{2+n}{n-4} = 3$$
$$2 + n = 3(n-4)$$
$$2 + n = 3n - 12$$
$$-2n = -14$$
$$n = 7$$

7. $\boxed{D}$ The graph of f crosses the x-axis at -2 and 2.

8. $\boxed{A}$ The graph approaches but never crosses the vertical line $x = -1$.

9. $\boxed{D}$ The absolute value turns all negative values of y into positive values, reflecting the negative portions of the graph across the x-axis. However, all positive values of y remain the same. Therefore, $|f(x)|$ has the graph shown in answer D.

10. $\boxed{C}$ If we let $y = g(x)$ for convenience, then $y = \sqrt[3]{x} - 2$. Swapping x and y, we get $x = \sqrt[3]{y} - 2$. Solving for y,

$$x = \sqrt[3]{y} - 2$$
$$x + 2 = \sqrt[3]{y}$$
$$(x+2)^3 = y$$

This "new" y is $g^{-1}(x)$. So, $g^{-1}(x) = (x+2)^3$.

11. $\boxed{C}$ First, $g(2) = -1$. Then, $f(g(2)) = f(-1) = 3$.

12. $\boxed{A}$ $f^{-1}(-3) = 2$ because $f(x)$ gives an output of -3 when $x = 2$. Then, $g(f^{-1}(-3)) = g(2) = -1$.

13. $\boxed{A}$ The easiest way to do this question is to graph $h(x)$:

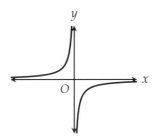

As you can see, h is increasing for $x < 0$ and increasing for $x > 0$.

14. $\boxed{C}$ Because the graphs of $f(x)$ and $g(x)$ intersect at 3 different points, $f(x) = g(x)$ has 3 solutions.

15. $\boxed{C}$

$$f(g(x)) = g(3x)$$
$$f(2x + k) = g(3x)$$
$$3(2x + k) - 8 = 2(3x) + k$$
$$6x + 3k - 8 = 6x + k$$
$$2k = 8$$
$$k = 4$$

16. $\boxed{B}$ We can factor $f(x)$ to be $2x(x^2 - 5)$. From here, we can tell the zeros are $x = 0, -\sqrt{5}$, and $\sqrt{5}$. That's one rational zero ($m = 1$) and two irrational zeros ($n = 2$). Therefore, $\dfrac{m}{n+1} = \dfrac{1}{3}$.

17. $\boxed{B}$ From the graph, it's easy to see that the function has two vertical asymptotes at $x = 0$ and $x = 2$. Therefore, those values are not in the domain. Mathematically, $f(x) = \dfrac{x-3}{x^2 - 2x} = \dfrac{x-3}{x(x-2)}$. Since $f(x)$ is undefined at $x = 0$ and $x = 2$, we've confirmed that those values are not in the domain.

18. $\boxed{B}$ Since the point $(-2, 3)$ lies on the graph, we can very easily test out each answer choice by plugging the point in. Only answers B and E give equations that are satisfied by the point. To decide between these two answers, we can test out another value like $x = 0$. When $x = 0$, answer B gives $y = 1$ and answer E gives $y = 6$. Because it's clear that the graph crosses $(0, 1)$ rather than $(0, 6)$, the answer is B. You could've arrived at the same answer through graph recognition. Because the graph opens downward, a negative should be out in front. Answer B has one, whereas E does not.

19. $\boxed{A}$ Because the zeros of $g(x)$ are $0, -1$, and 3, $b = 1$ and $c = -3$. Now we can use the point $(2, -30)$ to solve for a:

$$g(x) = ax(x+1)(x-3)$$
$$-30 = a(2)(2+1)(2-3)$$
$$-30 = -6a$$
$$a = 5$$

Finally, $a + b + c = 5 + 1 + (-3) = 3$.

20. $\boxed{B}$ If you recall your function transformations, $f(x-2) + 1$ means shift $f(x)$ to the right by 2 units and up by 1 unit. The graph that shows the correct result is B.

21. $\boxed{E}$ If $P(x)$ is a 4th degree polynomial, then it crosses the x-axis AT MOST 4 different times. Therefore, n cannot be 5.

22. $\boxed{D}$ First, graph the function:

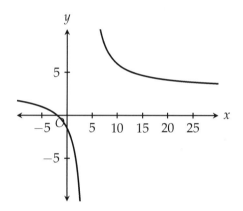

We can see that the horizontal asymptote is somewhere between $y = 0$ and $y = 5$. As the value of x gets larger, $g(x)$ gets closer and closer to the horizontal asymptote. So to find the equation of the horizontal asymptote, we can make up a large number for x, let's say 500, and use our calculator to see what the value of $g(x)$ is. It turns out that $g(500) \approx 3.04$. Therefore, we can be pretty certain the horizontal asymptote is $y = 3$.

Chapter 12: Lines

1. $\boxed{C}$ $\dfrac{4-2}{-2-4} = \dfrac{2}{-6} = -\dfrac{1}{3}$

2. $\boxed{B}$ When $t = 0, h = 120$. Only answers A and B contain that point. When $t = 1, h = 112$. Between A and B, only answer B contains this second point. Another way to do this question is to realize that 120 is the h-intercept and -8 is the slope.

3. $\boxed{B}$ A line parallel to the y-axis runs up and down, and 4 units to the left of the y-axis gets us to $x = -4$.

4. $\boxed{D}$ You have the option of testing each answer choice with both points or solving mathematically. We'll show you how to do it mathematically even though trial and error may be faster in this case. First, we find the slope: $\dfrac{2-(-4)}{2-(-1)} = \dfrac{6}{3} = 2$. At this point, it's clear that the answer is D because it's the only equation with a slope of 2, but for the sake of completeness, we'll get the slope-intercept form by using the point $(2,2)$:

$$y - 2 = m(x - 2)$$
$$y - 2 = 2(x - 2)$$
$$y - 2 = 2x - 4$$
$$y = 2x - 2$$

5. $\boxed{A}$ The slope of the graphed line is $\dfrac{3-0}{4-(-1)} = \dfrac{3}{5}$. A perpendicular line must then have slope $-\dfrac{5}{3}$.

6. $\boxed{A}$ First, we find the slope: $\dfrac{-3-(-6)}{-4-5} = \dfrac{3}{-9} = -\dfrac{1}{3}$. Next, we get the point-slope form of the equation using the point $(-4, -3)$:

$$y + 3 = m(x + 4)$$
$$y + 3 = -\dfrac{1}{3}(x + 4)$$
$$y + 3 = -\dfrac{1}{3}x - \dfrac{4}{3}$$
$$y = -\dfrac{1}{3}x - \dfrac{13}{3}$$

7. $\boxed{A}$ First, get the equation into slope-intercept form: $y = \dfrac{2}{5}x + 10$. Only answers A and B have y-intercepts of 10, and between them, only answer A has a slope less than 1.

8. $\boxed{C}$ Let's get the equation of line m in slope-intercept form: $y = \dfrac{3}{2}x - 4$. From this equation, we can see that the slope of line m is $\dfrac{3}{2}$ and its y-intercept is -4. Therefore, the slope of line n must also be $\dfrac{3}{2}$ and its y-intercept is $-4 + 4 = 0$. The equation of line n is then $y = \dfrac{3}{2}x$.

9. $\boxed{C}$ The equation for Town A is $y = 2x + 50$. The equation for Town B is $y = -2x + 70$. The graph of these equations is two intersecting lines. However, they are not perpendicular because their slopes are not negative reciprocals of each other.

10. $\boxed{B}$ Let's get two points that Lia mistakenly plotted and find the equation of the line from those two points. As mentioned in the question, the point $(3, 2)$ is on the correct line, but she plotted $(2, 3)$ instead. The point $(0, -4)$ is also on the correct line, but Lia plotted $(-4, 0)$ instead. The slope of the line that passes through $(2, 3)$ and $(-4, 0)$ is $\dfrac{3 - 0}{2 - (-4)} = \dfrac{3}{6} = \dfrac{1}{2}$. After getting the point-slope form with either of the previous two points, we can derive the slope-intercept form of the line:

$$y - 3 = m(x - 2)$$
$$y - 3 = \frac{1}{2}(x - 2)$$
$$y - 3 = \frac{1}{2}x - 1$$
$$y = \frac{1}{2}x + 2$$

11. $\boxed{A}$ Try to visualize the region. Hopefully, you see a triangle:

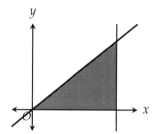

The base of the triangle is c. The height of the triangle is $4c$. Since the area of the triangle is 32,

$$\frac{1}{2}bh = 32$$
$$\frac{1}{2}(c)(4c) = 32$$
$$2c^2 = 32$$
$$c^2 = 16$$
$$c = 4$$

12. $\boxed{E}$ We get two distinct parallel lines when $a = 1$ and $b = 2$. We get two perpendicular lines when $a = -1$ (b can be any integer). We get a single line when $a = 1$ and $b = 1$.

13. $\boxed{B}$ The only possibility for l is a line that cuts the parallelogram through the "middle" as shown below.

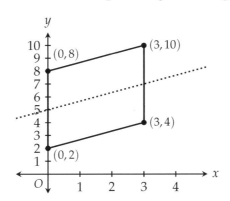

The y-intercept of this line is 5 (the midpoint of 2 and 8). The slope of this line is the same as the slope of either the top or bottom side of the parallelogram. For our calculation, we'll use the points from the top side: $\dfrac{10-8}{3-0} = \dfrac{2}{3}$. Therefore, the equation of line l is $y = \dfrac{2}{3}x + 5$.

Chapter 13: Quadratics

1. $\boxed{B}$ First, divide each side by 2.

$$x^2 = 3x + 18$$
$$x^2 - 3x - 18 = 0$$
$$(x - 6)(x + 3) = 0$$
$$x = 6, -3$$

2. $\boxed{B}$ The equation must have factors $(x + 2)$ and $(x - 5)$. The only answer choice that has those factors is B.

3. $\boxed{C}$ The axis of symmetry of the parabola crosses the midpoint of the two zeros, which is at $(2 + 8) \div 2 = 5$.

4. $\boxed{D}$ $-\dfrac{b}{a} = -\dfrac{-5}{2} = \dfrac{5}{2} = 2\dfrac{1}{2}$

5. $\boxed{B}$ First, move everything to the left side of the equation to get $2x^2 - x - 15 = 0$. Then use the quadratic formula:

$$x = \frac{-b \pm \sqrt{b^2 - 4ac}}{2a} = \frac{-(-1) \pm \sqrt{(-1)^2 - 4(2)(-15)}}{2(2)} = \frac{1 \pm \sqrt{121}}{4} = \frac{1 \pm 11}{4} = -\frac{10}{4} \text{ or } \frac{12}{4} = -\frac{5}{2} \text{ or } 3$$

6. $\boxed{B}$ For any parabola with equation $y = a(x - h)^2 + k$, the vertex is (h, k). Therefore, the vertex of $y = -2(x + 3)^2 + 1$ is $(-3, 1)$.

7. $\boxed{B}$ Let $f(x) = 2x^2 - 7x + 6$ for convenience. If $x - a$ is a factor of $f(x)$, then $f(a) = 0$. With this in mind, we test out each answer choice. For answer choice A, $f(3) = 2(3)^2 - 7(3) + 6 = 3$. For answer choice B, $f(2) = 2(2)^2 - 7(2) + 6 = 0$. Therefore, $x - 2$ is a factor.

8. $\boxed{E}$ Notice that 19 is prime (its only factors are 1 and 19). That means the only way the equation gives integer solutions is if it factors into $(x + 19)(x + 1)$ or $(x - 19)(x - 1)$. Of these two possibilities, $(x + 19)(x + 1)$ is the one that gives integer solutions that are negative.

9. $\boxed{E}$ From the graph, we see that the parabola has a vertex in the fourth quadrant and passes through $(0, -5)$. Remember that a parabola with equation $y = a(x - h)^2 + k$ has a vertex at (h, k). With this in mind, we inspect each answer choice. Only answer choices A, C, and E represent parabolas with a vertex in the fourth quadrant, $(3, -2)$. Among these options, only answer E passes through $(0, -5)$.

10. $\boxed{A}$ With x-intercepts at -3 and 5, the parabola must have an equation that looks like $y = a(x+3)(x-5)$. Using the point $(4, -14)$, we can solve for a:

$$y = a(x+3)(x-5)$$
$$-14 = a(4+3)(4-5)$$
$$-14 = a(-7)$$
$$a = 2$$

Therefore, $y = 2(x+3)(x-5)$. The x-coordinate of the vertex is at the midpoint of the two x-intercepts, $\dfrac{-3+5}{2} = 1$. When $x = 1$, $y = 2(3+1)(1-5) = -32$, so the vertex is at $(1, -32)$.

11. $\boxed{C}$ If a parabola crosses the x-axis at only one point, then its discriminant must be equal to 0.

$$b^2 - 4ac = 0$$
$$k^2 - 4(1)(8) = 0$$
$$k^2 = 32$$
$$k = \sqrt{32} = 4\sqrt{2}$$

12. $\boxed{E}$ For any quadratic expression $ax^2 + bx + c$, the sum of the roots is $-\dfrac{b}{a}$ and the product of the roots is $\dfrac{c}{a}$. In this question, the roots of the quadratic expression are 3 and -1, making the sum of the roots $3 + (-1) = 2$ and the product $3(-1) = -3$. Therefore,

$$-\frac{b}{a} = -\frac{m-5}{1} = -(m-5) = 5 - m = 2$$

which gives $m = 3$. The product of the roots is $\dfrac{m-n}{1} = m - n$, which equals -3.

$$m - n = -3$$
$$3 - n = -3$$
$$n = 6$$

Finally, $m + n = 3 + 6 = 9$. A second way of solving this question is to realize that the quadratic expression is equivalent to $(x-3)(x+1) = x^2 - 2x - 3$. We can then compare coefficients to find m and n.

Chapter 14: Coordinate Geometry

1. $\boxed{C}$ The y-coordinate of the midpoint is the average of the y-coordinates of the endpoints: $\dfrac{-8 + 20}{2} = 6$

2. $\boxed{D}$ $d = \sqrt{(y_2 - y_1)^2 + (x_2 - x_1)^2} = \sqrt{(1 - (-2))^2 + (7 - 5)^2} = \sqrt{3^2 + 2^2} = \sqrt{13}$

3. $\boxed{C}$ The hexagon is symmetrical about the y-axis, so the x-coordinate of Q must be $-a$. Now Q is twice as high up as vertex (b, c) so its y-coordinate must be $2c$. The coordinates of Q are then $(-a, 2c)$.

4. $\boxed{C}$ The center of the circle is at the midpoint of the diameter's endpoints, $\left(\dfrac{3 + 11}{2}, \dfrac{1 - 7}{2} \right) = (7, -3)$

5. $\boxed{B}$ The only way to do this question is to draw it out.

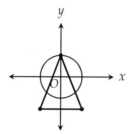

The triangle and the circle intersect at 3 points.

6. $\boxed{E}$ After a reflection across the y-axis, the x-coordinates are "flipped" but the y-coordinates stay the same. Therefore, the endpoints of $\overline{A'B'}$ are at (a, a) and $(-b, 2b)$.

7. $\boxed{A}$ In Judy's redesign, the logo is at $(4 - 6, -5 + 3) = (-2, -2)$. The center of the webpage is at $(0, 0)$. We can use the distance formula to find the straight-line distance between the two points:

$$d = \sqrt{(y_2 - y_1)^2 + (x_2 - x_1)^2} = \sqrt{(-2 - 0)^2 + (-2 - 0)^2} = \sqrt{(-2)^2 + (-2)^2} = \sqrt{8} \approx 3$$

8. $\boxed{A}$ Let the coordinates of C be (r, s). Using the midpoint formula, $\dfrac{2 + r}{2} = -4$ and $\dfrac{-1 + s}{2} = 3$. Solving for r,

$$\frac{2 + r}{2} = -4$$
$$2 + r = -8$$
$$r = -10$$

Solving for s,

$$\frac{-1 + s}{2} = 3$$
$$-1 + s = 6$$
$$s = 7$$

Therefore, the coordinates of C are $(-10, 7)$.

9. $\boxed{D}$ Another vertex of the square must have either 1) an x-coordinate that is 4 units away from 3, 2) a y-coordinate that is 4 units away from -2, or 3) both of the above. The following graph shows all the possibilities.

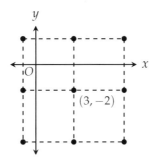

Answer A has #1. Answer B has #3. Answer C has #2. Answer E has #1. Answer D cannot be a vertex because its y-coordinate is 8 units away from -2.

10. $\boxed{E}$ If you know how reflection works, there isn't much to this question. $P'Q'R'S'$ is a reflection of $PQRS$ across the line $y = -x$, as shown below.

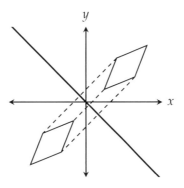

11. $\boxed{B}$ A' must have coordinates $(3,0)$. Since the length of $\overline{OA'}$ is 3, the length of $\overline{OA''}$ must also be 3 (the distance from the center does not change after a rotation). If we now draw a line from A'' to the x-axis, we get a $30 - 60 - 90$ triangle:

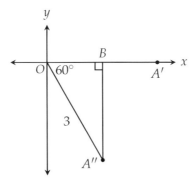

Using the $30 - 60 - 90$ triangle relationship, the length of $\overline{OB}$ is half the hypotenuse, $\dfrac{3}{2}$. Therefore, the x-coordinate of A'' is $\dfrac{3}{2}$.

12. $\boxed{B}$ To get the midpoint of $\overline{BC}$, we need to find the coordinates of B. The length of $\overline{AC}$ is $4-1=3$. Using the pythagorean theorem to find AB,

$$AB^2 + AC^2 = BC^2$$
$$AB^2 + 3^2 = 5^2$$
$$AB^2 = 16$$
$$AB = 4$$

By the way, the pythagorean theorem was unnecessary if you knew you were looking at a $3-4-5$ triangle. In any case, the coordinates of B are $(1, 0+4) = (1,4)$. Using the midpoint formula, the midpoint of $\overline{BC}$ is at $\left(\dfrac{1+4}{2}, \dfrac{4+0}{2}\right) = \left(\dfrac{5}{2}, 2\right)$.

13. $\boxed{C}$ A good way to picture this is to draw $\overline{OC}$ and perform the rotation on $\overline{OC}$, ignoring the triangle itself.

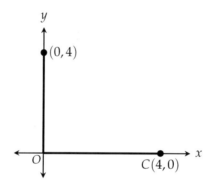

A well-drawn graph and your intuition are all you need to determine that the coordinates of the image are $(0,4)$. Note that the rotation was about the origin, NOT point A. If the rotation had been about point A, the image of C would've been at $(1,3)$.

14. $\boxed{D}$ Using the distance formula,

$$d = \sqrt{(y_2 - y_1)^2 + (x_2 - x_1)^2}$$
$$= \sqrt{(-k-k)^2 + (k - (k+1))^2}$$
$$= \sqrt{(-2k)^2 + (-1)^2}$$
$$= \sqrt{4k^2 + 1}$$

Chapter 15: Angles

1. $\boxed{D}$ Because the four angles add up to a full circle, we can set up the following equation:

$$(2y + 40) + 45 + y + 80 = 360$$
$$3y + 165 = 360$$
$$3y = 195$$
$$y = 65$$

2. $\boxed{A}$ Because $\overline{AD}$ is parallel to $\overline{BC}$, the measure of $\angle DAC$ is $40°$. The measure of $\angle D$ is then $180° - 25° - 40° = 115°$.

3. $\boxed{B}$ The minimum requirement for lines m and n to be parallel is the following two sets of equal angles: $a = d = e = h$ and $b = c = f = g$. This narrows down our answer choices to A and B. Answer A is insufficient because it only gives us the positioning of line m and doesn't guarantee anything about line n. Answer B, on the other hand, gives us the positioning of both lines.

4. $\boxed{A}$ Looking at right triangle ABD, we can calculate $\angle B$ to be $180 - 90 - 20 = 70°$. Now, we use triangle ABC to find the measure of $\angle BAC$: $180 - 50 - 70 = 60°$.

5. $\boxed{D}$ Because lines l and m are parallel, the third angle in the top triangle must also measure $65°$. Therefore, the sum of $\angle 1$ and $\angle 2$ is $180° - 65° = 115°$.

6. $\boxed{A}$ If we let the measure of $\angle GEH$ be x, then the measure of $\angle CEH$ is $2x$. Solving for x,

$$x + 2x = 180$$
$$3x = 180$$
$$x = 60$$

The measure of $\angle CEH$ is then $2 \times 60 = 120°$. Because $\angle FEH$ is a right angle, the measure of $\angle CEF$ is $120 - 90 = 30°$. Finally, $\overline{BC}$ and $\overline{EF}$ are parallel so $\angle BCE$ is also $30°$.

7. $\boxed{C}$ The total number of degrees in a hexagon is $180(6 - 2) = 720°$. In this particular hexagon, we have two angles of $80°$ and 4 angles of $x°$.

$$2(80) + 4x = 720$$
$$160 + 4x = 720$$
$$4x = 560$$
$$x = 140$$

8. $\boxed{B}$ We use the triangle in the lower right to find the desired angle. The angle to the left is $(180 - 120) \div 2 = 30°$. The angle at the top is then $180 - 30 - 112 = 38°$. Finally, the desired angle is $180 - 38 - 38 = 104°$.

9. $\boxed{A}$ The total number of degrees in a pentagon is $180(5 - 2) = 540°$. Because $\overline{AE}$ and $\overline{BC}$ are parallel, the measures of $\angle A$ and $\angle B$ sum to $180°$. Therefore, the measure of $\angle C$ is $540 - 180 - 150 - 90 = 120°$.

10. $\boxed{E}$ Because $\overleftrightarrow{BA}$ is parallel to $\overleftrightarrow{CE}$, $\angle BAE$ is also 129°. And because $\angle BAE$ is divided into thirds, $\angle BAC = \angle CAD = \angle DAE = 129 \div 3 = 43°$. Lastly, $\angle ADE$, the angle we're looking for, is equal to $\angle BAD$, which is $2 \times 43° = 86°$.

11. $\boxed{B}$ We draw a line from point C to a point F such that $\overline{CF}$ is parallel to $\overline{AB}$ and $\overline{ED}$.

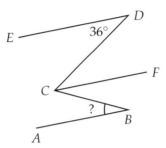

Using the properties of parallel lines, we see that $\angle DCF$ is 36° and $\angle FCB$ is $67 - 36 = 31°$. Since $\overline{CF}$ is parallel to $\overline{AB}$, the measure of $\angle ABC$ is also 31°.

Chapter 16: Triangles

1. $\boxed{C}$ First, draw the diagram:

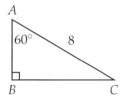

As we can see, $\triangle ABC$ is a $30 - 60 - 90$ triangle. Using the $30 - 60 - 90$ triangle relationship, $AB = 4$ and $BC = 4\sqrt{3}$.

2. $\boxed{D}$ First, draw a picture:

Answer A can't be true since $\overline{AB}$ is the hypotenuse. Answer B can't be true since $\overline{AB}$ is the hypotenuse, which is always the largest side in a right triangle. Answer C can't be true since $\angle C$ is already a right angle and a triangle can't have two right angles. Answer E can't be true since the 3 sides of a right triangle are never congruent (the hypotenuse has to be the largest side). However, answer D could be true if the triangle is $45 - 45 - 90$.

3. $\boxed{C}$ Since $AC = BC$, $\triangle ABC$ is isosceles with $\angle A = \angle B$. Since $\angle BCD$ is an exterior angle, the sum of $\angle A$ and $\angle B$ is $102°$. The measure of $\angle A$ is then $102 \div 2 = 51°$.

4. $\boxed{A}$ The diagonal of each rectangle creates two triangles that are similar to the triangles of the other rectangle. A pair of these similar triangles is shown in bold below.

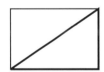

So if the ratio of the sides is 1:2, then the ratio of the diagonals must also be 1:2.

5. $\boxed{A}$ First we use the pythagorean theorem to find AB. $AB = \sqrt{AC^2 - CB^2} = \sqrt{13^2 - 5^2} = \sqrt{144} = 12$. Given that the 2 triangles are similar, $\overline{AB}$ corresponds to $\overline{EF}$ and $\overline{CB}$ corresponds to $\overline{DE}$.

$$\frac{DE}{CB} = \frac{EF}{AB}$$
$$\frac{DE}{5} = \frac{18}{12}$$
$$DE = \frac{18}{12} \cdot 5 = \frac{15}{2} = 7.5$$

6. $\boxed{A}$ If $\triangle ABC$ is isosceles with $AB = AC$, vertex A must lie on the line that runs through the midpoint of vertices B and C. Since the midpoint of B and C is $(1, 2)$, this line is $x = 1$. The only point with an x-coordinate of 1 in the answer choices is A.

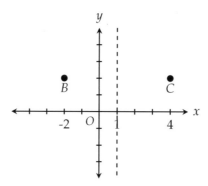

7. $\boxed{B}$ Draw it out.

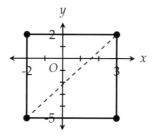

The width of the rectangle is $3 - (-2) = 5$ and the height is $2 - (-5) = 7$. Using the pythagorean theorem, the length of the diagonal is $\sqrt{5^2 + 7^2} = \sqrt{74} \approx 9$.

8. $\boxed{B}$ Let the measure of $\angle CAB$ be x. Then the measure of $\angle BCA$ is also x and the measure of $\angle ABC$ is $4x$. Since the angles of a triangle sum to $180°$,

$$x + x + 4x = 180$$
$$6x = 180$$
$$x = 30$$

Therefore, the measure of $\angle BCA$ is $30°$ and the measure of $\angle BCE$ is $90 - 30 = 60°$.

9. $\boxed{C}$ Draw lines from point B and point C straight downward to form two right triangles.

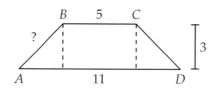

These two triangles are congruent and each has a base of $(11 - 5) \div 2 = 3$. Using the pythagorean theorem, $AB = \sqrt{3^2 + 3^2} = \sqrt{18} = 3\sqrt{2}$.

10. $\boxed{D}$ Since $AB > BC$, the angle opposite of $\overline{AB}$ must be greater in measure than the angle opposite of $\overline{BC}$. Therefore, $m\angle C > m\angle A$.

11. $\boxed{D}$ Because $\angle B \cong \angle E$, $\angle A \cong \angle D$, and $\angle BCA \cong \angle DCE$, $\triangle ABC$ and $\triangle DEC$ are similar. Therefore,

$$\frac{DE}{AB} = \frac{CE}{BC}$$

$$\frac{DE}{42} = \frac{20}{24}$$

$$DE = \frac{20}{24} \cdot 42 = 35$$

By the way, $\overline{CE}$ and $\overline{BC}$ are corresponding sides because they're opposite equivalent corresponding angles $\angle D$ and $\angle A$, respectively.

12. $\boxed{D}$ Because $\triangle KLO$ has angles that are congruent to those of $\triangle MNO$, the two triangles are similar. Therefore,

$$\frac{MO}{OK} = \frac{NM}{KL}$$

$$\frac{NO}{5} = \frac{12}{8}$$

$$NO = \frac{12}{8} \cdot 5 = 7.5$$

By the way, $\overline{NM}$ and $\overline{KL}$ are corresponding sides because they're opposite equivalent corresponding angles $\angle NOM$ and $\angle KOL$, respectively.

13. $\boxed{D}$ Both $\triangle ABC$ and $\triangle ACD$ are $30 - 60 - 90$ triangles. Applying the $30 - 60 - 90$ triangle relationship to both these triangles, we can first find that $AC = 2\sqrt{3}$ and then $AD = 2 \cdot 2\sqrt{3} = 4\sqrt{3}$.

14. $\boxed{A}$ We're looking for BD so let the length be x. Then the length of $\overline{AD}$ is also x using the $45 - 45 - 90$ triangle relationship and the length of $\overline{DC}$ is $x\sqrt{3}$ using the $30 - 60 - 90$ triangle relationship.

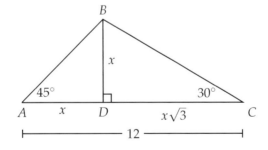

Now we can make an equation:

$$x + x\sqrt{3} = 12$$

$$x(1 + \sqrt{3}) = 12$$

$$x = \frac{12}{1 + \sqrt{3}} \approx 4.4$$

15. $\boxed{B}$ Draw a line from point C straight down to $\overline{AD}$ to form a $45-45-90$ triangle. Using the $45-45-90$ triangle relationship, $CE = 4$ and $ED = 4$ as shown below.

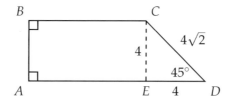

The area of $\triangle CDE$ is $\dfrac{1}{2}(4)(4) = 8$. Since the area of the trapezoid is 44, the rectangle must have an area of $44 - 8 = 36$. So,

$$4(AE) = 36$$
$$AE = 9$$

Finally, $AD = AE + ED = 9 + 4 = 13$.

16. $\boxed{B}$ Notice that $\triangle CDE$ is similar to $\triangle CAB$ because their corresponding angles are congruent. Since the length of $\overline{AC}$ is $\sqrt{90} = 3\sqrt{10}$, which is 3 times $\sqrt{10}$, the sides of $\triangle CAB$ are three times longer than the sides of $\triangle CDE$. So, $EC = 9 \div 3 = 3$ and now we can use the pythagorean theorem to solve for DE. $DE = \sqrt{DC^2 - EC^2} = \sqrt{(\sqrt{10})^2 - 3^2} = \sqrt{10-9} = \sqrt{1} = 1$. Finally, the area of $\triangle CDE$ is $\dfrac{1}{2}bh = \dfrac{1}{2}(3)(1) = \dfrac{3}{2} = 1\dfrac{1}{2}$.

17. $\boxed{E}$ Let the side length of the smaller equilateral triangle be x. Using the $30-60-90$ triangle relationship, we find that the height is $\dfrac{x\sqrt{3}}{2}$.

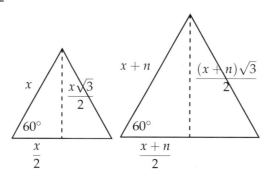

The side length of the larger equilateral triangle is $x + n$. Using the $30-60-90$ triangle relationship again, we find the height to be $\dfrac{(x+n)\sqrt{3}}{2}$. The difference between the two heights is then

$$\frac{(x+n)\sqrt{3}}{2} - \frac{x\sqrt{3}}{2} = \left(\frac{x\sqrt{3}}{2} + \frac{n\sqrt{3}}{2}\right) - \frac{x\sqrt{3}}{2} = \frac{n\sqrt{3}}{2}$$

Chapter 17: Circles

1. $\boxed{B}$ $C = \pi d = 30\pi$

2. $\boxed{A}$ Draw it out. The diameter of the circle must be 5.

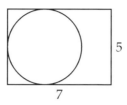

The circumference is then $\pi d = 5\pi$.

3. $\boxed{C}$

$$3(2x) = 6(4)$$
$$6x = 24$$
$$x = 4$$

4. $\boxed{A}$ Since $30°$ is $\dfrac{30°}{360°} = \dfrac{1}{12}$ of a full circle, arc $\overset{\frown}{AB}$ is $\dfrac{1}{12}$ of the circumference. Since arc $\overset{\frown}{AB}$ has a length of $\dfrac{\pi}{2}$, the circumference of the circle is $\dfrac{\pi}{2} \times 12 = 6\pi$. Solving for the radius, $2\pi r = 6\pi, r = 3$.

5. $\boxed{C}$ The general equation of a circle is $(x - h)^2 + (y - k)^2 = r^2$, where (h, k) is the center and r is the radius. Therefore, the center is at $(0, -3)$ and the radius has length $\sqrt{29}$.

6. $\boxed{B}$ Let the length of $\overline{CX}$ be x. The length of $\overline{BX}$ is then $10 - x$.

$$x(10 - x) = 8(3)$$
$$-x^2 + 10x = 24$$
$$-x^2 + 10x - 24 = 0$$
$$x^2 - 10x + 24 = 0$$
$$(x - 6)(x - 4) = 0$$
$$x = 4, 6$$

When $x = 4$, the length of $\overline{CX}$ is 4 and the length of $\overline{BX}$ is $10 - 4 = 6$, meeting the requirement that $BX > CX$. Although I just gave you an algebraic solution, this problem is best done through guess and check with the answer choices.

7. $\boxed{B}$ Minor arc $\overset{\frown}{CD}$ measures $40 \times 2 = 80°$. Because $\overline{BC}$ is a diameter, arc $\overset{\frown}{BDC}$ measures $180°$ (semicircle). Therefore, $\overset{\frown}{BD} = \overset{\frown}{BDC} - \overset{\frown}{CD} = 180° - 80° = 100°$.

8. ☐D If you trace out the path that the center of the circle travels, you'll notice that the path forms a rectangle with a base of 7 and a width of 3:

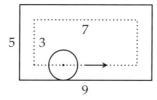

The perimeter is then $7 + 7 + 3 + 3 = 20$.

9. ☐B The circle in the coordinate plane has its center at $(1, 2)$ and a radius of $1 - (-2) = 3$. Therefore, the equation of the circle is $(x - 1)^2 + (y - 2)^2 = 9$.

10. ☐D The circumference of the pizza is $2\pi r = 2\pi(10) = 20\pi \approx 62.83$

We divide this value by 4 to get the maximum number of slices that can be cut out: $62.83 \div 4 \approx 15.7$

Since we only want full pizza slices, the answer is 15.

11. ☐B There are $360°$ in a circle and $60°$ is one-sixth of that. Therefore, the area of the sector is one-sixth the area of the circle. The area of the circle is then $6 \times 96\pi = 576\pi$. Solving for the radius,

$$\pi r^2 = 576\pi$$
$$r = 24$$

The circumference of the circle is $2\pi r = 2\pi(24) = 48\pi$. Arc $\overparen{AB}$ is one-sixth of the circumference:
$\frac{1}{6} \cdot 48\pi = 8\pi$

12. ☐D Draw it out. Notice that the center of the circle CANNOT be $(0, 1)$ because then the radius would be 3 (too short). This helps us come up with the following two circles:

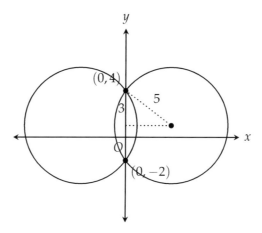

The y-coordinates of the centers must be 1 (the midpoint between -2 and 4). Drawing the right triangle shown above, we can see that it's a $3 - 4 - 5$ right triangle, which makes the x-coordinate 4 for the center of the circle on the right and -4 for the center of the circle on the left. Therefore, the possible centers are $(-4, 1)$ and $(4, 1)$.

13. $\boxed{B}$ The standard equation of a circle is $(x - h)^2 + (y - k)^2 = r^2$, where (h, k) is the center of the circle and r is its radius. Since the circle is tangent to the y-axis and the center of the circle is 5 units away from the y-axis, the radius must be 5. The equation of the circle is then $(x - 5)^2 + (y - 3)^2 = 25$.

14. $\boxed{A}$ The standard equation of a circle is $(x - h)^2 + (y - k)^2 = r^2$, where (h, k) is the center of the circle and r is its radius. To get the equation of the original circle into this standard form, we have to complete the square for x:

$$x^2 - 6x + y^2 + 8 = 0$$
$$[(x - 3)^2 - 9] + y^2 + 8 = 0$$

Completing the square for y is not necessary here because of the lone y^2 term. Combining like terms, we get

$$(x - 3)^2 + y^2 - 1 = 0$$
$$(x - 3)^2 + y^2 = 1$$

From this equation, we can see that the center of the circle is at $(3, 0)$. After the circle is translated 2 units to the right and 1 unit down, the new center is at $(5, -1)$. The radius stays the same. Therefore, the equation of the translated circle is

$$(x - 5)^2 + (y + 1)^2 = 1$$

Chapter 18: Area & Perimeter

1. $\boxed{E}$ The area of the square is $18^2 = 324$. For a rectangle,

$$A = lw$$
$$324 = 6w$$
$$54 = w$$

The perimeter is then $2l + 2w = 2(6) + 2(54) = 12 + 108 = 120$

2. $\boxed{C}$ The diameter of the circle is equal to the side length of the square. So the radius is $4 \div 2 = 2$.

$$\text{Area of 4 Corners} = \text{Area of Square} - \text{Area of Circle}$$
$$= 4 \times 4 - \pi(2)^2$$
$$= 16 - 4\pi$$

Because the four corners each have the same area, the area of the shaded corner is $\dfrac{16 - 4\pi}{4} = 4 - \pi$

3. $\boxed{D}$ Using the area of a trapezoid formula is fine, but we'll do this question without it. We can split up the trapezoid into a triangle on the left and a rectangle on the right.

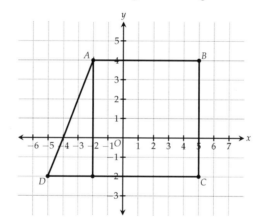

The sides of the rectangle are 6 and 7. The base of the triangle is 3 and the height is 6.

$$A = 6 \times 7 + \frac{1}{2}(3)(6) = 42 + 9 = 51$$

4. $\boxed{C}$ The shaded region is five squares and four half-squares, a total of 7 squares. The area of each square in the grid is then $28 \div 7 = 4$. The outer square $ABCD$ contains 9 squares, giving an area of $9 \times 4 = 36$.

5. $\boxed{E}$ There are 12 sides along the perimeter, so the length of each side is $60 \div 12 = 5$. The area of each square is then $5^2 = 25$, and the area of the entire figure is $5 \times 25 = 125$.

6. $\boxed{B}$ If we let the length of the rectangle be x, then its width is $x + 3$. Setting up an equation for the perimeter,

$$x + x + (x + 3) + (x + 3) = 94$$
$$4x + 6 = 94$$
$$4x = 88$$
$$x = 22$$

7. $\boxed{B}$ Let's start by graphing the lines:

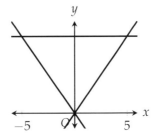

Let $y = 5$ (the top line) be the base and the portion of the y-axis below $y = 5$ be the height. The base is then 10 and the height is 5.

$$A = \frac{1}{2}(10)(5) = 25$$

8. $\boxed{D}$ For percentage problems such as these, one strategy is to make up some numbers. Let the width be 10 and the height also be 10 (a square is still a rectangle). Increasing the width by 10% gets us a new width of 11. Decreasing the height by 10% gets us a new height of 9. The area of the new rectangle is then $11 \times 9 = 99$, whereas the original area was $10 \times 10 = 100$.

$$\text{Percent Change} = \frac{\text{New} - \text{Original}}{\text{Original}} \times 100\% = \frac{99 - 100}{100} \times 100\% = \frac{-1}{100} \times 100\% = -1\%$$

The new area is 1% less than the original area.

9. $\boxed{B}$ Let the right side be the base. Let the height be the distance between the right side and the point $(-3, -2)$. The base is 11 (from -5 to 6) and the height is 6 (from -3 to 3).

$$A = \frac{1}{2}(11)(6) = 33$$

10. $\boxed{D}$ The side length of square A is $\sqrt{16} = 4$. The side length of square B is $\sqrt{25} = 5$. The side length of the outer square is then $4 + 5 = 9$. The left side of the shaded region is $9 - 4 = 5$. The top is 9. The bottom is also 9 (the top of A and the top of B). The right side is the same as the left side (think of the little vertical piece in the middle and the piece on the right as one). The perimeter is then $5 + 9 + 9 + 5 = 28$.

11. $\boxed{D}$ $15 + 20 + 15 + 20 = 70$.

12. $\boxed{D}$ The area of the inner rectangle (the pool) is $15 \times 20 = 300$. The base of the outer rectangle is $20 + 2 + 2 = 24$ and the height is $15 + 2 + 2 = 19$. The area of the outer rectangle is then $24 \times 19 = 456$. Subtracting the inner rectangle from the outer rectangle gives the walking area: $456 - 300 = 156$.

241

13. $\boxed{D}$ The area of $\triangle ABC$ is $\frac{1}{2}(12)(5) = 30$.

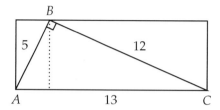

The area of $\triangle ABC$ is half the area of the rectangle. You can see this by drawing the dotted line from B to the base. On the left hand side, the two triangles are congruent. The same is true for the two triangles on the right hand side. The area of the rectangle is then $2 \times 30 = 60$.

14. $\boxed{A}$ The side length of the outer square is $\sqrt{64} = 8$. The radius of each circle is $8 \div 4 = 2$. Draw an inner square connecting the centers of each circle:

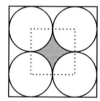

To get the shaded region, we need to subtract out the four quarter-circles from the inner square. The inner square has an area of $4 \times 4 = 16$. The four quarter-circles make up one circle with an area of $\pi(2)^2 = 4\pi$. The area of the shaded region is then $16 - 4\pi$.

15. $\boxed{B}$ Let the area of B be x. Then the area of A is $4x$.

$$4x + x = 80$$
$$5x = 80$$
$$x = 16$$

The area of B is 16 and the area of A is $4 \times 16 = 64$. The side length of square B is $\sqrt{16} = 4$. The base of A is $64 \div 4 = 16$ (the area divided by the height gives you the base). The perimeter is then $16 + 4 + 4 + 4 + 16 + 4 = 48$.

16. $\boxed{B}$ Given all rectangles with the same area, the one with the smallest perimeter is the one that's a square. In this case, a square would have a side length of $\sqrt{64} = 8$ and a perimeter of $4 \times 8 = 32$. Therefore, $P \geq 32$.

17. $\boxed{E}$ Let the length of a rectangle be x and the width be y. Notice that $y = 4x$:

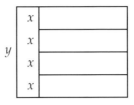

The perimeter of each rectangle is 30, which means

$$2x + 2y = 30$$

Substituting $y = 4x$,

$$2x + 2(4x) = 30$$
$$10x = 30$$
$$x = 3$$

which means $y = 4 \cdot 3 = 12$. The outer rectangle has a base of $x + y = 3 + 12 = 15$ and a height of $y = 12$. The area is then $15 \times 12 = 180$.

18. $\boxed{E}$ Each segment along the bottom of the rectangle has a length of $16 \div 8 = 2$. Each segment along the left of the rectangle has a length of $6 \div 6 = 1$. The base of triangle N is $3 \times 2 = 6$ and its height is 3. The base of triangle M is 2 and its height is $4 \times 2 = 8$. The area of triangle N is then $\frac{1}{2}(6)(3) = 9$ and the area of triangle M is $\frac{1}{2}(2)(8) = 8$. The ratio of M to N is 8:9.

19. $\boxed{E}$ Let the length of each of the congruent rectangles be x and the width be y.

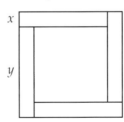

The perimeter of each of those rectangles is $2x + 2y = 20$. So, $x + y = 10$. Notice that $x + y$ is also the side length of the outer square. Therefore, the area is $10^2 = 100$.

20. $\boxed{B}$ The area of the trapezoidal wall is $\frac{1}{2}(b_1 + b_2)h = \frac{1}{2}(20 + 35)(20) = 550$. James will need $550 \div 50 = 11$ coats of paint, which is equivalent to $11 \div 3 \approx 3.67$ containers. Since James cannot buy 0.67 of a container, he needs to round up and buy a total of 4 containers.

21. $\boxed{A}$ Each triangle has one short side and two long sides. Let the length of a short side be x and the length of a long side be y. Each of the smaller triangles has a perimeter of $x + 2y$. The original triangle has a perimeter of $x + x + y + y + y + y = 2x + 4y$. The ratio is then $\dfrac{x + 2y}{2x + 4y} = \dfrac{x + 2y}{2(x + 2y)} = \dfrac{1}{2}$.

22. $\boxed{C}$ The diagonals of a rhombus intersect at right angles. Draw a line from point A to point B.

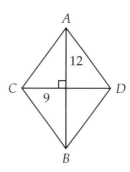

We end up with 4 triangles, each with a base of 9 and a height of 12. The area of each triangle is then $\frac{1}{2}(9)(12) = 54$. Finally, the area of the rhombus is $4 \times 54 = 216$.

23. $\boxed{A}$ The overlapping region is shared by both the circle and the rectangle. Taking that region away affects both the area of the circle and the area of the rectangle equally. The area of the circle is 30 square cm more than the area of the rectangle, whether the overlapping region is removed or not. Let x be the area of the rectangle. Then the area of the circle is $x + 30$. Since the area of the circle is 4 times the area of the rectangle,

$$x + 30 = 4x$$
$$30 = 3x$$
$$10 = x$$

The area of the rectangle is 10.

24. $\boxed{E}$ Each triangular strip has a base of 5, which means it takes 6 of them to cover the width of the poster:

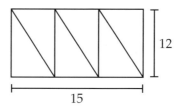

Think of the pattern above as one "layer." Now because we have 30 triangular strips and each of these "layers" requires 6 of them, we can stack $30 \div 6 = 5$ "layers" on top of each other. Since each layer has a height of 12, the maximum height that can be covered is $5 \times 12 = 60$.

Chapter 19: Volume

1. $\boxed{B}$ $V = s^3 = 4^3 = 64$

2. $\boxed{D}$ The volume of the cylindrical aquarium is $\pi r^2 h = \pi(6)^2(5) = 180\pi$ cubic feet. Therefore, it will take $\dfrac{180\pi}{20} \approx 28$ minutes to fill the aquarium.

3. $\boxed{E}$ The volume of one shipping box is $12 \times 15 \times 6 = 1{,}080$ cubic inches. The volume of one package is $4 \times 5 \times 2 = 40$ cubic inches. Therefore, one shipping box can fit a maximum of $\dfrac{1080}{40} = 27$ packages. Because each package contains 6 granola bars, one shipping box can deliver $27 \times 6 = 162$ granola bars.

4. $\boxed{B}$ Since there are 12 inches in a foot, the thickness of the tabletop is $3 \text{ inches} \times \dfrac{1 \text{ foot}}{12 \text{ inches}} = 0.25$ feet. The volume of the tabletop, in cubic feet, is then $36 \times 0.25 = 9$ (area of base $\times$ thickness).

5. $\boxed{C}$ If we let the radius of the first sphere be R, then the radius of the second sphere is $2R$. The volume of the first sphere is $\dfrac{4}{3}\pi R^3$ and the volume of the second sphere is $\dfrac{4}{3}\pi(2R)^3 = \dfrac{4}{3}\pi(8R^3) = 8\left(\dfrac{4}{3}\pi R^3\right)$. Therefore, the volume of the second sphere is 8 times the volume of the first sphere.

6. $\boxed{C}$ If we let the length be l, then the width is $2l$ and the height is $2(2l) = 4l$. Using the volume to set up an equation,

$$lwh = 2{,}744$$
$$l(2l)(4l) = 2{,}744$$
$$8l^3 = 2{,}744$$
$$l^3 = 343$$
$$l = \sqrt[3]{343} = 7$$

The width is then $2l = 2(7) = 14$.

7. $\boxed{D}$ We can find the length of $\overline{AB}$ by using the pythagorean theorem: $AB = \sqrt{10^2 - 8^2} = \sqrt{36} = 6$. The radius of the generated cone, AC, is 8 and the height, AB, is 6. The volume is then $\dfrac{1}{3}\pi r^2 h = \dfrac{1}{3}\pi(8)^2(6) = 128\pi$.

8. $\boxed{C}$ The resulting box has a length of $16 - 2 - 2 = 12$, a width of $12 - 2 - 2 = 8$, and a height of 2. Therefore, its volume is $12 \times 8 \times 2 = 192$ cubic inches. Since a cube with a side length of 1 inch has a volume of $1^3 = 1$ cubic inch, $192 \div 1 = 192$ of them can fit inside the box.

9. $\boxed{B}$ We can use the pythagorean theorem to find the length of the other leg: $\sqrt{15^2 - 9^2} = \sqrt{144} = 12$. The area of the triangular base is then $\dfrac{1}{2}bh = \dfrac{1}{2}(9)(12) = 54$. Finally, the volume of the solid is the area of the base times the height: $54 \times 4 = 216$.

10. $\boxed{D}$ Imagine the additional water sitting on top of the water already in the container. This additional water would form its own rectangular prism with a length of 5 and a width of 4 (equal to the container's length and width). Since this "prism" has a volume of 50, we can solve for its height h, which is equivalent to the rise in the water level.

$$lwh = 50$$
$$(5)(4)(h) = 50$$
$$h = 2.5$$

Therefore, the water level will rise by 2.5 inches.

Chapter 20: Systems of Equations

1. $\boxed{A}$ From the second equation, $x = 2y + 6$. Substituting this into the first equation,

$$-3x + y = 7$$
$$-3(2y + 6) + y = 7$$
$$-6y - 18 + y = 7$$
$$-5y = 25$$
$$y = -5$$

Now that we have y, $x = 2y + 6 = 2(-5) + 6 = -4$.

2. $\boxed{C}$ Multiply the first equation by 3 to get matching coefficients:

$$9x - 6y = 36$$
$$9x - 6y = 4k$$

For a system to have infinitely many solutions, both equations must be equivalent. Therefore, $4k = 36$ and $k = 9$.

3. $\boxed{D}$ A bagel is 2 more dollars than a cup of coffee so $b = 2 + c$. Three bagels cost $3b$ dollars and 2 cups of coffee cost $2c$ dollars. Altogether, that's $3b + 2c$ dollars. Since the total charge was 13.50, $3b + 2c = 13.50$.

4. $\boxed{D}$ Divide both sides by 3 in the first equation to get $x = -\dfrac{4}{3}$. Plugging this result into the second equation,

$$2x - 3y = -1$$
$$2\left(-\frac{4}{3}\right) - 3y = -1$$
$$-\frac{8}{3} - 3y = -1$$
$$-3y = \frac{5}{3}$$
$$y = -\frac{5}{9}$$

5. $\boxed{D}$ Don't get confused by the wording of the question. It's simply asking you to find the value of c for which there are an infinite number of solutions to the system. And for there to be an infinite number of solutions, the two equations must be equivalent. First, we multiply the first equation by $\dfrac{10}{6} = \dfrac{5}{3}$ to get the coefficients to match:

$$10x + 15y = 25$$
$$10x + cy = 25$$

Comparing the coefficients for y, $c = 15$.

6. $\boxed{A}$ Let's solve this system using elimination. Multiply the first equation by 3 and the second equation by 4.

$$12x + 15y = 27$$
$$12x - 16y = -128$$

Subtracting the second equation from the first, we get $31y = 155$, so $y = 5$. Plugging this result back into the original first equation,

$$4x + 5y = 9$$
$$4x + 5(5) = 9$$
$$4x + 25 = 9$$
$$4x = -16$$
$$x = -4$$

Finally, $x - y = -4 - 5 = -9$.

7. $\boxed{C}$ Translating words into math, $y = \dfrac{1}{2}x$ and $x + y = 12$. Substituting the first equation into the second and multiplying both sides by 2,

$$x + \frac{1}{2}x = 12$$
$$2x + x = 24$$
$$3x = 24$$
$$x = 8$$

And so $y = \dfrac{1}{2}x = \dfrac{1}{2}(8) = 4$. Finally, $xy = (8)(4) = 32$.

8. $\boxed{A}$ Yisel will order 40 buckets of paint so $s + m = 40$. There are s gallons of paint in s small buckets and $3m$ gallons of paint in m medium buckets for a total of $s + 3m$ gallons. Since the total number of gallons in Yisel's order is 100, $s + 3m = 100$.

9. $\boxed{B}$ Multiply the first equation by 2 so that the coefficients of y match up.

$$8x + 2y = 2a$$
$$x - 2y = 4a$$

Adding the two equations,

$$9x = 6a$$
$$x = \frac{6a}{9} = \frac{2}{3}a$$

10. $\boxed{C}$ Let the number of local passes they purchased be x and the number of express passes be y. Setting up a system of equations,

$$x + y = 20$$
$$18x + 24y = 432$$

To solve for y, we have to first eliminate x. We can do so by multiplying the first equation by 18 and then subtracting the two equations:

$$18x + 18y = 360$$
$$\underline{18x + 24y = 432}$$
$$-6y = -72$$
$$y = 12$$

11. $\boxed{B}$ The information gives us a system of equations. When $x = 4$, $rx + s = 40$. When $x = 2$, $rx + s = 50$. Putting everything together,

$$4r + s = 40$$
$$2r + s = 50$$

Subtracting the second equation from the first, we get $2r = -10$, $r = -5$. Substituting this result back into the first equation,

$$4(-5) + s = 40$$
$$-20 + s = 40$$
$$s = 60$$

12. $\boxed{D}$ Putting the given information together, we get $a + 2 = b$ and $5a = 2b$. Substituting b from the first equation into the second equation,

$$5a = 2b$$
$$5a = 2(a + 2)$$
$$5a = 2a + 4$$
$$3a = 4$$
$$a = \frac{4}{3}$$

Chapter 21: Inequalities

1. $\boxed{B}$

$$2(1 - 2x) < -3(x - 5)$$
$$2 - 4x < -3x + 15$$
$$-4x < -3x + 13$$
$$-x < 13$$
$$x > -13$$

2. $\boxed{E}$ First, multiply both sides by 2 to get rid of the fraction.

$$\frac{3y - 5}{2} > y$$
$$3y - 5 > 2y$$
$$y - 5 > 0$$
$$y > 5$$

Only values greater than 5.

3. $\boxed{C}$ Buying c candles will cost a total of $4.25c$ dollars. For Jacob to stay within his budget, the total must be less than or equal to his 200 dollars. Therefore, $4.25c \leq 200$.

4. $\boxed{D}$ The bold line segments imply that x can be greater than 4 or less than -3. Expressed mathematically, $x > 4$ or $x < -3$.

5. $\boxed{E}$

$$5x + 12 \geq 10x - 18$$
$$5x \geq 10x - 30$$
$$-5x \geq -30$$
$$x \leq 6$$

6. $\boxed{A}$ First, multiply both sides by 2 to get rid of the fraction.

$$-\frac{1}{2}x + 1 \geq 4$$
$$-x + 2 \geq 8$$
$$-x \geq 6$$
$$x \leq -6$$

On the number line, this solution set can be represented by an arrow that starts at -6 and goes left.

7. $\boxed{E}$ Since $x - y \leq 9$, isolating x gives $x \leq 9 + y$. From this inequality, we can see that x is at a maximum when y is at a maximum. The maximum value of y is 5, in which case x is less than or equal to $9 + 5 = 14$. Therefore, the greatest value x can have is 14.

8. $\boxed{A}$ The difference between a and b is c. The difference between a and d is larger since d is smaller than b. Therefore, $a - d > c$. It's worth noting that making up numbers and testing each answer choice is also a valid approach to this question. Sometimes it's hard to see the relationships algebraically.

9. $\boxed{B}$ Solving the inequality $2x + 9 < 5$ gives $2x < -4$ and $x < -2$. We then divide both sides of the inequality $-3x > 12$ by -3 to get $x < -4$ (remember to reverse the sign). To summarize, we have $x < -2$ and $x < -4$. For x to satisfy both of these inequalities, $x < -4$. After all, if $x < -4$, $x < -2$ is already satisfied.

10. $\boxed{C}$ The line has a rise of 3 and a run of 6, which means its slope is $\dfrac{3}{6} = \dfrac{1}{2}$. Its y-intercept is -3. The equation of the line is then $y = \dfrac{1}{2}x - 3$. Because the area above it is shaded, the graph illustrates the inequality $y \geq \dfrac{1}{2}x - 3$.

11. $\boxed{D}$ The best strategy here is to make up some numbers. If we let $x = 3$, then $(x - 5)(x + 2) < 0$ is satisfied. Testing each answer choice, the only one we can eliminate is A, since it evaluates to -3. The rest are positive. So that didn't help very much, but what if we try out $x = -1$, a negative value? In this case, $(x - 5)(x + 2)$ is still less than 0 and the only answer choice that results in a positive value is D, $x + 3 = -1 + 3 = 2$. It's safe to assume at this point that $x + 3$ is the one that's always positive.

12. $\boxed{D}$ The best strategy for weird "choose the graph" questions is to find some points and narrow down the graphs by process of elimination. For example, the point $(0, 1)$ is in the solution set since $|1| \geq |0|$. This eliminates choices C and E. The point $(1, 0)$ is not in the solution set since $|0| \ngeq |1|$. This eliminates A. Finally, the point $(-1, 0)$ is not in the solution set since $|0| \ngeq |-1|$. This eliminates B, which means the answer must be D.

13. $\boxed{B}$ Since $m > n$, $m - n$ is positive. This fact is important in the following steps.

$$m^2 - n^2 > 2(m - n)^2$$
$$(m + n)(m - n) > 2(m - n)^2$$
$$m + n > 2(m - n)$$
$$m + n > 2m - 2n$$
$$-m > -3n$$
$$m < 3n$$

In the first step, we factored $m^2 - n^2$ into $(m + n)(m - n)$. Then we divided both sides by $(m - n)$. We did NOT have to reverse the sign because $m - n$ is positive. Then we continued to simplify until the last step, where we multiplied both sides by -1 to isolate m. For this step, we did have to reverse the sign.

14. $\boxed{C}$ First, we must figure out the equations of the lines. The line that goes up and to the right (let's call this line a) must have a slope greater than 1 because it goes up 2 units over a run of less than 2 units (this is easy to see if you look at the intercepts). From the answer choices, we can infer that its slope is $\dfrac{3}{2}$. The line that goes down and to the right (let's call this line b) must have a slope less than -1 because it goes down 5 units over a run of less than 5 units (again, this is easy to see if you look at the intercepts). From the answer choices, we can infer that its slope is -2. Since the shaded region is above line b but below line a, $y \geq -2x - 5$ and $y \leq \dfrac{3}{2}x + 2$.

15. $\boxed{A}$ When $x - a$ is positive, $|x - a| = x - a$. In this case,

$$|x - a| \leq 3$$
$$x - a \leq 3$$
$$x \leq a + 3$$

When $x - a$ is negative, $|x - a| = -(x - a)$. And in this case,

$$|x - a| \leq 3$$
$$-(x - a) \leq 3$$
$$-x + a \leq 3$$
$$-x \leq 3 - a$$
$$x \geq a - 3$$

Putting these two cases together, $x \leq a + 3$ and $x \geq a - 3$. On the number line, this solution set can be represented by a line segment between $a - 3$ and $a + 3$.

Chapter 22: Trigonometry

1. $\boxed{A}$ Relative to θ, we're given the opposite side and the hypotenuse. Because sine relates the opposite and the hypotenuse, $\sin\theta = \dfrac{12}{30}$.

2. $\boxed{B}$ BC is the hypotenuse and AC is adjacent to $\angle C$. Therefore, $\cos\angle C = \dfrac{AC}{BC}$, which means $\dfrac{BC}{AC} = \dfrac{1}{\cos\angle C}$.

3. $\boxed{D}$ Because $\sin J = \dfrac{4}{9}$, we can let $KL = 4$ (opposite) and $JK = 9$ (hypotenuse). The pythagorean theorem gives $JL = \sqrt{9^2 - 4^2} = \sqrt{65}$. Finally, $\sin K = \dfrac{JL}{JK} = \dfrac{\sqrt{65}}{9}$.

4. $\boxed{B}$ From the graph, we can see that it repeats every π units along the x-axis. For example, the graph from 0 to π is the same as the graph from π to 2π. Therefore, the period is π.

5. $\boxed{D}$ Because $\sin^2\theta + \cos^2\theta = 1$, $3 - \sin^2\theta - \cos^2\theta = 3 - (\sin^2\theta + \cos^2\theta) = 3 - 1 = 2$.

6. $\boxed{B}$ Given that $\tan\alpha = \dfrac{9}{12}$, we can create a right triangle with angle α such that the opposite side has length 9 and the adjacent side has length 12.

The pythagorean theorem gives $BC = \sqrt{9^2 + 12^2} = 15$. Therefore, $\sin\alpha = \dfrac{\text{opp}}{\text{hyp}} = \dfrac{9}{15}$.

7. $\boxed{E}$

$$\tan\angle E = \frac{CD}{DE}$$
$$\tan 40° = \frac{120}{DE}$$
$$(DE)\tan 40° = 120$$
$$DE = \frac{120}{\tan 40°}$$

8. $\boxed{A}$ A full circle measures 2π radians (this is worth memorizing). So, $\dfrac{\text{Area of Shaded Sector}}{\text{Area of Circle}} = \dfrac{\text{Central Angle}}{\text{Full Circle}} = \dfrac{\frac{2\pi}{5}}{2\pi} = \dfrac{1}{5}$.

9. $\boxed{B}$ Using the following identity,

$$\frac{\sin\theta}{\cos\theta} = \tan\theta$$

$$\sin\theta = (\tan\theta)(\cos\theta)$$

$$\sin\theta = \left(\frac{35}{12}\right)\left(\frac{12}{37}\right)$$

$$\sin\theta = \frac{35}{37}$$

With the given values of $\cos\theta$ and $\tan\theta$, we instead could've created a right triangle with θ in order to find $\sin\theta$ but that would've taken longer.

10. $\boxed{A}$ The amplitude of $a\sin Z$, no matter what Z represents, is $|a|$. Therefore, the amplitude of $y = \frac{1}{3}\sin(2x + 1)$ is $\frac{1}{3}$. Another way to see this is to realize that the maximum of sine is always 1 and the minimum is always -1. Therefore, the maximum of $\frac{1}{3}\sin(2x + 1)$ is $\frac{1}{3}$ and the minimum is $-\frac{1}{3}$. The amplitude is then $\frac{1}{2}(\text{Max} - \text{Min}) = \frac{1}{2}\left(\frac{1}{3} - \left(-\frac{1}{3}\right)\right) = \frac{1}{3}$.

11. $\boxed{B}$ Let the height of the utility pole be h.

$$\tan 26° = \frac{h}{150}$$

$$h = 150\tan 26° \approx 150(0.488) \approx 73$$

12. $\boxed{E}$ Because $\cos\alpha = \frac{AC}{2}$, $AC = 2\cos\alpha$. Since AD is a radius, its length is 2. Finally, $CD = AD - AC = 2 - 2\cos\alpha$.

13. $\boxed{A}$ Use the law of sines and cross multiply.

$$\frac{\sin\angle T}{h} = \frac{\sin\angle SRT}{ST}$$

$$(ST)(\sin\angle T) = (h)(\sin\angle SRT)$$

$$ST = \frac{h\sin\angle SRT}{\sin\angle T}$$

14. $\boxed{E}$ The maximum of $\cos Z$, no matter what Z represents, is 1 and the minimum is -1. Therefore, the maximum of $3\cos(\pi x)$ is $3(1) = 3$ and the minimum is $3(-1) = -3$. The range is then $-3 \le y \le 3$.

15. $\boxed{C}$ Because $\overline{AB}$ is a radius, $AB = 6$. Now draw the height of the triangle from B to $\overline{AC}$.

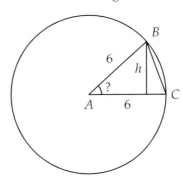

The area of $\triangle ABC$ is 12, so $\frac{1}{2}(6)(h) = 12$, $h = 4$. Relative to $\angle BAC$, we now have the opposite side and

the hypotenuse. Therefore, the measure of $\angle BAC$ is $\sin^{-1}\left(\frac{4}{6}\right) = \sin^{-1}\left(\frac{2}{3}\right)$.

16. $\boxed{D}$ Use the identity $\tan \theta = \dfrac{\sin \theta}{\cos \theta}$.

$$\frac{\tan \theta}{\sin \theta} = \frac{\dfrac{\sin \theta}{\cos \theta}}{\sin \theta} = \frac{\sin \theta}{\cos \theta} \times \frac{1}{\sin \theta} = \frac{1}{\cos \theta} = \frac{1}{\dfrac{3}{4}} = \frac{4}{3}$$

17. $\boxed{C}$ Using the law of sines,

$$\frac{PQ}{\sin 68°} = \frac{40}{\sin 34°}$$

$$PQ = \frac{40 \sin 68°}{\sin 34°} \approx \frac{40(0.927)}{0.559} \approx 66$$

18. $\boxed{C}$ Draw the height of the triangle from B to $\overline{AC}$. Let the point of intersection, which has coordinates $(4,3)$, be E.

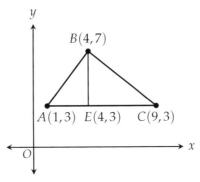

$BE = 7 - 3 = 4$ and $EC = 9 - 4 = 5$. Looking at right triangle $\triangle BEC$, $\tan \angle C = \dfrac{BE}{EC} = \dfrac{4}{5}$.

19. $\boxed{A}$ Using the identity $\sin^2 x + \cos^2 x = 1$ along with the given ones,

$$\sec x - \sin x \tan x = \frac{1}{\cos x} - \sin x \left(\frac{\sin x}{\cos x} \right) = \frac{1}{\cos x} - \left(\frac{\sin^2 x}{\cos x} \right) = \frac{1 - \sin^2 x}{\cos x} = \frac{\cos^2 x}{\cos x} = \cos x$$

20. $\boxed{C}$ Using the law of cosines,

$$QR^2 = 15^2 + 21^2 - 2(15)(21)\cos 39°$$
$$QR^2 \approx 666 - 630(0.78)$$
$$QR^2 \approx 174.6$$
$$QR \approx \sqrt{174.6} \approx 13.2$$

21. $\boxed{E}$ For the sake of simplicity, let $X = \cos\alpha$ so that it's clear we have a quadratic we can factor.

$$2\cos^2\alpha - 5\cos\alpha = -2$$
$$2X^2 - 5X = -2$$
$$2X^2 - 5X + 2 = 0$$
$$(2X - 1)(X - 2) = 0$$
$$(2\cos\alpha - 1)(\cos\alpha - 2) = 0$$

So, $\cos\alpha = \dfrac{1}{2}$ or $\cos\alpha = 2$. However, $\cos\alpha$ can never equal 2 since the maximum of cosine is 1. Therefore, $\cos\alpha = \dfrac{1}{2}$. From here, $\alpha = \cos^{-1}\left(\dfrac{1}{2}\right) = \dfrac{\pi}{3}$ radians, and $\sin\alpha = \sin\left(\dfrac{\pi}{3}\right) = \dfrac{\sqrt{3}}{2}$.

Instead of finding the value of α, we could've drawn a right triangle such that $\cos\alpha = \dfrac{1}{2}$ and used that to find $\sin\alpha$.

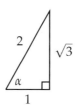

Note that this is a very tough question. A brute force way would be to backsolve for possible values of α by taking the $\sin^{-1}$ of each of the answer choices. Then we would plug each of those values into the given equation to see if both sides match.

22. $\boxed{E}$ You can compare the graphs or look at the equations. Relative to $f(x)$, $g(x)$ is shifted $\dfrac{\pi}{2}$ units left and 2 units down. If you can't see these transformations from the equations alone, review the section on function transformations in the chapter on functions.

Chapter 23: Permutations & Probability

1. $\boxed{D}$ The number of red or purple jellybeans is $6 + 5 = 11$. Therefore, the probability is $\dfrac{11}{18}$.

2. $\boxed{C}$ Out of 8 sectors, there are 3 with stars. Therefore, the probability is $\dfrac{3}{8}$.

3. $\boxed{E}$ The set contains the even numbers from 2 to 20. If you divide each number in the set by 2, you get $1, 2, 3, \ldots, 10$, which means there are 10 numbers in the set. Of the numbers in the set, the ones divisible by 3 are 6, 12, and 18. That's 3 numbers out of 10, giving a probability of $\dfrac{3}{10}$.

4. $\boxed{B}$ The probability of drawing a black card from the first stack is $\dfrac{5}{5+5} = \dfrac{1}{2}$. The probability of drawing a black card from the second stack is $\dfrac{4}{3+4+5} = \dfrac{4}{12} = \dfrac{1}{3}$. Because the two drawings are independent, the probability that both cards are black is $\dfrac{1}{2} \times \dfrac{1}{3} = \dfrac{1}{6}$.

5. $\boxed{E}$ Multiply the number of choices she has for each item: $6 \times 3 \times 2 \times 3 = 108$.

6. $\boxed{B}$ Multiply the number of answer choices for each question: $5 \times 5 \times 5 \times 5 = 5^4$.

7. $\boxed{C}$ There are 7 choices for the first digit. Once the first digit is set, there are 6 remaining choices for the second digit. Once the second digit is set, there are 5 remaining choices for the third digit. Altogether, there are $7 \times 6 \times 5 = 210$ possible order numbers.

8. $\boxed{D}$ If the probability of drawing a white marble is $\dfrac{3}{7}$, then the probability of drawing a blue marble must be $1 - \dfrac{3}{7} = \dfrac{4}{7}$. From here, we can let the number of blue marbles b be 4 and the number of white marbles w be 3. $\dfrac{w}{b} = \dfrac{3}{4}$.

9. $\boxed{B}$ Let x be the total number of gumballs in the jar. If the probability of selecting an orange gumball is $\dfrac{1}{6}$, then the probability of selecting a red or purple gumball is $1 - \dfrac{1}{6} = \dfrac{5}{6}$. So, five-sixths of the gumballs in the jar must be red or purple.

$$\frac{5}{6}x = 42 + 33$$

$$x = \frac{6}{5}(42 + 33) = \frac{6}{5}(75) = 90$$

The number of orange gumballs is then $90 - 42 - 33 = 15$.

10. $\boxed{C}$ Let x be the number of oatmeal cookies that must be added. Once they're added, the number of oatmeal cookies increases to $8 + x$ and the total number of cookies increases to $36 + x$. Now we can set up an equation and cross multiply.

$$\frac{8 + x}{36 + x} = \frac{1}{3}$$

$$3(8 + x) = 36 + x$$

$$24 + 3x = 36 + x$$

$$2x = 12$$

$$x = 6$$

11. $\boxed{B}$ Syed has to roll the dice 4 more times. The probability that he gets one of the remaining numbers (1, 3, 4, or 6) on the first roll is $\frac{4}{6}$. Once he rolls that target number (whichever one it is), 3 target numbers remain. The probability that he gets one of those on the second roll is $\frac{3}{6}$. The probability is $\frac{2}{6}$ on the third roll and finally $\frac{1}{6}$ on the fourth roll. Multiplying these probabilities together,

$$\frac{4}{6} \times \frac{3}{6} \times \frac{2}{6} \times \frac{1}{6} = \frac{24}{1,296} = \frac{1}{54}$$

There is another way using permutations. There are $6 \times 6 \times 6 \times 6 = 1,296$ total possible combinations of roll outcomes (6 choices for the first roll, 6 choices for the second roll, ...). Of them, $4 \times 3 \times 2 \times 1 = 24$ meet the requirement that no numbers repeat (4 choices for the first roll, 3 choices for the second roll, ...).

Therefore, the probability is $\frac{24}{1,296} = \frac{1}{54}$.

Chapter 24: Data & Statistics

1. $\boxed{C}$ Putting the numbers in order, we get $8.1, 8.4, 9.3, 9.5, 9.7, 10.8, 11.1$. The median is the 4th term, which is 9.5.

2. $\boxed{D}$ The sum of the scores for his first 4 tests is $89 + 84 + 92 + 97 = 362$. The sum of the scores for his last 5 tests is $5 \times 86 = 430$. Altogether, that's 792 points. The average of all 9 of his scores is then $792 \div 9 = 88$.

3. $\boxed{B}$ $\dfrac{240 + 230 + 242 + 225 + 235 + 244}{6} = 236$

4. $\boxed{B}$ From the 21st to the 22nd, the ticket price decreased by 10. From the 22nd to the 23rd, the ticket price increased by 12. From the 23rd to the 24th, the ticket price decreased by 17. From the 24th to the 25th, the ticket price increased by 10. From the 25th to the 26th, the ticket price increased by 9. The biggest increase in price occurred between the 22nd and the 23rd.

5. $\boxed{C}$ A price of \$16 is $28 - 16 = 12$ dollars below the mean. That's equivalent to $12 \div 5 = 2.4$ standard deviations.

6. $\boxed{B}$ Remember that when an operation is applied to every number in a list, it is also implicitly applied to the median. Therefore, we can work backwards by reversing the operations on the median. The median of the second list is $37 + 12 = 49$. The median of the first list is $\sqrt{49} = 7$.

7. $\boxed{B}$ According to the graph, Abigail was 20 miles away from City A at time 0. Because she started in City B, City B must be 20 miles from City A.

8. $\boxed{C}$ The two graphs intersect at about 22.5 minutes into the commute. This intersection means that they were both the same distance from City A at that moment in time, and thus passing each other on the highway.

9. $\boxed{C}$ Abigail's graph has two horizontal line segments, the first from 10 to 15 minutes and the second from 25 to 30 minutes. These horizontal line segments indicate that she did not travel any distance during those times. Therefore, Abigail stopped 2 times during her commute.

10. $\boxed{A}$ According to the graph, Jeff arrived in City B after 50 minutes. Abigail arrived in City A after 40 minutes. Jeff's commute took $50 - 40 = 10$ minutes longer.

11. $\boxed{D}$ Speed is represented by the slope of the graph. Throughout his commute, Jeff drove at a constant speed of $\dfrac{2}{5}$ (2 miles every 5 minutes). From 0 to 10 minutes, Abigail drove at a speed of $\dfrac{20 - 18}{10 - 0} = \dfrac{2}{10} = \dfrac{1}{5}$ (slower than Jeff). From 15 to 25 minutes, she drove at a speed of $\dfrac{18 - 6}{25 - 15} = \dfrac{12}{10} = \dfrac{6}{5}$ (faster than Jeff). From 30 to 40 minutes, she drove at a speed of $\dfrac{6 - 0}{40 - 30} = \dfrac{6}{10} = \dfrac{3}{5}$ (faster than Jeff). In summary, Abigail drove faster than Jeff from 15 to 25 minutes and from 30 to 40 minutes.

12. $\boxed{D}$ The curve gives a value of 90 for Wednesday.

13. $\boxed{E}$ Because the curve passes through the actual number for Saturday, that's when it comes closest to fitting the actual data.

14. $\boxed{B}$ Listing out the actual values from the graph, we get $60, 80, 100, 90, 60, 50, 30$. Putting these in order gives $30, 50, 60, 60, 80, 90, 100$. The median is the 4th term, which is 60.

15. $\boxed{E}$ The stem-and-leaf plot gives 5 students who own more than 15 books (16, 21, 21, 21, and 28). Since there are 14 students in total, the probability is $\dfrac{5}{14}$.

16. $\boxed{B}$ The class starts out with 14 students who own a total of $2 + 2 + 3 + 5 + 11 + 11 + 12 + 12 + 12 + 16 + 21 + 21 + 21 + 28 = 177$ books. After the new student joins (now 15 students), the total for the class increases to $15 \times 13 = 195$ books. Therefore, the new student must own $195 - 177 = 18$ books.

17. $\boxed{D}$ The median of a list of 7 numbers is the 4th number. Therefore, we have a few possible cases:

$$a, b, c, \boxed{x}, x, x, d$$

$$a, b, x, \boxed{x}, x, c, d$$

$$a, x, x, \boxed{x}, b, c, d$$

where a, b, c, and d are placeholder numbers, the boxed number is the median, and the numbers are ordered from left to right. If we add 4 numbers greater than x to the first case,

$$a, b, c, x, x, \boxed{x}, d, e, f, g, h$$

the median becomes the 6th term and is still x. This is not true for the second and third cases. Therefore, there must be 3 numbers in the list less than x (represented here by a, b, and c).

18. $\boxed{E}$ If you're stumped and have no idea what the graphs of various equations look like, then make up a number for a and graph each answer choice on your calculator. In this case, the points most closely resemble an exponential function. Therefore, the answer is $y = a^x$. If you plot $y = 2^x$ on your calculator, you can see how closely the shape of the graph matches up with the given data points.

19. $\boxed{B}$ For 8 to be the mode, two of the integers in the data set must be 8. Note that there can't be three 8's because then the median would be 8 instead of 7. So our data set currently looks like

$$x, y, 8, 8$$

Because there are 4 elements, the median is the average of the middle two. Therefore, 7 CANNOT be in the data set because then the median would be 7.5 (average of 7 and 8). Instead y must be 6. That way, the median is the average of 6 and 8, which is 7. So now our data set is

$$x, 6, 8, 8$$

Because the mean is 6, the sum of the integers in the data set must be $4 \times 6 = 24$. Therefore, $x = 24 - 6 - 8 - 8 = 2$, which is the smallest integer in the data set.

20. $\boxed{B}$ Let $a = b = 19$ and $c = 35$. After these 3 numbers are added, the new data set contains 10 terms and the median becomes the average of the 5th and 6th terms.

$$15, 19, 19, 19, 25, 29, 33, 33, 35, 41$$

The 5th term is 25. The 6th term is 29. The average of these two terms is 27. This is always the median of the new data set no matter what values we choose for a, b, and c.

21. $\boxed{C}$ The cost per box decreases in a stepwise fashion as the number of boxes in the order increases. From 1 to 19 boxes, the cost per box stays constant at $50. From 20 to 39 boxes, the cost per box stays constant at $46. From 40 to 59 boxes, the cost per box stays constant at $42. Finally, from 60 to 79 boxes, the cost per box stays constant at $38. Answer C is the only graph that accurately reflects this pricing model with its decreasing stepwise horizontal line segments.

Chapter 25: Logarithms

1. $\boxed{D}$ By the definition of a log, $\log_4 x = 3$ is equivalent to $4^3 = x$. Therefore, $x = 64$.

2. $\boxed{D}$ By the definition of a log, $5^a = 3$ and $5^b = 4$. Multiplying both equations, we get

$$5^a \cdot 5^b = 3 \cdot 4$$
$$5^{a+b} = 12$$

3. $\boxed{E}$ By the definition of a log, $c^{\frac{1}{2}} = 9$. Squaring both sides, $c = 81$.

4. $\boxed{C}$ By the definition of a log, $5^x = 4$. Now,

$$5^{2-x} = 5^2 \cdot 5^{-x} = \frac{5^2}{5^x} = \frac{25}{4}$$

5. $\boxed{A}$

$$\log_3 x^2 = c$$
$$2\log_3 x = c$$
$$\log_3 x = \frac{c}{2}$$

6. $\boxed{B}$ $\log_2 63 = \log_2(7 \cdot 3^2) = \log_2 7 + \log_2 3^2 = \log_2 7 + 2\log_2 3 = p + 2q$

7. $\boxed{C}$ $\log\left((3x)^2\right) = 2\log(3x) = 2(\log 3 + \log x) = 2\log 3 + 2\log x$.

8. $\boxed{D}$ By the definition of a log, $x = \log_a b$ and $y = \log_a c$. Therefore, $xy = (\log_a b)(\log_a c)$.

9. $\boxed{A}$

$$\log_4(x+3) + \log_4(x-3) = 2$$
$$\log_4\left((x+3)(x-3)\right) = 2$$
$$(x+3)(x-3) = 4^2$$
$$x^2 - 9 = 16$$
$$x^2 = 25$$
$$x = 5$$

10. $\boxed{A}$

$$\log_b 40 - \log_b 5 = 3$$
$$\log_b 8 = 3$$
$$b^3 = 8$$
$$b = \sqrt[3]{8} = 2$$

Chapter 26: A Mix of Algebra Topics

1. $\boxed{D}$ If we let the smaller number be x, then the larger number is $x + 8$. Since these two numbers sum to 30,

$$x + (x + 8) = 30$$
$$2x + 8 = 30$$
$$2x = 22$$
$$x = 11$$

The larger number is then $x + 8 = 11 + 8 = 19$.

2. $\boxed{E}$ The driver must pay \$50 for the first violation and \$80 for each of the remaining $(n - 1)$ violations. Therefore, $d = 50 + 80(n - 1) = 50 + 80n - 80 = -30 + 80n$.

3. $\boxed{B}$ Let h be the number of hours of court time. The total fee at Sportsmen's is then $20 + 8h$ and the total fee at Midtown is $12h$.

$$20 + 8h = 12h$$
$$20 = 4h$$
$$h = 5$$

4. $\boxed{D}$ Setting up an equation to solve for n,

$$t = 2n^{\frac{2}{3}} + 3$$
$$21 = 2n^{\frac{2}{3}} + 3$$
$$18 = 2n^{\frac{2}{3}}$$
$$9 = n^{\frac{2}{3}}$$
$$(9)^{\frac{3}{2}} = (n^{\frac{2}{3}})^{\frac{3}{2}}$$
$$n = 9^{\frac{3}{2}} = 27$$

5. $\boxed{E}$ $F = \frac{9}{5}C + 32 = \frac{9}{5}(85) + 32 = 153 + 32 = 185°$.

6. $\boxed{C}$ Based on the given information, $a = b - 3$ and $c = a + 6$. Substituting the first equation into the second, $c = a + 6 = (b - 3) + 6 = b + 3$. Since $ac = 135$,

$$ac = 135$$
$$(b - 3)(b + 3) = 135$$
$$b^2 - 9 = 135$$
$$b^2 = 144$$
$$b = \sqrt{144} = 12$$

7. $\boxed{C}$ Let the number of shelves be s. Then the number of books on each shelf is $s + 5$. Since there are 126 books in total,

$$s(s + 5) = 126$$
$$s^2 + 5s = 126$$
$$s^2 + 5s - 126 = 0$$
$$(s + 14)(s - 9) = 0$$

Since s cannot be negative, $s = 9$. If you had trouble with the factoring, consider graphing the equation on your calculator or using the quadratic formula.

8. $\boxed{E}$ We need to solve for R_2 when $R_T = 5$ and $R_1 = 6$.

$$\frac{1}{R_T} = \frac{1}{R_1} + \frac{1}{R_2}$$
$$\frac{1}{5} = \frac{1}{6} + \frac{1}{R_2}$$
$$\frac{6}{30} = \frac{5}{30} + \frac{1}{R_2}$$
$$\frac{1}{30} = \frac{1}{R_2}$$

Comparing both sides, $R_2 = 30$.

9. $\boxed{C}$ Set up an equation and then simplify it to a quadratic.

$$14 = 50 - 6t - 2t^2$$
$$-36 = -6t - 2t^2$$
$$2t^2 + 6t - 36 = 0$$
$$t^2 + 3t - 18 = 0$$
$$(t + 6)(t - 3) = 0$$

Since t cannot be negative, $t = 3$.

264

10. $\boxed{A}$ Let x be the number of dollars he withdraws the first day. Then he will withdraw $x + 20$ dollars on the second day, $x + 40$ on the third day, $x + 60$ on the fourth day, $x + 80$ on the fifth day, $x + 100$ on the sixth day, and $x + 120$ on the seventh day. Adding all these amounts up, we get $7x + 420$. Equating this expression to the amount in his bank account,

$$7x + 420 = 546$$
$$7x = 126$$
$$x = 18$$

11. $\boxed{E}$ In maximum/minimum questions like this one, the maximum/minimum always occurs at one of the vertices. In this case, the vertices are $(0, 6000)$, $(3000, 5000)$, $(6000, 2000)$, and $(6000, 0)$. The vertex $(0, 6000)$ gives a profit of $0.10(0) + 0.20(6000) = \$1,200$. The vertex $(3000, 5000)$ gives a profit of $0.10(3000) + 0.20(5000) = \$1,300$. The vertex $(6000, 2000)$ gives a profit of $0.10(6000) + 0.20(2000) = \$1,000$. The vertex $(6000, 0)$ gives a profit of $0.10(6000) + 0.20(0) = \$600$. Comparing these values, we can see that the maximum possible profit is \$1,300.

Chapter 27: Miscellaneous Topics I

1. $\boxed{D}$ There must be $14 - 6 = 8$ students who are only on the math team and $19 - 6 = 13$ students who are only on the science team. The number of students who are on at least one team is then $8 + 13 + 6 = 27$. Therefore, $31 - 27 = 4$ students are on neither team.

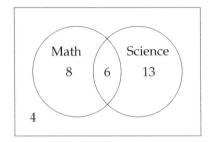

2. $\boxed{D}$ The common difference of the sequence is $2\frac{5}{8} - 1\frac{1}{2} = 2\frac{5}{8} - 1\frac{4}{8} = 1\frac{1}{8}$. The next term in the sequence is then $3\frac{3}{4} + 1\frac{1}{8} = 3\frac{6}{8} + 1\frac{1}{8} = 4\frac{7}{8}$.

3. $\boxed{B}$ Use the answer choices to guess and check. For example, 33 gives a remainder of 3 when divided by 6, but a remainder of 5 when divided by 7. So the answer isn't A. Moving on to B, which turns out to be the answer, 39 gives a remainder of 3 when divided by 6 and a remainder of 4 when divided by 7.

4. $\boxed{C}$ This question requires some guessing and checking. Let's say Freddie spent all his money on large candles. Then he would be able to buy $\frac{53.00}{3.25} = 16$ of them with $53.00 - 16(3.25) = \$1$ left over. That's not enough left over to buy 1 small candle. Remember that he has to buy at least one of each size. So, 16 is too many. Let's try 14, answer choice D. If he bought 14 large candles, Freddie would have $53.00 - 14(3.25) = \$7.50$ left over. That's definitely enough to buy at least one small candle but then he would still have \$1.50 left over in change. Because the question specifies that he must spend exactly \$53.00, 14 large candles is not the answer. Let's try 12, answer choice C. If he bought 12 large candles, Freddie would have $53.00 - 12(3.25) = \$14.00$ left over. That's enough to buy 7 small candles with no change left over. This is our answer.

5. $\boxed{E}$ The common ratio is $\dfrac{\frac{1}{3}}{-\frac{2}{3}} = -\frac{1}{2}$. The 6th term is then $\frac{1}{12} \times -\frac{1}{2} \times -\frac{1}{2} = \frac{1}{48}$.

6. $\boxed{C}$ Guess and check. If $x = \frac{1}{2}$, then we get $\frac{1}{4} < -\frac{1}{2}$, which is not true, eliminating A. If $x = 2$, then we end up with $4 < -2$, which is not true, eliminating B. If $x = -\frac{1}{2}$, then we get $\frac{1}{4} < \frac{1}{2}$, which is true and proves C is the answer.

7. $\boxed{B}$ The difference between the fourth term and the second term is $6 - (-8) = 14$, and since there are $4 - 2 = 2$ steps between them, the common difference of the sequence must be $14 \div 2 = 7$. The first term is then $-8 - 7 = -15$.

8. $\boxed{D}$ We can either list the terms out and count or use the formula for the nth term of an arithmetic sequence. I'll show you the latter. The nth term of an arithmetic sequence is given by $a_n = a_1 + (n-1)d$, where a_n is the nth term, a_1 is the first term, and d is the common difference, which is 2 in this case.

$$a_n = a_1 + (n-1)d$$
$$31 = -5 + (n-1)(2)$$
$$36 = (n-1)(2)$$
$$18 = n-1$$
$$n = 19$$

Since 31 is the 19th term, there are 18 terms in the sequence less than 31.

9. $\boxed{E}$ $10 + 15 + 26 + 9 = 60$ tourists.

10. $\boxed{B}$ List the terms out and count: $-3, -7, -11, -15, \underline{-19}, \underline{-23}, \underline{-27}, \underline{-31}, \underline{-35}, \underline{-39}, -43$. There are 6 terms between -15 and -43.

11. $\boxed{B}$ Let's use a pentagon (5 sides) as an example of how to count diagonals. First, pick a vertex. We can't draw diagonals from this first vertex to itself or its neighboring vertices. We can only draw 2 diagonals to 2 other vertices. For the next vertex, another 2 diagonals can be drawn. For the third vertex, only 1 diagonal can be drawn. At this point, we're done. No more diagonals can be drawn. So for a 5-sided polygon, the number of diagonals is $2 + 2 + 1 = 5$.

Perhaps you already see the way this works, but if not, let's count the diagonals of a hexagon (6 sides). Again, pick a vertex. We can't draw diagonals from this first vertex to itself or its neighboring vertices. We can only draw 3 diagonals to 3 other vertices. For the next vertex, another 3 diagonals can be drawn. For the third vertex, only 2 diagonal can be drawn. For the fourth vertex, only 1 diagonal can be drawn. At this point, no more diagonals can be drawn. So for a 6-sided polygon, the number of diagonals is $3 + 3 + 2 + 1 = 9$.

For a decagon, the number of diagonals is $7 + 7 + 6 + 5 + 4 + 3 + 2 + 1 = 35$.

12. $\boxed{B}$ This question requires some guessing and checking. Let's see if we can have 10 teams that each contain exactly 4 people. The 10 teams would account for $10 \times 4 = 40$ people and the 6 remaining teams would have to have $90 - 40 = 50$ people in total. This scenario is impossible since 6 teams can have at most $6 \times 7 = 42$ people.

How about 9 teams? The 9 teams would account for $9 \times 4 = 36$ people and the remaining 7 teams would have to have $90 - 36 = 54$ people in total. This scenario is impossible since 7 teams can have at most $7 \times 7 = 49$ people.

How about 8 teams? The 8 teams would account for $8 \times 4 = 32$ people and the remaining 8 teams would have to have $90 - 32 = 58$ people in total. This scenario is impossible since 8 teams can have at most $8 \times 7 = 56$ people.

How about 7 teams? The 7 teams would account for $7 \times 4 = 28$ people and the remaining 9 teams would have to have $90 - 28 = 62$ people in total. Since 9 teams can have at most $9 \times 7 = 63$ people, this scenario is possible.

13. $\boxed{C}$ Let the first term of the sequence be a and the common ratio be r. Then the second term is ar. Since the first two terms sum to 60,

$$a + ar = 60$$
$$a(1 + r) = 60$$

Since r is a positive integer, a must be a factor of 60 less than 60. Therefore, a cannot be 8, which is answer C.

14. $\boxed{A}$ The minimum of 10 occurs when all the students receiving leadership awards also get community service awards and all the students receiving academic excellence awards also get community service awards.

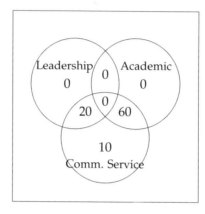

Chapter 28: Miscellaneous Topics II

1. $\boxed{C}$ To become a member, a player has to be invited by at least 3 current members. Therefore, Tony received at least 3 invitations, not less than 3.

2. $\boxed{E}$ The first row gives $b - 3 = 5, b = 8$. The second row gives $a - b = 2, a - 8 = 2, a = 10$.

3. $\boxed{D}$ The bottom of the cube is square #3. Squares #2 and #4 then fold up and #5 folds to the left. Therefore, the square opposite #2 is #5.

4. $\boxed{B}$ After a 90° clockwise rotation around A, the triangle looks like this:

Once it's reflected over $\overline{AC}$, the final orientation is

5. $\boxed{C}$ $(x)(2y) - (-w)(z) = 2xy + wz$

6. $\boxed{B}$ You can get 0 intersection points if the horizontal line is below the x-axis. You can get 2 intersection points if the line is near the top of the graph. You can get 3 intersection points if the line crosses the "tip" that is on the y-axis. You can get 4 intersection points if the line crosses the y-axis below the "tip" and above the x-axis. You cannot, however, get 1 intersection point.

7. $\boxed{E}$ Using the determinant to set up an equation,

$$(y)(y) - (y)(6) = -9$$
$$y^2 - 6y = -9$$
$$y^2 - 6y + 9 = 0$$
$$(y - 3)^2 = 0$$
$$y = 3$$

8. $\boxed{D}$ Draw out the different cases.

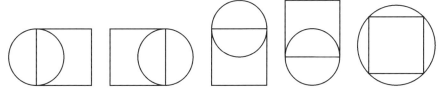

There are 5 of these circles.

9. $\boxed{A}$ The standard equation of an ellipse is $\dfrac{(x-h)^2}{a^2} + \dfrac{(y-k)^2}{b^2} = 1$, where (h,k) is the center, a is the "horizontal radius," and b is the "vertical radius." The graph of the equation is a "fat" ellipse with center at $(0,0)$, a "horizontal radius" of $\sqrt{49} = 7$, and a "vertical radius" of $\sqrt{25} = 5$. Therefore, the ellipse has y-intercepts at $(0,-5)$ and $(0,5)$.

10. $\boxed{D}$ Remember that a translation is just a shift in the graph, either in the x-direction, y-direction, or both. Comparing the matrices, the point $(-1,8)$ was shifted to $(3,3)$. That's $3 - (-1) = 4$ units in the x-direction and $3 - 8 = -5$ units in the y-direction. In other words, 4 units to the right and 5 units down. Applying this same translation to $(2,5)$, we get $(6,0)$. Therefore, $c = 6$.

11. $\boxed{D}$ The only logical equivalent is the contrapositive: "If you have not passed the 7th grade, then you are not learning algebra in school."

12. $\boxed{E}$ Draw them out. There are 18 possible triangles.

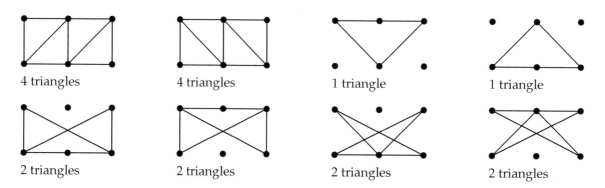

| 4 triangles | 4 triangles | 1 triangle | 1 triangle |

| 2 triangles | 2 triangles | 2 triangles | 2 triangles |

13. $\boxed{C}$ Matrix A is a 2×2 matrix. For AB to be defined, matrix B must have 2 rows (equal to the number of columns in matrix A). For AB to result in a 2×3 matrix, matrix B must have 3 columns. To show this visually,

$$\begin{matrix} A & & B \\ 2 \times \boxed{2} & & \boxed{2} \times 3 \end{matrix}$$

The boxed numbers have to match up for matrix multiplication to be possible. The outer numbers represent the dimensions of the resulting matrix AB:

$$\begin{matrix} A & & B \\ \boxed{2} \times 2 & & 2 \times \boxed{3} \end{matrix}$$

Choice C is the only matrix that has 2 rows and 3 columns. Note that both B and product AB are 2×3 matrices.

14. $\boxed{C}$ The standard equation of an ellipse is $\dfrac{(x-h)^2}{a^2} + \dfrac{(y-k)^2}{b^2} = 1$, where (h,k) is the center, a is the "horizontal radius," and b is the "vertical radius." The graph in question is a "skinny" ellipse with a center in the second quadrant. Because it's a "skinny" ellipse, the vertical radius is longer than the horizontal radius ($b^2 > a^2$). Only choice C gives an equation of an ellipse with a center in the second quadrant, $(-4,3)$, and $b^2 > a^2$ ($16 > 4$).

Made in the USA
Columbia, SC
25 July 2018